D1593834

Relating to Ancient
Culture

Relating to Ancient
Culture

And the mysterious agent changing it

Gary W. Wietgrefe

GWW Books
Sioux Falls, SD

GWW Books *GWW*
401 E. 8th St., Suite 214-730
Sioux Falls, SD 57103-7011
www.relatingtoancients.com

Ordering Information
Quantity sales. Special discounts are available on quantity purchases by corporations, associations, and others. For details, submit a request through the website www.relatingtoancients.com.
Individual sales. GWW Books publications are available through most bookstores and on-line retailers. They can also be ordered directly from the website www.relatingtoancients.com.
Orders for college textbook/course adoption use. Please make contact through the website www.relatingtoancients.com.
Orders by U.S. trade bookstores and wholesalers. Please contact BCH Fulfillment & Distribution, 33 Oakland Avenue, Harrison, NY 10528; Orders: 1 (800) 431-1579, Email: orders@bookch.com; Tel: (914) 835-0015; Fax (914) 835-0398; Website: www.bookch.com.

Production management: Michael Bass Associates, www.bass-books.com
Cover Design: Julie Gallagher at Michael Bass Associates with photo design by Chad Philips with microphone and headset images with permission from Istock Photo Images inserted by Chad Phillips Photography, 1908 W. 42nd St., Sioux Falls, SD 57105; www.chadphillipsphotograpy .com. Gila River New Mexico cliff-dweller photo supplied by author.

Names: Wietgrefe, Gary W., 1953– author.
Title: Relating to Ancient Culture and the mysterious agent changing it/Gary W Wietgrefe, Sioux Falls, South Dakota: GWW Books, 2018.

Identifiers: Library of Congress Control Number: 2017916589 / ISBN 9780999224908 - hardcover; ISBN 9780999224915 - paperback; ISBN 9780999224922 - e-book

Subjects: Non-fiction: Social Science–Culture

Classification: BISAC Codes: 1. SOC 005000 Social Science/Customs & Traditions; 2. HIS 037080 History/Modern/21st Century; 3. FAM 034000 Family & Relationships/Parenting/ General; 4. EDU 021000 Education/Non-Formal Education; 5. BUS 069030 Business & Economics/Economics Theory; 6. EDU 016000 Education/History

First Edition   Printed in the United States of America

*This is dedicated to my loving wife, Patricia,
our children, grandchildren, and future
generations that seek the
best culture.*

CONTENTS

ACKNOWLEDGMENTS

Getting books proofread, edited, produced, printed, and marketed is a pleasing effort when working with talented professionals. First, my dear wife, Patricia, I cannot thank enough for all the years she has endured my reading, notetaking, and day and night writing. It is also with heartfelt thanks that I pass on my gratitude to Michael Bass Associates who took both books, *Relating to Ancient Culture* and *Relating to Ancient Learning*, through the many facets of the book production process. Thankfully, Lori Cavanaugh worked tirelessly editing again, again, and again. Thanks also to Martha Ghent for proofreading and Julie Gallagher for text design and production. Linda Hallinger did an amazing job indexing. Eli Wietgrefe and Chad Phillips I thank dearly for their imagination in photo production and manipulation. Scott Jordan, using his years of experience in book publishing, did a fantastic job developing my website **www.relatingtoancients.com**. Last, but certainly not least, I thank Becky Phillips for the many years I have worked with her in marketing, coordinating too many loose ends, and scheduling.

Thank you all so much ... Gary

INTRODUCTION

Culture is survival. Memory is culture. Society is losing all three.
Survival is in jeopardy when memory, books, and clouds disappear.

It is never the job of others to remember your memories.
Relating to Ancient Culture can only be accomplished through
memories. Past thoughts create cultural understanding.

Human culture is changing, but why? Who has a vested interest in
the status quo? Who cares about the apathetic subject? Wietgrefe.

Idling through memories, get irked. Become exasperated. Yearn.
Laugh. Learn. Question societal infections for better or worse.

Twenty riddles throughout this book reveal a common, yet
mysterious, cultural agent of change.

Be shocked at what must change to survive.

1

Cultural Shift

What is culture? What changes it?

Many archeologists, anthropologists, ecologists, ethologists, etiologists, historians, kinesiologists, linguists, physiologists, polyglots, psychologists, sociologists, theologians, and others have studied ancient cultures.[1] Fossils, structures, landscapes, mummies, scripts, and even deoxyribonucleic acid (DNA) provide clues, but clues are merely inklings.

How do you know culture if you have not lived it?

I will offer an inkling of how this book is *Relating to Ancient Culture.*

Culture for most people develops around family and always has. Daughters learned from their mothers and grandmothers, and boys until they come of age tagged along behind their fathers and grandfathers. Historically, children followed the career of their parents.

Establishment of culture for the lifetime of most individuals is approximately one hundred to one hundred and fifty years. How can establishment of culture last longer than a person's lifetime? Assuming you were socially connected with your parents, grandparents, great grandparents, and great aunts and uncles, your initial culture develops from them.

---

[1] Archeologists study artifacts; anthropologists study biological and physical remnants; ecologists study organism interaction; ethologists study behavior; etiologists study disease origin; historians are chroniclers; kinesiologists study human movement; linguists study languages; physiologists study physical functions; polyglots study multilinguistic peoples; psychologists study behavior; sociologists study social interaction; and theologians study religions.

A quick example would be that your grandmother was twenty when your mother was born and she was around your family when your mother was twenty and you were born. If they lived to the current life expectancy of about eighty, your lifetime cultural experience would be one hundred and twenty (20 + 20 + 80) years.

For thousands of years, most people benefited from the cultural experiences of their family.

Other than family, what established cultural experience?

MONEY: WANTS VERSUS NEEDS

Money changed agriculture. Families and tribes gathered food, built shelter, and when sick or injured, members were treated in their community. Bartering allowed for exchange of goods. Fish for grain or salt for meat were exchanged with varying values depending on needs. Hand weapons provided security. A nonconsumable medium of exchange developed, but authority to standardize was lacking.

Civilizations developed independently under larger protectorates with wild the rule on borders. Ancient Greeks were one of the first to coordinate written edits.

> ... Draco, one of the nobles, was appointed in 621 B.C. to codify the hitherto unwritten and unorganized law ... (and) embodied the customary law of the land. Money, however, was not plentiful, and only a few could get possession of it ... Peasants had been unable to keep pace with the other classes ... (as) the whole system of transacting business had changed. Debtors ... were liable to forfeit their freedom on the failure to satisfy the usurers.[2]

Human culture developed around food accumulation and establishment of shelter. Until recently, all cultures were primarily rural and survived off of natural resources alone.

It wasn't until the late 1850s that the United States shifted from primarily rural to a developing urban economy, facilitated largely by the standardization of weights, measures, and money. The 1860 U.S. Census

---

[2] Wolfson, Arthur Mayer, *Essentials in Ancient History, from the Earliest Records to Charlemagne,* 1902, American Book Company, pp. 91–92.

estimated 48.2 percent of the population lived on farms.[3] This was the first time in U.S. history that the farming population dropped below half. A century and a half later, very few farmers fed nearly all of the population.

When *Relating to Ancient Culture*, old is a term defined by comparing to recent social functions. Because agriculture was the primary economic activity, it is relevant then to compare the 1800s transition to the twenty-first century.

Over the centuries, an organized flow and availability of money created population shifts.

By 2007, approximately 85 percent of U.S. agricultural production came from less than 200,000 largely family-owned farms. The United States Department of Agriculture (USDA) considers 91 percent of all farms to be "small farms." Those living on economically viable farms account for less than 1 percent of the population. Small farms control more than half the land in farms, and because of tax laws and regulations small farms receive 46 percent of government support payments. Very small farmers, 60 percent of all U.S. farms, sell less than $10,000 per year. (Obviously, they are not economically viable farms.)[4] The urges of rural life represented in the smaller farms are the link between thousands of years of natural history and today's increasingly artificial society (a society dependent on non–life-sustaining needs).

Through efficiencies created from a lack of available labor, rural living in the United States switched from necessity to a lifestyle choice. Seldom is it the best economic choice to live in rural areas, causing many to tend toward urban life.

Additionally, universal availability of money further facilitated urbanization and caused an addiction to wants throughout "developed" culture.

As the oldest son of parents raised on farms during the 1930s Great Depression, I was taught to spend on needs before wants. After I became an adult and left home at eighteen, my brothers occasionally repeated a story to exemplify lessons our parents instilled in us.

---

[3] *Growing a Nation, The Story of American Agriculture, Ag In the Classroom,* http://www.agclassroom.org/gan/timeline/1860.htm (Sourced February 9, 2017)

[4] *2007 Census of Agriculture, Small Farms,* United States Department of Agriculture, https://www.agcensus.usda.gov/Publications/2007/Online_Highlights/Fact_Sheets/Farm_Numbers/small_farm.pdf (Sourced March 13, 2017)

I was fourteen and a freshman in high school in the fall of 1967. One fall day after the school bus dropped five of my siblings and me in our farmyard, I began asking our parents to allow me to go to Kansas City, Missouri, for a week to attend the Future Farmers of America (FFA) national convention. Our parents had never been south of South Dakota, nor had they ever traveled six hundred miles away from the farm. However, since our family had always been farmers, I was the oldest boy and likely to take over the family farm. Also, since my father had to quit school at age 14 to run the farm for my disabled grandfather, my parents knew it was a good idea for me to attend the convention. The problem was I had no money, and they could not afford to send me. Although the transportation and lodging were sponsored by local agricultural businesses and our high school's Vocational Agricultural (Vo-Ag) program, food was not.

Perhaps they heard me trying to memorize the first sentence of the FFA Creed:

> I believe in the future of agriculture, with a faith born not of words but of deeds–achievements won by the present and past generations of agriculturists; in the promise of better days through better ways, even as the better things we now enjoy have come to us from the struggles of former years.[5]

The FFA motto provides a simpler lesson in culture and economics: "Learning to Do, Doing to Learn, Earning to Live, and Living to Serve."

I had been driving our team of horses, tractors, and a pickup truck for years, so at fourteen our parents knew I was responsible enough to keep out of trouble and get by with what I had or had been given. On a Monday morning in late October, I left for Kansas City with all my parents' cash, $20, and I excitedly jumped into our local Vo-Ag instructor's car with four other students and headed south.

Fast-forwarding five or six years found me in the U.S. Air Force in Italy. My parents would teach the same lessons to my siblings. While sitting at the supper table, they described my first trip from home and how

---

[5] Erwin Milton "E.M." Tiffany of Lyndon, Kansas, wrote the original FFA Creed and the current version was adopted by the organized body of delegates in 1991 as chartered by the United States Congress.

they fretted day after day about how Gary would have to eat all week on $20. Parents teach lessons in many ways. The lesson that night was: "When Gary returned he gave us back the money he did not spend, $12 and some change."

As I was writing this book, one of my brothers brought up the story, and asked me how I ate all week on less than $8. He asked, "Did you cut out pop (our colloquial term for carbonated soda or soft drink)?" I responded: "Pop is never a necessity."

Divergence of ancient to modern culture is as simple as understanding the difference between a "want" and a "need." Money is the denominator.

When money becomes scarce, a migration occurs from urban to rural as it did during the 1930s' U.S. Great Depression. Shortly thereafter, the trend toward urbanization continued. Following Mao Tse-Tung's (a.k.a. Zedong) (1893–1976) failed experiment of collective farms as a Communist dictator, China's economy awakened to the late twentieth century with rural migrants seeking employment as city construction and factory workers. Operating from a base of unlimited low-cost labor, China built its twenty-first-century economy on exports. As Chinese exports softened in the early 2000s, unemployment rose, and older temporary migrants (remembering their survival skills on the farm) returned to their rural villages where sustenance replaced wages. Those who grew into adulthood fed by money, lost their ability to feed themselves. They remained in cities addicted to money, which was not a life-sustaining need. Hence, money initiated an artificial society.

Since the Industrial Revolution (1760–1840) with distributed currency, other countries, beginning in Western Europe, shifted from rural to urban. China only recently made the shift between 2010 and 2015 with an urbanization rate at 3 percent per year with 55.6 percent considered urban in 2015.[6] China, like other developing countries given the distribution of money, is experiencing a cultural shift of confusing wants and needs.

---

[6] China, The World Factbook, United States Central Intelligence Agency (CIA), https://www.cia.gov/library/publications/the-world-factbook/geos/ch.html (Sourced February 13, 2017)

Until my great-grandparent's generation (born in the 1860s into 1880s), world cultural experiences developed from family and agriculture. What other phenomenon affected a person's cultural experiences?

RELIGION: WHERE ART THOU?

Religion is as old as human history. Religion, or the lack of it, has shaped cultures and still does. China currently is about 18.2 percent Buddhist, 5.1 percent Christian, 1.8 percent Muslim, and a few minor religions with 52.2 percent considered "unaffiliated" with a religion.[7] U.S. colonies, beginning with the Mayflower Pilgrims (1620), were founded on religious (Christian) separatism. The percentage of U.S. citizens unaffiliated with any religion is growing with current estimates at 78.4 percent Christian, 4.7 percent non-Christian (the largest segment being 1.7 percent Jewish) with about 16.1 percent "unaffiliated" with religion (including about 1.6% atheist).[8]

The lack of a personal religion is growing and affects culture. When a society blurs the distinction of morality, ethics, and personal responsibility taught through religion, inevitably crime and dependency results.

Since the advent of script, more has been written about religion than any other topic. Hence, I will keep the religion category short.

Besides family, agriculture, money, and religion, what else through the centuries affected culture?

CONFLICT: PERSONAL TO IMPERSONAL

Into the twenty-first century, militarization shaped the culture of human history. Human conflict has been recorded since Moses wrote in the Pentateuch nearly 3500 years ago, ". . . Cain rose up against Abel his brother and killed him."[9]

---

[7] Ibid.

[8] Americans Changing Religious Landscape, May 12, 2015, Pew Research Center, http://www.pewforum.org/2015/05/12/americas-changing-religious-landscape/ (Sourced February 13, 2017)

[9] Genesis 4:8, *The Holy Bible, New King James Version (NKJV)*, Thomas Nelson, Inc. 1994, p. 5. The first five books of the Holy Bible's Old Testament have been historically referred to as the Pentateuch.

Historically, man fought man. Eventually, man used tools and machines to fight against other men and their equipment. It remained an interpersonal[10] relationship until the mid-twentieth century when intercontinental ballistics and twenty-first-century drones intercepted human relations allowing cultures to divorce physical, abutting contact between combatants. Thereafter, women were phased into the military labor pool.

In a period I can relate to from the time my grandfather was born (1891), the United States fought many wars. First with Native Americans (e.g., Apache–1851–1900; Yaqui–1896–1918) then the Spanish-American War (1898), Philippine-American War (1899–1902), Moro Rebellion (1899–1913), Boxer (China) Rebellion (1899–1901), Mexican Border War (1910–1919), and World War I (WWI, 1917–1918).

My great-grandfather, Henry, was born before the Civil War. After the Civil War (1861–1865) nearly everyone in the United States was touched by conflict. "The War to end all wars" was supposedly WWI. Native uprisings were past, borders were secure, expansionism was over. Roman literature indicates Europeans had been fighting for thousands of years. U.S. isolationism after World War I prevailed for years. One of my grandfathers in 1911 escaped the Soviet Bolshevik uprising in South Russia (now the Ukraine), and the other also just wanted to farm in peace. Another massive skirmish in the late 1930s into the 1940s was one the United States wanted to avoid at all cost.

It was not to be so. Expansionist Japan decided China, Korea, and other Pacific Rim countries were not satisfying its appetite for control. Their next target would be the United States. Most think Japan's bombing of Hawaii's Pearl Harbor (December 7, 1941) was only a massive military success. Wars are not won by only exchanging bullets. Determining culture, the minds of the controllers and the controlled must be at peace.

Two things happened that terrible December day (less than twelve years before I was born). Japan not only thought it could destroy the U.S.'s Pacific fleet and control the strategic Hawaiian Islands, but also

---

[10] Interpersonal refers to relationships between persons, whereas impersonal means without a personal connection with another.

that it could further suppress the United States' will to fight. Pearl Harbor's Sunday surprise attack was therefore both a geographic move and a psychological one.

Bombs were successful in destroying most of the American ships in the Harbor, and Japan had control of more people than lived in the United States. However, "the war to end all wars" was no longer a dream. Japan's psychological strike on Pearl Harbor was not the last attempt at mind control of the American public. Utilizing the west-to-east jet stream that brings volcanic particles and airborne pollutants from Japan, China, and other volcanic, populous Far-Eastern countries was converted to a psychological jet-stream weapons system carrying dangerous balloons. During World War II, Japan lofted over 9000 hydrogen balloons into the jet stream, each carrying more than a hundred pounds of anti-personnel explosives accompanied by incendiary bombs and devices. They were designed to kill people, but were primarily psychological weapons to create massive fear of unstoppable forest and prairie fires. Several hundred explosive hydrogen balloons reached Canada and the United States with only six deaths from one incident and limited physical collateral damage. Psychological collateral damage was limited as a result of military and media suppression of the massive balloon attack.

Japan's strategy was not a new one. Balloons had been used in the Far East for war support for a couple thousand years. The Han Dynasty (2006 B.C. to 220 A.D.) invented the Kongming paper lanterns. For later reference, please note that the paper "sky lanterns" were used 2000 years before American schools used toilet paper. It seems like a digression but remember history, inventions, and culture connect. Additionally, Chinese military strategist, Zhuge Liang (a.k.a. Kongming 181–234 A.D.), used paper lanterns for battle signals.

However, Japan's hydrogen balloons were the first intercontinental weapons. What started as a signal system, began impersonal wars.

The United States fought in World War II (1941–1945), the Korean War (1950–1953), the Vietnam War (1965–1975), the Gulf War (1990–1991), the war in Afghanistan (2001–present), the war in Iraq (2003–2011), and the ongoing battle with Islamic State of Iraq and the Levant (ISIL) from 2014 to the present. Other countries have their own involvement list of international conflicts, civil wars, rebellions, and uprisings.

Throughout the twentieth century, most of the world's population has been involved in wars either by fighting on the front lines or as support. Women and disabled men left at home had to produce food and maintain shelter for their children, aging parents, and for fighting men and boys. Even children learned lessons of war. Those warring person-to-person have no time to produce food. Families, though abandoned for a time, or permanently, are affected by national and international conflict.

Travesties of war were personal and acted as a natural resistance to entering the next conflict. *Impersonal* battles have turned blood and mayhem into a video game.

Interpersonal wars required discipline and responsibilities that had a lasting cultural impact on families and communities, much more so than impersonal wars fought with incendiary bombs, intercontinental ballistic missiles (ICBM), drones, and electronic and cyber warfare.

As with agricultural efficiency mentioned earlier, military efficiencies requiring less people shifted from personal contact to remotely operated impersonal infliction during my lifetime.

"Cybernation" was a term coined by D.N. Michael (1923–2000) of the Peace Research Institute in 1961 which led to the term "cyberculture" for its manufacturing and process changes as well as social, political, military, and cultural impact on people. Impersonal "cyber" warfare did not even enter military lexicon until the late twentieth century.

With the development of digital technology, cyber incursions became more frequent on companies, universities, governments, militaries, and infrastructure with December 23, 2015, being the first successful international cyber attack on a country's electrical power grid. (Russia blacked out part of the Ukraine.) Computerized cyber conflicts have become impersonal as evidenced by today's social media causing stress and even suicide on innocent participants.

Throughout human history, family, agriculture, money, religion, and interpersonal militarization were the five major factors that shaped family and community culture. When did these historic factors get realigned?

As pointed out above, countries have urbanized as adult children moved into cities with decreasing emphasis on religion and the phasing out of man-to-man military conflict. Invention of telecommunications (telegraph–1837) allowed regular contact without physical presence. Similarly, transportation changed with the invention of the internal combustion engine (1790s) and the airplane (1903), allowing families to increasingly separate upon adulthood.

As family, agriculture, and religion played decreasing roles in cultural development, replacing person-to-person warring has lowered the percent of a country's population directly affected by wars. What then has been replacing and shaping family and community culture the last few generations?

Personal, family, and public responsibilities are reverting to a new paradigm. It is a cultural riddle. For clues, please continue to follow me on my journey *Relating to Ancient Culture.*

2

Ancient

Riddle: What delays maturity, can take two decades to ferment, and consumes, but is not consumable?

Are things different today compared with ancient times? Ancient is relative. A scholar of history considers the Iron Age ancient. Teenagers may be overheard calling their parents "ancient." Ancient has many definitions but no age.

XVIII AMENDMENT

At the end of the 1920s my paternal grandfather was nearly forty years old. He thought the 1920s generation was "going to hell in a hand basket" with their music, dress, and worst of all their drinking. He was a prohibitionist.

The XVIII Amendment to the U.S. Constitution (that's 18th Amendment for those not schooled in Roman Numerals like we were) took effect January 17, 1920. During prohibition, all forms of alcohol were illegal to sell, transport, or produce, except for personal medical or religious use. For the only time in U.S constitutional history, in 1933, enough states approved the XXI Amendment to completely repeal an entire former amendment, the XVIII. My grandfather was never happy about the reversal.

My father, Walter F. Wietgrefe Jr., passed away nearly forty years ago, but he told a story about my grandmother, Minnie, making some homemade wine in the basement from excess fruit when she had no more fruit jars in which to can it. My parents, who lived on a farm a half-mile north, were at my grandparents one evening. Grandmother asked if they wanted to try her homemade wine. In the fall of 1951, being twenty and twenty-two, my parents agreed they would try some.

My grandmother went to her dirt basement, brought up an old clear-glass gallon vinegar jug of wine. It was hush-hush as she didn't want my grandfather to know about it. Apparently, it was quite good. After a couple glasses, everyone was very "spirited." My grandfather, listening from the bedroom, eventually "blew a cork." The party ended. My folks went home. Grandma likely slept on the couch that night.

In the mid-1960s my grandfather left the Lutheran Church to become Baptist. It is highly unlikely for a man in his seventies, to change churches. Lutherans served wine at communion; Baptists served grape juice. Grandfather was a prohibitionist to the end.

As anecdotes often indicate, many things are learned at home, from religious interaction, and cooperating or opposing civil authority.

LEGAL AGE

When I turned eighteen, in February 1971, I could not vote. I could drink 3.2% beer, but not hard liquor or wine until I was twenty-one. I was a wrestler in high school. To keep fit, I did not smoke or drink, although I do admit to having a half-can of nonalcoholic orange pop when I was a senior. The Vietnam War was going full blast. During World War II, thirty years earlier, President Roosevelt lowered the "conscription" age (military draft) to eighteen. Mainly as a voter response to war protests of President Lyndon Johnson's (1903–1978) escalation in Vietnam, the XXVI Amendment (the right for 18-year-olds to vote) was approved by enough states to take effect July 1, 1971, exactly one hundred days after Congress sent it to the states for ratification. It remains the quickest amendment ever ratified. "If you are old enough to fight, you are old enough to vote" was the popular slogan across the country, especially college campuses when I was in high school.

Voting was important, but so was drinking. The axiom expanded to: "If you were old enough to fight, you were old enough to vote, and if you were old enough to vote, you were old enough to drink."

By the fall of 1971, I had volunteered to join the U.S. Air Force. After Basic Training, as a service member, I could drink alcohol on base even though states like Kansas still had "dry counties." The military allowed alcohol under regulation. For example, in 1973 when I was stationed in Misawa, Japan, the "chow hall" had a beer machine in the entryway. It was the same as a soda machine, except the beer cost more—a quarter a can.

Times were different then. We could even talk about God on government property. My job was a printer systems intercept operator. Without revealing our top secret work, our motto, which hung on a bare concrete block wall, summarized our work: "In God we trust; all others we monitor. We haven't found God's frequency yet, but we are still searching." Nearly every document we handled was classified "Secret" or "Top Secret." Operational policy was that we should not have more than two cans of beer during lunch when working.

I've been voting and drinking since July 1, 1971—of course in moderation.

Even when not consuming alcohol, individuals of each generation tend to think they are more advanced, more understanding, smarter, and more educated than previous generations. Those assumptions make us better people than our ancestors, especially societies, a century or more ago. Those who lived four thousand years ago are therefore in an ignorant category that is hard to fathom how dumb and technologically inept they were. Some Stone Age people lived in caves, hence the term "caveman," which is a slang reference for someone dumb because these people were so much less advanced than we are today. Right?

Let us compare generational knowledge. Can you make iron?

You can ask your friends for help. No looking on the Internet.[1] Any idiot born before 1969 A.D. knows the Internet was not around before iron.

---

[1] Schneider, Gary, Jessica Evans, Katherine Pinard, "The Internet—Illustrated"; Four universities in 1969 developed the Advanced Research Projects Agency Network, (ARPANET), the first shared computer network from which the public Internet was developed. Cengage Learning, 2009 https://books.google.co.uk/books?id=Y HwQ9WpvHfEC&pg=PA6&dq=ARPANET&hl=en&sa=X&ved=0CEAQ6AEwBjg KahUKEwiUh5yyhKvHAhVKF9sKHessDV0#v=onepage&q=ARPANET&f=false (Sourced August 22, 2015)

How about this: Can you and your friends make bronze?

OK, I will give you an easier problem. Can you and your friends make copper?

What? You can't.

If not, you and your friends are dumber than a caveman.

People in the Stone Age were smelting copper. Paleolithic and Neolithic Stone Age people[2] only lived into their twenties, maybe early thirties, and they invented copper tools followed by bronze, a harder metal, made from a combination of several metals. Life was hard. Life expectancy was only thirty when iron was developed.

One sometimes shakes his head in disbelief. Have societies advanced?

People are certainly maturing later. Minds are developing at a slower pace than previous centuries.

Many American children are living at home, in their mid-twenties, going to school, and qualify as children under their parents' health insurance. Technically, they are adults, but politically they are treated as children.[3] Most consider themselves smart, some have master's degrees, but they cannot support themselves. Stone Age people were senior citizens at that age.

In 2014, life expectancy in the United States was 78.8 years (76.4 for men and 81.2 for women).[4]

Is someone living at home mature?

If the parents are paying university tuition, the house payment/rent, utilities and food, providing a car to their twenty-five-year-old live-at-home student, the student is not mature and the parents are incompetent. At least they are incompetent at weaning. At the current rate of immaturity, the United States may have to amend the Constitution again to raise the minimum voting age to twenty-six.

---

[2] Age of Paleolithic, Neolithic, Stone Age. https://en.wikipedia.org/wiki/Bronze_Age (Sourced August 22, 2015)

[3] Adult: "A person who has reached an age set by law that qualifies him for full legal rights, in common law generally 21 years," *Webster's New World Dictionary*, Second College Edition, Simon and Schuster, 1982, p. 19.

[4] Murphy, Sherry L., Kenneth D. Kochanek, Jiaquan Xu, Elizabeth Arias, "Mortality in the United States, 2014," National Center of Health Statistics, Centers for Disease Control and Prevention, U.S. Department of Health and Human Services, Data Brief No. 229, December 2015, http://www.cdc.gov/nchs/data/databriefs/db229.pdf (Sourced August 20, 2016)

At what age does a person have the maturity to expect someone else to respect his or her opinions?

Someone going through puberty may expect to be respected, but it is legitimate to write off his or her opinions as a hormone imbalance. Someone not living off their own income should not be expected to be respected; therefore, they can be written off as financially imbalanced.

He, who does not contribute to a family's financial sustenance, certainly is not competent to provide for the country's sustenance. Thus, their voting rights should be denied—in the family and country. Right?

Am I being too crass to the incompetent? At what point is someone competent to speak for others? Each society must establish that criteria. Some have done it through dictatorships, monarchies, and many forms of nonrepresentative government. When incompetence rules society or a culture, the bell tolls signaling change.

We are not cavemen, but few today can make metal even though many ancient civilizations in diverse geographies had metallurgy. Metal was better than stone tools. Even the Stone Age cavemen, without books, developed and passed on technology and art. Do we pass on knowledge early in life with the same efficiency? It's questionable.

Ancient learning systems relied on memorization—a lifelong asset. Writing, a pseudo-retrospection, was the first invention to replace memory.

Bronze (<3000 B.C.) was developed after copper, and iron succeeded bronze when technology spread using memory. So, one may say our learning efficiency, retained development, and perhaps our natural intelligence, is less developed now than those living 5000 years ago when a leap of technology appeared.

Could it be that many parents are not smart enough, or too lazy, to teach their preschoolers? Academics think so. Are there other reasons?

Though often attributed to the ever-witty Benjamin Franklin (1706–1790), truth is apparent no matter who said:

"We are all born ignorant, but one must work hard to remain stupid."

3

Family Learning

Riddle: What does not give birth, does not love, is carnal, but before celebrating the end serves as the family undertaker?

Not everyone has the privilege of being a father or mother. Some of us have been fortunate to be stepfathers and stepmothers. When my paternal grandfather was in his thirties he married a divorcee who had two boys and a girl, the youngest. The boys were old enough to remain and help their father. The girl, raised by her mother, was adopted by my grandfather and carried the Wietgrefe name throughout high school, graduating in 1939 ten years after my father was born.

My grandfather's formal education ended at grade 8. My father had to quit school during grade 10 to help farm. His only other sister completed high school in a private Lutheran academy in 1951 a year after my mother. Fortunately, after the two girls met, my father and mother were introduced and produced seven children.

With lots of cousins and step cousins, all were treated like grandchildren by my grandfather and grandmother.

Shortly after I started first grade, my grandmother passed. At age twenty-three I was selected administrator of my grandfather's estate. I can testify that my cousins and I received several times more inheritance than my father. Why? Did my grandfather like his grandchildren and step-grandchildren more than my father? Likely not.

My grandfather sold the family farm to my father, which allowed my grandfather to have an estate to distribute. Did my father feel badly? If he did, he never showed it. That is character. One never knows the will of someone, but that will and knowledge passed on is worth more than money.

Money earned is worth more than inheritance. Physical and mental work is a process of learning. Inheritance is not love. Similarly, it does not pass on knowledge.

Often we hear "schools need more money," "it's for the children," or "let's not deprive them." If more money is needed to build a bigger school, at what point is learning optimized?

Grades 1 through 4 I spent in one-room country schools with about fifty square feet total per student. Is fifty square feet per student adequate or optimum? If fifty were adequate, given a hundred square feet would I have increased my knowledge a hundred percent? It takes money to build, maintain, and staff larger schools. Where is learning optimized?

Imagine how smart kids must be now in schools with two or three hundred square feet per student.

It is not money that educates children, just like it is not an inheritance that transfers knowledge to the next generation to establish culture.

Those born in the mid-twentieth century into the twenty-first century are unique. In the history of the world, a significant percentage of children in our generation were old enough to know and learn from their great-grandparents, great-uncles, and great-aunts. Previously, few children have ever had three living generations to pass on cultural knowledge, also known as the generational record.

GENERATIONAL RECORD

What is the generational record?

According to Guinness World Records' store of knowledge called *Officially Amazing*,[1]

---

[1] "Most Living Generations (ever)," Officially Amazing, Guinness World Records, http://www.guinnessworldrecords.com/world-records/most-living-generations-(ever)/ (Sourced December 9, 2015)

The most generations alive in a single family has been seven. The youngest great-great-great-great-grandparent being Augusta Bunge (USA) age 109 years 97 days, followed by her daughter age 89, her grand-daughter age 70, her great-grand-daughter age 52, her great-great grand-daughter age 33 and her great-great-great grand-daughter age 15 on the birth of her great-great-great-great grandson on 21 January 1989.

Each generation conceived when they were young. Interestingly, the oldest, Augusta Bunge, was twenty when her daughter was born. One might say those ladies have seen a lot of water passed under the generational bridge in 109 years. What did the water under the bridge contain? Who knows, but it passed with each generation and culture remained through generational interaction.

Augusta Bunge was eleven when my grandfather was born, and he died at age eighty-five. If he had lived to one hundred nine like Ms. Bunge, grandpa would have only seen a few of his great-great grandchildren—five generations.

To increase the chances of passing on three generations of knowledge, there must be generational interaction, long life expectancy, retention of intellect, and couples must bear children when young. This no longer seems to be happening. Why? Distance of families from each other, age of childbearing, and level of formal education are all contributors to this cultural shift.

Now, early in the twenty-first century, couples or children move great distances from where they were born, get married when they are older, and begin having children later. For example, my oldest nephew was forty-one when he had his first child; his wife gave birth about a week before she turned forty. They are not unique. Consequently, the chance of their children knowing and learning from three or four previous generations is diminished as the older die or are segregated preventing interaction of old and young.

Disease, accidents, sustained nutritional deficiencies, and dementia are examples of how age increases the chances of losing mental skills. Communication and transportation technology has also segregated generations. Without intimate progression through mental and physical contact, future generations are losing the ability to pick up cognitive skills from their living ancestors, but a great-great-aunt can pass on her hugs. The very youngest may learn the most from the way she hugged. If she lives on the opposite coast, without personal contact she can pass on a bit of her knowledge, but understanding, feelings, or hugs are not electronically transferable. Simply, you cannot hug viewing grandma on a computer or smartphone or receive the same cultural benefit from her.

One should never underestimate what children learn from aunts, uncles, and grandparents.

For example, I was out of grade school when my paternal great-grand-mother died and out of high school when my maternal great-grand-mother passed. I knew them. Until the mid-twentieth century life expectancy was too short to have a large percentage of four living generations. Before Internet became widely used (late 1990s) photo albums throughout the country were packed with pages of four, five, even six generations of photos. Also, into the mid-twentieth century parents followed custom and began having children when they were young–late teens to early twenties. Those grandparents and great grandparents often lived nearby for regular personal contact.

Social skills, word usage, accents, career interests, physical movements, and care for others are examples of learning through close family contact.

Lesson XIV in a fourth-grade school *Reader* published in 1885 entitled "Humanity Rewarded" hints at how information is passed from generation to generation. The short story is about Joseph II (1741–1790), Emperor of Germany. He was twenty-four when his father died, but was co-regent (domain rulers) of the Habsburg area with his mother until she died in 1765 when he became Holy Roman Emperor. Joseph II died at forty-eight but outlived two wives and had no living children. That did not keep him from observing the vigilant and teaching, caring for others, and passing on aspects of culture.

Although he became sole ruler 263 years after Dr. Martin Luther began the Christian Reformation in 1517 (A.D.), Joseph II remained an extension of the Catholic Church, but he was also a reformer allowing more religious freedom for Jews, Protestants, Lutherans, and Greek Orthodox.

Lesson XIV: Humanity Rewarded:[2]

1. Joseph Second, Emperor of Germany, once received a petition in favor of a poor and superannuated officer, with a family of ten children, who was reduced to the utmost poverty.

2. After making inquiries respecting the man, and satisfying himself of his worth, the emperor determined to judge of his necessities by personal observation.

3. Accordingly, he went alone to the house of the officer, whom he found seated at table, with eleven children around him, dining upon vegetables of his own planting.

4. The Emperor, who was disguised as a private citizen, after some general conversation with the officer, said: "I heard you had ten children, but I see here eleven."

5. "This," replied the officer, pointing to one, "is a poor orphan, whom I found at my door. I have endeavored to obtain for him the assistance of persons who could better afford to provide for him, but have not been able to succeed; and of course I could do no better than to share my little portion with him."

6. The Emperor, admiring the generous humanity of the poor man, immediately made himself known to him, and said, "I desire that all these children may be made my pensioners, and that you will continue to give them examples of virtue and honor.

7. "I grant you one hundred florins per annum, for each and also, and addition of two hundred florins to your pension. Go tomorrow to my treasurer, where you will receive the first quarter's payment, together with a lieutenant's commission for your eldest son. Henceforth I will be the father of all the family."

Are children today required to read such wisdom? Who is passing it on?

Countries have always had struggles, broken apart, reformed. The same can be said for families and marriages. It is the innocent subsequent generations that learn from the rights and wrongs of the past. Albert Pike died in 1891, eighty-nine days before my grandfather was

---

[2] Embury, Emma C., "Lesson XIV: Humanity Rewarded," *Sheldons' Modern School Fourth Reader*, Sheldon and Company, 1885, pp. 46–47.

born, but Pike, the soldier, Civil War veteran, lawyer, and writer passed on his wisdom: "What we have done for ourselves alone dies with us; what we have done for others and the world remains and is immortal."

Knowledge relayed by a parent, aunt, grandfather, or great-grandmother is not always verbal. A hug or the smell of grandma's banana bread is not spoken or heard, but it is deeply felt. Feelings are passed on through more hugs and memories of cooking, tinkering in the woodshed, or learning other intangible things. Little things like setting the table or how to cook sauce are educational.

My great-grandma Wagner had a very small home—too small for our large family. Our stops were often only for a few hours and we generally played outside. On the corner of the house was her water cistern fed from the house downspout. When Selby, South Dakota, built a water tower only the wealthier people could afford running water in their house. Like many others, great-grandma collected and rationed cistern water for her daily needs. To avoid falling through the top, us kids learned danger by command: "Stay off the cistern."

The cistern was like an established life lesson: When digging yourself a hole, stop digging before you cannot crawl out. Don't play on the cistern as you might drown from your own foolishness.

Great-grandma had a drop-leaf table, perhaps a foot wide and a yard across. Folded, it was too small for one person to comfortably eat from. With both sides flipped up, it made a comfortable setting for four with children tucked between.

Two hinges connected the drop leaves. The center support board under the table had a small cutout that pivoted on a nail. By lifting a side, the pivoted wood rotated horizontally and rested in place on a beveled piece of wood to hold up each side, thus defying gravity. The lesson: "Move the beveled wood strip in to make the leaves level." Likewise, a twelve-inch table could be converted into a thirty-six-inch circumference dining table in a few seconds.

When we ate there, my sister, eleven months older than me, could help great-grandma by putting the tablecloth on the table. The square, approximately thirty-inch cloth did not cover the table. Why have a tablecloth if the plates do not sit where four people do?

"Turn the cloth like this."

Each corner of the thirty-inch cloth hung over the edge of the thirty-six-inch diameter table exactly where each plate was set.

How can that be? The cloth was too small.

Square cloth napkins would be folded in a triangle with a fork, knife, and spoon placed in order on the napkin next to the plate on the edge of the tablecloth that should have been too small. Somehow they all fit perfectly.

Ten years later in geometry class I would learn that the square napkins were folded forming an isosceles triangle of two equal sides with the long side called the "hypotenuse" (opposite the right angle). The small tablecloth fit under the plates because the measurement from one corner to the far corner across the cloth was longer than the sides of the cloth. Had the thirty-inch square tablecloth been folded like the napkin, the hypotenuse would have been 42.4 inches long, which was enough for corners to droop over the edge under each place setting of the thirty-six-inch diameter table.

When great-grandma told my five-year-old sister and me to "Set the table," we had already learned how to follow directions, proper placement and manners for setting a table, plus some carpentry, engineering, physics, and geometry. That information is simply not passed on by interfacing with a grandma over today's computers.

As great-grandma Wagner aged, her mind faded into dementia and she completed her years in a rest home. My younger brothers cannot remember sitting at her table. Her knowledge was not lost. Great-aunt Clara, the middle daughter, outlived two husbands, had always lived nearby, and cared for great-grandma Wagner's house into her nineties.

Great-aunt Clara, while downsizing her two homes, sold her mother's drop-leaf table to my wife, Patricia, and me. We used it regularly. Patricia hosted tea for Darleen (great-aunt Clara's only child) using Clara's pink flowered dishes.

Darleen asked her mother on her ninety-ninth birthday if she was going to live to one hundred. With clarity of mind, she responded, "Oh, I suppose." She died not knowing the teaching tool (drop-leaf table) passed to her great-great-great-grandniece.

Passed from generation to generation, we often learn from elders what may never be taught in school. Table settings were learned and passed to each generation. It is more customary now to eat on the run or separately in front of the television. Formality, discipline, tradition, and "family time" are being lost to electronic devices.

School always began around September first and ended in late May. It still does. Once I asked a teacher why schools had a summer break. I was told that back when the school system was being set up our country was mostly agrarian. The break allowed farm children to help plant and harvest. That sounded logical to a teenager. As I got older I realized the teacher fed me a bunch of malarkey. She obviously never grew up on a farm.

Farm kids, like us, had chores morning and night—before school, after school, or no school. Furthermore, how could we plant and harvest? Field and garden planting was completed across the country, north-to-south, east-to-west before children got out of school in late May. Except for cool-season crops, like radishes and small grain, the fall harvest of most crops did not begin until after fall classes started.

Even harvest holidays are celebrated at different times based on latitude and harvest schedules. In the United States, we celebrate Thanksgiving on the fourth Thursday of November. The original holiday was a three-day celebration of the harvest by the Pilgrims in1621. Crops differ and harvest closes earlier in Canada. Canadians celebrate the fall harvest blessing the second Monday in October.

If the school year was initially established to educate an agrarian economy, why are we still using the same system with less than 1 percent of our country's children living on viable farms?

Likely, the school year was determined and maintained for some other purpose. Were schools too hot? No air-conditioning then? Were teachers exhausted? Had student learning peaked?

Now children are told they need more classroom time. School learning, as explained in my book *Relating to Ancient Learning*, was more efficient when societies were mostly rural and agrarian. Historically, family learning consumed far more time than formal training. Independence was encouraged. During the twentieth century, a significant transition occurred to decrease family interaction and increase organized learning. Are children now spending too much time in school and organized activities? What is the proper balance?

The quest for knowledge is of higher value if not constantly exposed to it. Perhaps that is one reason why our ancestors set the school year at nine months rather than twelve. Summer, Christmas/New Year, and spring breaks allow students and teachers to rejuvenate and increase learning in more worldly environments.

A short weekend break is good, but not the same as a two-week vacation. Summer break was an efficient interlude. Likewise, it is more exciting to learn from grandpa or grandma if they are not around all the time. At least that's how it was when I was a kid.

4

Basic Training

Riddle: What hunts, calls the shots, offers bounty, and can be a military substitute?

Our family has been hunters for several generations. Grandpa Wietgrefe used to lean against his 1940-something car with his 12-guage Winchester pump-action shotgun as we flushed pheasants from his one hundred acres of Soil Bank[1] in the 1950s and early 1960s.

My father bought his first single-shot .22 caliber rifle for $12.98 as a teenager in the 1940s. Guns were affordable then and it was not unusual for a teenager to purchase one.

Growing up on the South Dakota Missouri River bluffs north of Akaska (not Alaska) in the 1930s and 1940s my mother learned to be quite a shot. With a single small .22 bullet from my father's rifle, mother killed several skunks that wandered into our farmyard. Sometimes, she would open the kitchen window to shoot. She did not want potentially rabid skunks around us kids and farm animals.

---

[1] Soil Bank (Title I of the Agricultural Act of 1956) was a U.S. Department of Agricultural program to "... increase net farm income (by) ... reducing production of basic crops, maintaining farm income, and conserving soil ... (through) voluntary land retirement through acreage rental payments to farmers." See: "Brief History of the USDA Soil Bank Program," Natural Resources Conservation Program, U.S. Department of Agriculture, http://www.nrcs.usda.gov/wps/portal/nrcs/detailfull/national/about/history/?cid=stelprdb1045667 (Sourced September 18, 2015)

Shooting out the kitchen window is not a big deal. However, as revealed in the next chapter, even for a farm family, a maturing girl seldom gets a rifle for her fourth birthday. Of course, we did not grow up in central Alaska.

It was also not unusual for our family to carry bullets. Shells have shown up in places that surprise people.

BASIC BULLETS

My brother, Mark, joined the U.S. Air Force in the summer of 1972–a year after I entered. He had a few hours to kill before he flew out of Aberdeen, South Dakota, so he took Dad's .22 and went to the pasture gopher hunting.

I'm not sure when or why the gopher bounty started, but since us six Wietgrefe boys were old enough to trap, we have been after pasture gophers. They are pests whose digging created mounds of dirt and gravel in the pasture and hay fields which would break the hay mowers. Each minute not mowing was time the farm wasn't making money, especially during harvest. Additionally, cows from our beef or dairy herd would step into a gopher hole and go lame. Pasturing a lame cow is an unwelcome expense to a farmer.

In the 1960s and early 1970s gopher tails were worth a nickel each when delivered to our Edmunds County Courthouse Treasurer's office. Nickel a tail was good cash bounty for poor farm boys.

Tails were the smallest, easily identifiable, least smelly portions of the gopher to claim the bounty. Although fresh gopher tails kept in a baby-food jar could get a bit ripe after a couple weeks, we did punch nail holes in the lid for aeration.

Another good thing about gopher tails is that if we forgot to take the tails out of our pants pockets before Mom or sister, Susan, would wash our blue jeans, the tails would not disintegrate. We could claim a clean bounty on our valuable five-cent tails.

No one really knew why the gopher bounty started but let's get back to Mark: He was a good shot and picked off several gophers before flying to San Antonio, Texas, to start Air Force Basic Training.

If you had been through military basic training, you understand how drill sergeants can, and will, look for opportunities to intimidate you. Their voices are amazingly clear to me, even today.

During my first hour of basic training, our squadron had about five minutes to open our suitcases and put our civilian clothes, shoes, rings, watches, and anything civilian into it for six weeks of storage.

Unfortunately for me, I had a thumb-sized padlock on the zipper. I'll be darned if my key would open it. About fifteen seconds into my struggle, a muscular 5'5" 210 lb. Sergeant Cervantes was standing over my suitcase and me SCREAMING: "Open it NOW you F---ing idiot! What do you think? Don't trust us? Open that F---ing thing NOW or I'll Jap slap the hell out of you boy."

Sixty other guys likely did not look up for fear of being "Jap slapped."

Brother Mark tells of a similar experience in his basic training. Before he could put his "civvies" into his suitcase, Mark had to empty his pockets onto his bunkbed's olive green wool blanket that could bounce a dime.

Given 19-year-old wisdom, before Mark entered the Air Force, I told him not to ask his drill sergeant any questions. Unfortunately, I did not tell him about the likely basic training prohibition against .22 shells and gopher tails.

Upon seeing these items removed from Mark's pocket, it was obvious that Mark's drill sergeant was not a gopher hunter. He did, however, recognize .22 bullets.

"What the F–K! You going to shoot somebody!"

It was the military, but bringing bullets in your pockets to basic training is not a good idea.

HUNTING BACKPACK

Dateline: Friday, February 21, 2014: Guatemala City, Guatemala:

The next morning, our daughters, Michelle and Charmion, sons-in-law Kirk and Mike, plus Patricia and I were going to fly back to the States from a two-week trip to Guatemala.

That Friday evening, Michelle decided to repack her backpack before facing another hassle with airport screening. On the way out of the States, Kirk passed easily through airport security. Michelle was pulled aside and put into a room with a desk and chair.

Michelle tends to enjoy her last minutes at the airport. Following someone else's schedule is a pain when on vacation, but since 9-11-2001, Americans do not test airport security schedules.

They went through different security lines. Kirk did not know where Michelle had been taken. Michelle could not see Kirk nor could she communicate with him. Their flight departure was approaching.

Time after time, Michelle calmly asked why she was pulled aside. No answer. No answer. No answer.

Finally, minutes before their flight left, Michelle urgently, but pleasantly, asked the third security person:

"Why am I being held here?"

"Well, miss," the security agent said, "we have detected gun powder on your backpack, but we have failed to find any reason to hold you."

"Why didn't you ask me?" Michelle responded. "This is the backpack I use when hunting with my son. Sure, it is likely to have traces of gunpowder."

They let her go.

Two weeks later, back in the Guatemalan hotel room: Michelle completely emptied her backpack, and lo and behold, out drops a live .22 caliber bullet. We are certain that it is illegal for an American tourist to possess a rifle bullet in Guatemala–only a short decade or so after their bloody civil war. Likely, the bullet will remain secure in a Guatemalan garbage dump well into the twenty-fifth century.

Timing is everything. Had she not found that one bullet the night before our departure flight, Michelle might still be sitting in a Guatemalan prison trying to find someone that would believe her story that she mistakenly carried live ammo through U.S. airport security, traveled throughout Guatemala with at least one lethal shell, and why she should not rot in a Guatemalan prison.

We all should learn whether in the military, during international travel, under the guidance of parents, or sitting in a classroom, church, or courtroom, authorities should be respected.

Those of us who have lived many years know and teenagers who have many years to live will know, there is a time for everything.

Nearly 3000 years ago (~935 B.C.) King Solomon wrote in the book of Ecclesiastes:

> To everything there is a season, a time for every purpose under heaven: A time to be born, and a time to die; A time to plant ... to pluck; A time to kill ... to heal; A time to break down ... to build up; A time to weep ... to dance; A time to cast away stones ... to gather; A time to embrace ... to refrain; A time to gain ... to lose; A time to keep ... to throw away; A time to tear ... to sew; A time to keep silence ... to speak; A time to love ... to hate; A time of war, And a time of peace. God has made everything beautiful in its time. Also, He has put eternity in their hearts.[2]

Youth is the time for parenting.

---

[2] Ecclesiastes 3: 1–8, 11, NKJV, pp. 954–955

5

Preschool

Riddle: What can nurse, functions as a pacifier, and it is not unusual to publicly observe two abreast?

In the fall of 2003, my nephew, Seth Wietgrefe, passed through South Dakota heading to Alaska. Seth, a U.S. Army IED[1] explosives expert who later served in the Second Persian Gulf War (2003–2011) in Iraq and the Balkans, had recently married his musically talented wife, Liesl. With a small pickup truck loaded with all their earthly belongings and dog, Winnie, they headed to Alaska.

Through my brother, Wayne, I heard stories of my nephews' fishing and hunting exploits. His other son, David, also an Army veteran of the Gulf War, has made a living for years, in Georgia and surrounding states, as a cell phone tower expert. In his spare time, David fishes for bass and is considered a sponsored semi-professional on the Pro-Bass circuit. On the extreme other side of the country, Seth and Liesl, are raising their three girls, and now thirteen-year-old Winnie, in North Pole, Alaska.

Shortly after his oldest granddaughter turned four, Wayne told me about how Seth gave Adelaide a real .22 caliber rifle for her fourth birthday.

---

[1] IEDs (Improvised Explosive Devices), better known as "road-side bombs," were non-conventional bombs, often buried on roads, during the Iraq War to prevent, slow, or scare troops from using the road.

Parents are responsible for their children. At age four, Seth and Liesl thought their girls were old enough to be responsible with their personal gun.

I asked my nephew, Seth, to send me a few notes so that I do not mess up his rendition of teaching his girls about guns. Rather than paraphrasing, with his permission I hereby quote Seth's letter verbatim—emphasis is his.

Raising our children (letter dated July 16, 2015),

I honestly feel that we started the teaching process as soon as Adelaide was born. Liesl and I had many discussions about the rearing of our future children and how to teach safety around tools such as firearms and knives.

From the day Adelaide was born, we had *empty* firearms throughout the house. This was to teach the child that the firearm was not something mysterious, but a tool just as though it was a hammer or screwdriver.

Even as infants, the children were accompanying us as we would walk through the woods hare hunting or grouse hunting.

As Addie became a toddler, we bought her a plastic toy shotgun. We treated this toy replica as though it was the real deal. It was kept in my gun case when not in use and was only used for pretending to shoot moose in the yard or the taxidermy animals on my walls. Again, this was to build upon the concept that guns were not toys, but tools.

At age four we had purchased a youth model .22 caliber rifle for each girl.

We had many opportunities to practice safe firearm handling. It is a tradition for me to take each girl out on her birthday—either fishing or hunting.

As Addie turned seven, she harvested her first animal, a squirrel. The next year we focused on grouse and together we harvested quite a few.

We absolutely eat the animals we harvest. Not only because we harvested it, but also because the meat is healthier than the store meat (leaner, no additives, most importantly, fresher).

The meat in the stores here in Alaska is mostly shipped in from the Lower 48. The quality is mediocre at best.

Does it save money to harvest our own meat?

Crunching the numbers, it's hard to tell, because of all the variables.

We also try to harvest berries in July and salmon throughout the summer. Most of the salmon comes from a subsistence fishery available only to Alaskan residents. These are the world-famous Copper River Red (Sockeye) salmon.

Our household (of five), can harvest up to 500 salmon if we saw fit to do that. Usually, 20–30 fish (40–60 fillets) is more than enough for the year.

We do not choose to eat wild game as a political or social statement. We ultimately just like it more than the options in the store.

We have also raised poultry and had the girls be involved in every part of the process from chicks, to laying hens, egg harvest to butchering a turkey in the fall.

The girls are not traumatized in the least bit. In fact, it's hard to keep their fingers out of the way when butchering the animals. They are so curious about everything, and we treat it as a natural thing so they have no learned behaviors of disgust or repulsion towards the process. They always want to see the hearts and brains and 'guts'. And, if I don't share the works, they are greatly disappointed.

This fall I am hoping to be able to bring Adelaide along with me on my annual moose hunt. She will turn nine years old while at moose camp. We are both very excited. She asks constantly if it's time to go. It is my hope that conditions will allow for her to harvest a moose on my tag–which is permitted in Alaska.

We feel that this 'teaching' provides a more practical and logical insight to the workings of life. We believe the animals and plants were put on earth by God to provide us with the necessities to maintain our health and well-being.

Ultimately, we live this way because we can, and it's fun. It is a very prominent and accepted way of life in Alaska. In fact, I find it amusing that our way of life seems extreme to some, because compared to many here in this state, we are city slickers.

September 18, 2015, I called Seth to thank him for his summary of how he and Liesl were raising their three girls in North Pole, Alaska. At 2:30 p.m. Alaska time, he said,

What impeccable timing. I am almost finished packing our gear for moose hunting. The weather was too bad last weekend to take Addie, but my friend and I did bag one moose. I didn't fill my tag, so Addie and I are leaving as soon as she gets out of school.

I have our tent and most of the gear loaded, including Addie's .22 rifle. Obviously, she is not going to down a moose with it, but she might get a shot at smaller game. After a short, two-and-half to three-hour drive, we'll have to pack our things in as far as she can hike. We'll set up camp and hopefully have a successful weekend.

"Addie excited?" I asked.

"Oh, she can't wait to hit the road." Seth continued, "I still find it humorous that people in the Lower 48 think we are some kind of Hillbillies training our daughters to hunt. Alaska is different. We are certainly not unusual up here. Shoot! We live in town."

"No." I continued, "Not at all. They don't think you are Hillbillies—they find your story intriguing. Most parents down here think their seven-year-olds are still babies."

In fact, my wife received a message a week before I wrote this about some of our friends who were apprehensive about sending their five-year-old to kindergarten. The mother, who messaged, was so excited to report that their daughter wanted to feel grown-up before going to school, so she potty-trained herself the week before she started school. Ditched her own diapers . . . at five!"

It seemed ironic that the child could change her own diaper yet wasn't potty trained.

Recently, my wife and I rented a bungalow from a Danish couple that had immigrated into Canada. Their daughter joined our conversation about training children. Danish mothers, we were told, pride themselves on getting their babies potty trained early. The mother in her beautiful north-European accent commented on how her daughter was potty trained at six months. The key was to sit the baby on the pot twenty minutes after eating; once completed, the baby was clothed again in clean diapers.

A few minutes later, the daughter who was in her late forties, brought up a recent comment from her own twenty-year-old daughter:

"Mother, stop trying to be my friend—I need you to be a mother. I have plenty of friends, but I need to be able to call on you for a mother's guidance."

I had to smile at the progression of how the grandmother's wisdom of teaching personal responsibility at six months of age was being passed on to her granddaughter several decades later. Was it any different 5000 years ago?

God intended humans to not only reproduce but to be responsible for rearing offspring.[2] It was not the preschool or any teacher's job. Parents and children have a unique relationship that is not possible with nonbiological substitutes. Here is a personal example. My father passed away when I was twenty-seven. Unfortunately, I did not learn everything he knew, but at times we thought alike.

One day after I got out of the U.S. Air Force in the mid-1970s, my father and I were just sitting and chatting, which was unusual because my father seemed to be always working to provide for his family and his father (who lived with us until grandpa died in 1976). Anyway, someone had been sick, so I brought up the topic of a dream that I had when I was young. The dream only occurred when I was sick.

The same dream happened multiple times when I was in grade school. I seldom remember my dreams, but this one recurred when I was sick sleeping and even when simply closing my eyes again after waking. I was dizzy and the dream would make me dizzier.

In the dream, I was rolling down a long steep hill trapped in a large cotton or soft Styrofoam[3] ball. There was no end. The longer I dreamed, or kept my eyes closed, the ball accumulated more, making it bigger, rolling faster, and making me dizzier.

My father looked at me puzzled but did not interrupt while I was telling the story. When I finished, he said, "That is the same dream I had when I was a kid. It only happened when sick or getting sick."

Nobody I've ever told that story knew of an instance where father and son, or mother and daughter, had the same dream when they were the same age and unbeknownst previously. When I told dad my

---

[2] "Train up a child in the way he should go, and when he is old he will not depart from it." Proverbs 22:6, NKJV, p. 936

[3] Styrofoam is a registered trademark of Dow Chemical Company, Midland, Michigan, USA.

dream, it had been a decade since I had had that dream and likely thirty years since my father dreamed the same dream. All I can say is biological parents and children have phenotypic traits and similar unobserved thoughts.

Children learn different things from friends than what parents should teach. Parents are a link to reality. Many empty-nester mothers apparently have an urge to befriend their children.

Spending a couple years traveling around the United States in an RV (recreational vehicle), we realized, when removed from their adult children and grandchildren, many senior RVers fill their confined space with dog(s). Some had four.

Given the free-living lifestyle of RVing, it was hard for me to fathom why someone would want to get up early, haul their barking dog(s) out the door, and clean up shit first thing in the morning, during the day, and before heading to bed at night. Our Danish landlord took care of that chore when her only daughter was six months old. The military would call that shortened training technique "basic training."

Dogs are amazing. They can train their masters to pick up their shit. In a major cultural shift, children also have trained their parents, especially mothers, to feed them, wash their clothes, and pick up after them well into adulthood. It further proves the immaturity and irresponsibility of many "adult children" in their mid-twenties and complex immature psychological needs of retirees. Like a puzzling riddle, something caused the shift.

FISHING

When our granddaughter and both grandsons were two and three I started taking them out fishing. I made light long poles out of willow. Six-pound monofilament fishing line was tied to the end tipped with a small hook, weight, and worm.

Before we went fishing, each time I grabbed a spade and an empty two-pound coffee can with a plastic lid and headed to our backyard. Around and under a pile of raked leaves where moisture allowed angleworms and soil organisms to break down lignin and other carbohydrates, we found plenty of worms and occasionally night crawlers. At age two and three even our granddaughter dug in the dirt for the evasive wigglers.

An oxbow lake of the Big Sioux River would flood in the spring and had enough flow to sustain populations of bluegill and bullheads–perfect fish for youngsters to catch. Biting was generally fast and furious. I would start baiting with the youngest (Emily, our granddaughter, if I had all three of them that day) and before I finished threading a worm on Austin's pole, Willie or Emily would often be holding a fish bouncing from a weeping willow stick.

Sitting on the riverbank, the kids would lift fish after fish with homemade poles. The monofilament length was just long enough to reach the water and when vertical the pole would bend enough for each to grab their own fish. Sometimes it would slap them in the face. Bluegill and bullhead's dorsal fin can easily penetrate the hand, but bullhead maxillary barbels contain a pointed, sharp, yet jagged protective bone projecting horizontally near the mouth. Both poke. By age three my grandchildren wanted to bait their hook with worms and remove their fishhooks. They wanted to be responsible for their own fish.

Fish swallow other fish head-first so the fin bones do not penetrate gut lining during digestion. Bullheads have few predators because the bony barbel and pointed dorsal fin does not fold back when swallowed. Young children learned dangers from apparently innocent fish.

A time limit was not set. Sometimes fishing was slow. That taught patience. Usually it was good. We would set a fish limit–usually thirty to forty, which would allow each to score multiple times and keep their own count. Most fish were too small and were released, according to the grandchildren's guidelines. Each was responsible for their line, watching their bobber and feeling the fish tug. Some were cleaned and eaten as fresh fried fish for our evening dinner.

I like to fish. Nieces, nephews, young brothers, and all our children and grandchildren have gone fishing with me and had wonderful experiences. Never once was one of my fishing mates endangered beyond a fish fin poke.

When fishing, I often tell the story of when a friend, Alan, and I were spring fishing Hayes Lake in Stanley County, South Dakota, after an "ice out." As spring sun warms the water, fish, especially northerns, become more active–attacking anything that moves. In the Northern Plains, early spring is the best time to catch the native aggressive northern pike (*Esox lucius*).

Alan and I were catching a northern every few minutes, each usually eighteen to twenty inches long using flashy casting spoons. After an hour catching and releasing perhaps twenty fish, I pulled an unusual one to shore.

"Al, look at this," I shouted. We had fished together often so simply observing the other's fish was no big deal. I held up a northern, probably 18 inches long. Al could not see why I bothered him.

Moving closer, I asked Al to look below my silver spoon (lure). The tail of another northern was sticking out the mouth of the fish on my lure. I dissected my catch immediately. The cannibal at the end of my line had eaten a fish approximately the same size. Head, gills, and part of the stomach were already dissolving in the gut of my keeper.

It is easy for a young child to understand survival as "dog eat dog" (in this case fish eat fish) with a silver spoon in its mouth. As if it were a fable, it has a moral: Unfortunately, some people have it tough and may go hungry; others have too much and want more.

One late spring day when our grandchildren were staying with us on their two-week vacation, I took Emily and Austin to my favorite Big Sioux oxbow lake. The riverbank dropped about four feet to the water. Emily could not have been older than three, meaning Austin would have been about five.

I was afraid they would slip off the bank into the water. Emily's spot was sitting on my tackle box, and I packed the grass and hacked the weeds a few feet away for Austin to sit on the grass so they could flip their lines with ease into the water.

Fishing was active the first half-hour, but Austin was scratching himself and had a hard time focusing on fishing. Chiggers! Chiggers! We packed up quickly when I realized the grass was harboring thousands of unseen mites (*Trombiculidae*). I felt so bad for Austin. He was imbedded with mites from his waist down. Emily, sitting on the tackle box, had only a few.

What do these experiences teach?

Their grandfather could interact with them—tell stories, have fun, get dirty, fight pests, and put food on the dinner table. Two, three, four, or five is not too young to learn food produced from your own labor may be time-consuming and unpleasant but was also rewarding. Looking back, getting dirty, slimy, and enduring a poke or two from a fin or mite was fun when not called "work."

Not everyone is fortunate to live as well as our society. With a full stomach, it is hard to understand survival. Most people accumulate more than they need. There are extremes. Workaholics and lovers of money go beyond need and take on more than they can chew—not much different from the cannibalistic fish mentioned above. Those who were never taught responsibility feed off others.

Parents wait too long or may never apply this old proverb: "Give a man (or child) a fish and you feed them for a day. Teach a man (or child) to fish and you feed them for a lifetime."

The world developed around water. For thousands of years, seafood likely was, and still is, feeding more people than hunting. Historic evidence of population centers developing along seas and waterways indicate seafood provided sustenance and nutrient balance; meanwhile, fowl and animals were domesticated as wild game was depleted near developments. Fresh water was needed for survival and seafood is still highly valued, especially where it enters a sea or ocean providing nutrients and sustainability of sea life. On every continent, population centers developed where coastal rivers entered salt water.

It was common for children to accompany parents, who taught them how to repair nets, catch fish, pry open oysters without getting cut, dig for clams, and prepare and preserve them. Seafood was a protein staple to supplement leafy vegetables, seaweed, roots, fruits, and nuts. Food was sourced for survival while satisfying cravings for balanced nutrients. The young see their parents fish, hunt, and gather and they learn to do it themselves. Humans are not unique. Throughout history, they established a natural maturity cycle. It is interesting to watch the parallel in wildlife with hatchlings following their parents searching for food and learning how to extract, dissect, select certain parts and swallow based on particle size. However, in the wild nature forces maturity. If the young do not learn hunting and feeding techniques, their growth does not match the natural weight gain, migration, and weather cycles, they die.

A modern child can watch television, play computer games, or chat with friends, which produces very little that helps sustain life; however, if a child can catch a fish, she has learned the basic lessons of patience, tenacity, responsibility, enjoyment, and providing food.

If parents do not give children chores (a mistake), they should at least teach them a life skill—even if it is a hobby, like fishing. Kids will get in trouble if left idle. The older they get, the more serious the trouble. Alternatively, others idle their life away without learning to preserve, prepare, or cook a meal, clean their domicile (for health purposes), or produce financial resources (a must as civilizations urbanized).

About three thousand years ago, around 950 B.C., King Solomon wrote:

> The soul of a lazy man desires, and has nothing; but the soul of the diligent shall be made rich.[4]

A thousand years later, 61 A.D., Saint Paul sent a letter to his followers in Ephesus stating:

> Let him who stole steal no longer, but rather let him labor, working with his hands what is good, that he may have something to give him who has need.[5]

It is good to teach children while growing to provide for themselves; if they reach maturity and are slothful, their soul will always be troubled. No parent wants that.

Mentally preparing a child for adulthood takes responsibility, not physical strength of the child or parent. As American essayist, Ralph Waldo Emerson (1803–1882) suggested:

> Great works are performed not by strength but by perseverance.

Dead fish float. They go nowhere. That's it! Except, like children, they spoil quickly when not properly prepared.

WHO NEEDS TRAINING?

By age three, my grandchildren could all catch their own fish. By four, our nephew's girls were responsible for their own gun. Some children

---

[4] Proverbs 13:4, NKJV, p. 921
[5] Ephesians 4:28, NKJV, p. 1665

do not wait for their parent's training. If not held back, by nature they know what is right. Our Danish landlord potty trained her daughter at six months. A friend's daughter shed her own diaper at age five before heading to school. What a contrast in parenting!

Who is right?

For perspective, let me frame the diaper (nappy) timeline. Cotton into cloth has been traced back nearly 7000 years to isolated finds in Mexico and India. In the late 1500s, after mechanical cloth production by looms, diapers allowed mothers to care for infants during intercontinental organized colonization. Maria Allen has been credited with mass producing cloth diapers in the United States in 1887—four years before my grandfather was born. Money availability when women entered the workforce in World War II created a childcare need for someone other than the mother to change the baby, including longer times between changing, and the need for increased efficiencies at home. After the war, rubber coating allowed fitting to prevent leaking (called "rubber pants"). Mass-produced disposable diapers quickly followed.

Do disposable diapers begin to expose a cultural transition? In trying to make things more efficient and easier for us, have we created a disposable society?

My nephew's girls each received and were trained on their own rifles at age four. At six, they were bringing home, cleaning, and helping dress their own game (grouse), and catching fish destined for the freezer and a winter meal. Meanwhile, children the same age were walking around messing their diapers. Children grow and learn responsibility or irresponsibility. Those that only watch television or play computer games as children and expect others to provide for them as they grow become society's problem.

Developed countries provide societal feeding options. In underdeveloped countries, providing daily food is a survival skill. Children learn quickly—like puppies lapping a fresh bowl of milk or sucking the bitch.

Public utilities in developed urbanized areas have removed some individual responsibilities by supplying clean water and chlorinating to minimize bacteria load. For health purposes, those are expected services. Public sewer and designated garbage disposal dates back to at least ancient Babylonia, Persia, Pakistan, and Rome where hunting and fishing for survival was ancient history to them.

Just because modern urbanites do not have to stalk their food, carry their water, and dispose of their sewage does not exempt parents from training their children to make their bed, buy supplies, and prepare a meal. Cleaning a living area and self has also slipped from individual responsibility. Otherwise, why would restaurants post signs to staff to "wash hands before returning to work"?

How many parents in developed countries are training their children to live independently? It has never been the schoolteachers' job.

Has the Western world matured? Not close. Some irresponsible parents, at age forty, can't potty train. Many parents fail to give responsibilities at any age. Has it become a public necessity to train individual responsibility?

6

Spectator

Riddle: What is justified by social grouping where children, teenagers, and adults can be seen playing?

FREE-RANGE PARENTING

In December 2014, a Maryland couple, Danielle and Alexander Meitiv, allowed their daughter, six-year-old Dvora, to walk about a mile home from their suburban playground with her ten-year-old brother, Rafi. Someone, seeing the children walking, called police. The police picked up the children, promising to take them home, but instead drove them ten miles away and held them for two-and-a-half hours in a process to turn them over to Child Protective Services.[1]

The Meitivs were charged with neglect.

Child Protective Services was called to step in on behalf of the children to protect them from their supposed irresponsible parents.

Although the Meitivs had previously taught their children the route and where to cross streets, Child Protective Services found them incompetent.

---

[1] McCarren, Andrea, "Parents in trouble again for letting kids walk alone," WUSA-TV, Washington, April 13, 2015. http://www.usatoday.com/story/news/nation/2015/04/13/parents-investigated-letting-children-walk-alone/25700823/ (Sourced September 18, 2015)

"Free-Range Parenting" is a term used to classify parents who try to teach their children responsibilities. Government agencies think they should determine when children are old enough to play and return from the park.

TOO OLD AT ONE

After my sister turned sixty, our mother told her this story about having three children under three. Mark was a few months old, Susan was two, and I was one.

All of us were bottle trained early. Mark, born big, always cried, and was always hungry. One day, mom said, I went to Mark's crib shortly after she gave him a bottle. Mark was crying because my sister and I were under his crib sharing his bottle.

At age one, mother taught me to grow up. I was too old, at one, to be sucking a bottle.

Before the British prisoner ships, known as the First Fleet, landed on the Australian shore in 1788 A.D., aboriginals roamed their continent for thousands of years. There was no central government. Before French General de Trobriand arrived on American's Northern Great Plains in the 1860s, organized in tribes, the Natives taught their children how to hunt. Before Judean Desert Bedouin shepherds discovered the Dead Sea Scrolls in a cave near Qumran in 1946 A.D., their youth tended sheep.

Most children stayed and carried on the family's profession. Some moved. Some became leaders.

In sociological terms, a cosmopolite is cosmopolitan "... not bound by local or national habits or prejudices; at home in all countries or places...."[2] Localite is "a native or resident of the locality under consideration."[3] Language changes. It is interesting to note that cosmopolite can be found in Webster's 1982 dictionary, but localite is not listed. Although localites were discussed in a sociological context before 1982, throughout thousands of years of civilization localites were assumed to be standard, normal people. They did not need a term defining their status to an outsider. Cosmopolite, once defined, needed the flipside.

---

[2] Cosmopolite, *Webster's New World Dictionary*, p. 321
[3] Localite, http://www.merriam-webster.com/dictionary/localite (Sourced November 5, 2015)

It is not wrong to be a localite or a cosmopolite. Neither term should be considered derogatory or belittling. However, both types of people exist in every society and play different roles in adopting technology.

It is assumed that those whose lives revolve around their immediate contacts and surroundings (localites) share incoming technology brought in by those with outside social interests (cosmopolites), but insiders provide more clout to adopt change. All societies have both types of people.

Natives of the North American Plains went through dramatic change with the introduction of previously unseen (guns and horses), untasted (wheat), and unfelt (alcohol) articles brought in after Columbus.

After the American Civil War, a nationalized American of French descent, Philippe Régis Denis de Keredern de Trobriand,[4] became commander of Fort Stevenson, Dakota Territory (now North Dakota). Besides keeping peace in that area of the United States and being well read with aristocrat heritage, de Trobriand, a cosmopolite, worked diligently to bring progressive ideas to Native Americans confined to reservations.

de Trobriand obviously did not have access to modern-day understanding of localites and cosmopolites with implied differences in technology adoption. From his cultural background, he assumed by giving a man a hoe, he would hoe. Giving a man seed meant he would plant it to raise food for himself, his family, and his tribe.

Through de Trobriand's personal journal, we know the personal deprivation of Natives, especially during the winters of 1867–1870, and their need for a sustainable food supply. Hunting was waning; de Trobriand attempted to convert hunters into farmers. Operating carte blanche, mass conversion was, and still is, unlikely. Following protocol, he met with various tribal leaders (all men), rather than selecting individual leaders that would have been more likely to adopt agriculture.

de Trobriand assumed explaining the purpose and giving farm supplies before the planting season would convince tribesmen to establish an agricultural protectorate producing corn, wheat, oats and other edibles they could consume or trade.

---

[4] de Trobriand, Philippe Regis Denis de Keredern, *Army Life in Dakota, 1867–1870*, translated by George Francis Will, 1941, The Lakeside Press, R.R. Donnelly & Sons Co., pp. 223–225.

Native men were hunters in their paternal society. Women produced and gathered seed, cooked and cared for tribal functions when the men were off, sometimes weeks hunting or fighting. Tribal women were always working and on the new reservations men were not. Girls learned from their mothers, boys from their fathers.

de Trobriand was militarily successful but failed sociologically. Men do not, and will not, do what is considered women's work, especially if suggested to do so by an outsider. European men farmed; it was assumed Natives would also. Changing perception, especially gender roles, was a cultural shift.

Consider another society that had converted to herdsmen from hunters; Mongolian herdsmen roamed the highlands and plains before Genghis Khan became leader of united tribes in 1206 A.D. Through his leadership and horsemanship, the Mongol dominance expanded to become the largest Empire in world history and lasted for more than 160 years (1206–1368).[5]

Government is like a chair. Making rungs, seat, back, and legs creates a chair. Is it a chair if not assembled? Sitting only on a rung is a pain in the ass. The Great Khan said:

There is no value in anything until it is finished.

Rapidly the Mongol empire stretched from the Pacific Ocean (Sea of Japan) north to Siberia and south through China across to Iran and Arabia into Central Europe. Genghis Khan's grandchildren and descendants should have heeded his wisdom:

Conquering the world on horseback is easy; it is dismounting and governing that is hard.

I doubt the Mongols under Genghis Khan waited for their children to potty train themselves. It would have been too uncomfortable to ride a horse in messy diapers.

Eight hundred years ago, a Mongol boy of ten, Temüjin, supported his family with the father absent. The Khan government likely only had "free-range" parenting.

---

[5] Mongol Empire, https://en.wikipedia.org/wiki/Mongol_Empire (Sourced September 19, 2015)

Culture has changed. When did it become the government's responsibility to take care of single parents? Why are teenagers now not expected to help support the family? Why were teenagers old enough to work eight hundred years ago, but not today?

Parents no longer use their authority and give responsibility to their children.

How many children no longer are expected to do chores around the house? After a long day at work and picking up groceries, is it the mother's responsibility to come home, make dinner, and do laundry while washing the day's dishes? In a single-parent household, how many ten-year-old boys and girls are expected to have dinner ready when the mother returns from work?

Born as Temüjin, Genghis Khan's father arranged his marriage. It has been recorded:

> ... At nine years of age he was delivered by his father to the family
> of his future wife, Borte, who was a member of the tribe Khongirad.
> Temüjin was to live there in service to Dai Setsen, the head of the
> new household, until he reached the marriageable age of 12.[6]

Genghis Khan's empire, originator of the largest centralized government ever established, had no evidence of a "child service agency." His government was lean and especially mean. How ludicrous would it be to think, after returning from a conquest, Emperor Khan would scold free-range parents of a ten-year-old who returned his six-year-old sister from a city park.

Think back eight hundred years:

News Flash: Dateline Qingyang, China 1198 A.D.: With a long history dating to the Western Zhou Dynasty (1100–771 B.C.), Qinyang has hosted armies for over two thousand years. Qinyang, a thousand miles from Ulaanbaatar, will be the overnight stop for Genghis Khan and his mounted army.

Mid-afternoon the press corps dismounts, as the Great Khan pulled to a halt on a low bluff. His army, by rank, gathers below. All positioned–the Khan never interrupted.

---

[6] Temüjin, his life's summary as Genghis Khan, https://en.wikipedia.org/wiki/Genghis_Khan (Sourced September 28, 2015)

"Mongols! Great men you are! Mongols!" he shouts with his booming voice. "Our ride has been hard; journey long. Dust, everlasting dust, adrift toward our future–a guide to lands directing us to conquer. Conquer we will!!!

"Why? Why here? Why nomads stop so early in the day you ask. My Mongols, you know we have a reputation of conquest. Conquest–not caring. Conquer we will! Before we slaughter the brassards of Qingyang tomorrow, we will inquire with compassion today in the village of Yimazhen. There look: Yimazhen on the narrow plain of Qingyang.

"Though a thousand miles a hoof, I vision the village of my youth. Village Yimazhen. Quiet. Yimazhen–nomad's respite.

"Youth. What is youth? I was a man at nine and was to marry at 12. Four years I had to delay that honor.

"Our advance scouts looking, always looking. Keen. Keen they are at sighting slightest hints of inconsistency.

"It has come to my ears that a boy of ten was playing with his six-year-old sister in the Yimazhen village park.

"Park! What park? Why isn't that land a garden producing food?

"Mongols! Great men you are! Mongols!" The Great Khan shouts with his booming voice, "Find out! Find out! I command you to find the pipsqueaks! What the hell is going on in Yimazhen that a ten-year-old has time to go to the park and not garden!"

It is not good to underestimate my readers, but I want to be clear: Genghis Khan was an international thug. Imagine his style. To my knowledge Khan never had a press corps, but he had a system to communicate to the populace he controlled.

With media, especially political propaganda from the U.S. White House broadcast every day, most people likely assume every U.S. president since George Washington had a press secretary. Wrong! President Herbert Hoover appointed the first presidential press secretary, George Akerson,[7] in March 1929. Before then, the nation was not meshed with electricity nor radio stations, and certainly not television stations that

---

[7]Jurkowitz, Mark, "7 facts about White House press secretaries," Fact Tank, June 19, 2014, http://www.pewresearch.org/fact-tank/2014/06/19/7-facts-about-white-house-press-secretaries/ (Sourced September 30, 2015)

required electricity. Consequently, before then, broadcasting the president's every move was not news.

Development of twentieth-century radio, television, and newsprint media used "wire services" which required electricity.[8] Although electricity was not invented, it is a natural occurrence. It took a couple thousand years after discovery to develop a nationwide electrical network.

Everything has a history. Based on archeological evidence, Persians and Romans likely used copper to form a battery to produce light before Christ.[9]

Twelve hundred years after Christ, Genghis Khan traveled light. No evidence indicates he carried it. Khan used small, rugged horses for his escapades, enhancing his reputation of lightning fast raids. Teams of horses could carry more, but they would have slowed his movement. His supply chain was short—local resources were available to feed his mounts and men.

Consider the news release above fictitious. Enough is known of Genghis Khan to give a comparison between his early years and modern-day children. In the words of French novelist, Anatole France (1844–1924):

To know is nothing at all; to imagine is everything.

Relating to Ancient Culture is hard for many to imagine. Likewise, until indoctrinated children became adults, society did not accept, or expect government to babysit their children. Today, it is hard to imagine a society without cradle-to-grave government services.

In my youth, neighbors expected kids to walk home from the park. Is it any wonder now that kids are twice the weight they should be? Perhaps a spinster down the block did not have enough chips and pop to feed the munchkins. Instead, she calls the cops. "Rescue. Rescue the children," she demands as she screams down the block at free-range parents.

---

[8] News Wire Services, "A news wire is an organization of journalists established to supply news reports to news organizations: newspapers, magazines, and radio and television broadcasters ... referred to as a wire service...." http://assignmenteditor.com/news-wires/ (Sourced September 30, 2015)

[9] Atkinson, Nancy, "Who Discovered Electricity?," Universe Today, March 3, 2014, http://www.universetoday.com/82402/who-discovered-electricity/ (Sourced September 30, 2015)

Has life changed so much parents lack compassion for their off-spring? No.

It is not the competence of the free-walking ten-year-old, nor his parents I question. Incompetent are institutions and those that believe their prattle. Basically, schools teach children to suck parents into senility before sucking the everlasting public trough. It seems the biggest suckers are now defining compassion.

I hear critics screaming: "What garbage! Who is this crazy guy?" Take a deep breath. Although many of my statements are cringeworthy to some, my goal is not to insult but to point out these potential absurdities so that we can improve as a society.

Many are unaware of the predicament our culture is in as a result of our government assuming responsibility for parenting. Subsidized childcare, child protective services, free preschool through high school, free school lunches, free milk and cookies before free teen condoms, and subsidized college tuition are all a grand burlesque show for many parents to observe rather than participate in the raising of their children.

SPORTS

After babysitters, sports is often the next place where parents turn responsibility of their child over to someone else—a coach. As mentioned before, many parents observe their children growing rather than participate in it.

Parents or grandparents that sit on bleachers and cheer for their daughter or grandson, week after week, year after year and say "I don't miss a game" aren't actually participating or interacting with their child.

Sorry to be so blunt, but "sport" is activity. No definition of "sport" is there inactivity. Flat-assed on bleachers is not "sport." Sunken into an oversized chair, gut bulging from snacks and a brew, hours-on-end watching weekend games on television is not "sport." It may be relaxing, reclining, resting, debilitating, out of shape, gut busting, a destination for the morbidly obese, or even taking another breather before half-time or seventh inning stretch, but it is not "sport"–it's "watching."

You ask: How do free-range parenting, Genghis Khan, government social programs, and sports tell a cultural story?

Children used to be taught life skills. Youth used to be called the "springtime of life" or an "awkward age" as they learned to live independently. Plants grow before they flower. Spring brings new growth and natural timing creates budding, flowering, and fruit.

A plant cannot sit in an artificially lit schoolroom for twenty years and expect to produce when released into nature. Why are children? Ancient life followed nature.

It reminds me of the plant, bittersweet (*Solanum dulcamara*) often referred to as nightshade. Like kindergarten, it is native to Europe but became an invasive species in the United States. Enchanting, but toxic berries, appeal to children.

Stark reality of ancient life compared to societies today is unconnected. The current definition of "youth" is as corrupted as the definition of "sport." When does "youth" end and "adult" begin? Neither have any relationship to any previous society I have studied.

Is it any wonder that children do not respect their elders, when elders have not trained their children?

I should tread lightly on this topic but I feel it is too important. Many, perhaps most, believe I do not understand that children should be protected into their mid-twenties.

Perhaps I don't understand reality. More likely, as I age I am less patient understanding understanding.

Sports are satisfying; they have a purpose. I like sports. As a former athlete in later years I enjoy being a spectator at my grandsons' football and basketball games and wrestling matches and watching nieces, nephews, and our granddaughter play soccer.

When he was nine years old, I took my grandson to wrestling practice. I did not just watch. I taught him moves. My other grandson played basketball; as he was growing I spent hours playing "HORSE" and just shooting hoops. It was family time afterward when we all gathered. Patricia and I never went to every game—never intended to. It would not have been special if we did. Our grandchildren were too special to have that relationship destroyed by hard, impersonal bleachers.

Sports used to be boys and girls playing kickball in a backyard or park. As they matured, sports was a group of men and boys shedding suit jacket and tie after church for a round of baseball before the wagons headed home. In the 1920s my grandfather enjoyed such games with his immigrant family, large enough for a team. With all nations living mostly in rural areas into the twentieth century, people did not have to organize teams to get exercise. People had to grow food to eat and haul water and wood; that was enough exercise for most.

With less than1 percent of Americans making a living farming, very few Americans have ever had a farm job. Even farm labor is now often sitting in an air-conditioned machine. Backbreaking work like picking fruit and cotton, stacking hay, and milking cows is now mechanized or turned over to immigrant labor. Walking to the snack bar in a corporate office is not exercise—it's called a "break." At one time the squeaky wheel got the grease. Now it surrounds the belly of the office gossip.

Working in offices is not new. America's third president, Thomas Jefferson (1743–1826), certainly had office hours, but he advised:

> The sovereign invigorator of the body is exercise, and of all the exercises walking is the best.

And it does not require a team.

While in Italy, I played football and wrestled on an Air Force wrestling team in Rota, Spain, and England. I was not that good, but did take fourth Air Force Europe in 1973. While in Japan the following year, I set a world endurance record playing softball continuously for seventy-four hours and five minutes. They called me "Ironman Wietgrefe." Hundreds participated in the nine-day game. Those that were not on the field were sponsors and donated for each hour their individual played. Most satisfaction came from the thousands of dollars raised for "Operation Eyesight" which helped disadvantaged children see. Trophies are just thrown in a box, if I still have them, but those given eyesight should still be able to see forty years later.

Envision a successful program.

For years, our daughter, Charmion, sponsored a young girl in Guatemala so she could go to school. For three consecutive years, our family visited the Mayan village in the Guatemalan mountains helping to replace dirt houses with mostly concrete block. Our son, Wyatt, helped and returned several years to give family support.

In late winter 2016, our whole family (my wife, our son, both daughters, granddaughter, a friend, and two of my wife's sisters) worked together constructing four homes. Before going each year, our family accumulated bags of items to give to each family (i.e., shampoos, lotions, soaps, tooth brushes, used clothes, notebooks, nutrition bars, and so on).

The third year, before flying to Guatemala, I stopped at a discount store and bought most of the available reading glasses for about three dollars each. Trying to imagine what would be beneficial, I realized in the two previous years I had never seen one person wearing eyeglasses in the village, San Pablo la Laguna, with an estimated population of 14,000. They either had great eyesight, or lacked optical care. Our intention was to give the local medical clinic the whole batch of glasses.

A couple days before delivering the eyeglasses to the clinic, we helped replace an eighty-four-year-old widow's eight-by-ten rusted tin metal shack with an eco-friendly bamboo and dried cane home. That day we had given the widow and five other families we had been working with our bag of items including a pair of off-the-shelf reading glasses.

The following day, after work, we stopped on the way home at a little corner market to have a beer or soda which we consumed sitting on the sidewalk as there are no cafes or bars in the poor village. A five-year-old Mayan boy sat down by us. He wanted nothing other than to visit with strangers to his town. Before leaving, my wife gave him one Q (quetzal) worth about fourteen U.S. cents. The little guy walked back and forth checking in several shops to find a certain candy he wanted.

Meanwhile, a middle-aged Mayan lady in traditional dress came down the hill, apparently looking for our group. She stopped to chat in broken Spanish (as her traditional language was one of many Mayan dialects). After the introductory exchange, it became apparent that the lady had talked to one of the families who received our bag and she wanted a pair of reading glasses. My sister-in-law, who needed glasses to read measurements, happened to have a pair of the cheap glasses in her pants pocket, which she promptly gave the lady. It is hard to imagine a happier soul.

The little boy was happy to have a candy sucker that lasted less than ten minutes. The middle-aged lady was far more permanently content with a pair of glasses she could use daily for the rest of her life—a permanent solution like the eighty-four-year-old's new home.

My readers, please consider your actions, your gifts, and the culture you are establishing. Are you creating a fleeting culture—one that satisfies a temporary want, or a long-term need?

Life's treasures do not have to be expensive gifts. The exercise of imagining, planning, and delivering is the satisfying vision.

After retiring, I bicycled more than a thousand miles a year and hiked hundreds of miles yearly in many states and countries. At sixty-two, biking more than a hundred miles per day was invigorating. My longest hike from Port Macquarie, Australia, following the Pacific's sandy beach to Kempsey was 62 kilometers (more than 37 miles) in ten and a half hours. It, like many, was a wonderful, natural experience. That to me is sporting and it does not take a team.

Teams devalue individuality. Youth need to learn to live independently and take personal responsibility.

A cultural shift has occurred. What is causing it?

Why would someone want to restrict parents or a child's freedom? When one can participate, why would one settle for observing? When one sees people who need help, why would one be satisfied sitting at home watching a box?

"Watching" is a multibillion-dollar industry. It would be an interesting statistic to know how many people are addicted to watching.

7

Teams

Riddle: Where is timing critical, leaders compensated, and team members are paid nothing?

In the last two decades, I've notice business management has changed. What one individual used to do, now takes a team. Teams make decisions. Projects are team projects. Committees determine corporate direction. Why?

Society transferred individual responsibility. Children are not given responsibility. Parents are not responsible for their children. Team effort has replaced individual effort. Managers cannot or refuse to make decisions without team consensus.

Genghis Khan and his ancestors did not use teams of horses to master and maintain control of the world's largest empire. Why?

Simple. Horse teams were too slow. An individual on a horse can travel twice as far and twice as fast as a team. Teams, like horses, are organized to carry heavy loads. They are slow to react, slow to change direction, use a lot of resources, and hard to get them to change from an established pattern. People teams are the same as horse teams. Smell may be the only difference as office teams camouflage their pits with deodorant. Horses do not use deodorant; they sweat when working–people try to avoid sweating.

When I lived for eighteen months outside of San Vito dei Normanni, Italy, in the early 1970s, every day throughout the year (except Sunday),

I would see horses, carts, and farmers head to their fields in the morning and return to San Vito in the late afternoon.

Often, the farmer was slouched in his wagon seat dozing after a hard day, while his trusted horse, or team, headed home. For centuries life changed little for farmers like Giovanni, Antonio, and Santino into the 1970s. Friends, neighbors, and rare San Vito visitors never questioned where the horses were going. Horses knew the route to the correct field in the morning and the route home at night.

Not to criticize 1970s Italian farmers, but they followed the team. They did not lead them. Poor managers hide behind teams. To paraphrase Howard Fast,[1]

> A team manager is a eunuch working in a harem. He watches it, but
> he knows he can't do it.

It is easy to get teams confused with responsible individuals and working groups that organize, often quickly, to investigate, start, and drive an initiative. When satisfied with direction, they move into the implementation stage.

BULK SEED

In 1998 when I was a business development agronomist for a seed company, an experienced sales representative asked me if some of his customers could get our soybean seed in bulk. At the time he had a couple of large farmer-dealers licensed to sell our soybean seed. They were also looking at other suppliers that would sell patented soybean seed in bulk.

As a good salesperson with over two decades of selling soybeans, to save good customers he devised a plan in 1988 to sell his customers soybeans in large woven bags weighing 2000 pounds, called totes. Although totes had to be handled by forklift, each tote would fill a planter and replace forty paper bags each weighing fifty pounds. Totes allowed farmers to fill their planters quickly without manually opening, dumping, and disposing of forty paper bags.

---

[1] Fast, Howard, "A critic is a eunuch working in a harem. He watches it, but he knows he can't do it." Brainy Quote, http://www.brainyquote.com/quotes/keywords/failed.html (Sourced September 30, 2015)

In the 1990s totes became quite popular, but they still required another piece of planting equipment, a forklift in the field that served no other function. Original totes, even though they were delivered on wooden pallets, like paper bags, were very dangerous to stack thereby requiring at least twice the storage space as paper bags. Seed must be at the farmers' place at planting otherwise planting is delayed. However, farmers wanted to use their storage buildings, called machine sheds, to store expensive machinery like combines costing more than $300,000 each rather than waste space storing seed bags.

By the late 1990s soybean acres were moving west into traditional wheat country. As a nitrogen-producing legume, soybeans were a good fit in a wheat-soybean, or a wheat-soybean-corn rotation. Consequently, the salesman asked me to help develop a system that farmers could use to deliver soybeans to the field in bulk like wheat seed was handled.

With new soybean varieties receiving individual patents to protect the developer's intellectual property, the processing and packaging division of seed companies, like ours, refused to sell soybean in bulk. Only package seed would have the necessary legal tags to meet state and federal purity and identity-preservation regulations.

In November 1998 in the days immediately after meeting with that sales representative, I had a few phone exchanges with our innovative soybean manager. Within a week I arranged a meeting with the soybean manager, sales representative, and two of his good customers who desired to purchase our soybean seed in bulk.

After meeting with the four of us, the soybean manager with his soybean knowledge and solid reputation with our seed processing division, helped us devise a plan to deliver our proprietary, patented soybean seed to farmers in bulk (without any packaging).

Without another meeting, by April 1999 our ad hoc working group negotiated legal hurdles to get nine seed dealers in various states to invest about $100,000 each to install our newly designed bulk system, trade named "TruBulk.®"[2]

As the TruBulk® soybean system spread across the United States into Canada, our competitors jumped on the bulk wagon for several reasons, including decreased packaging costs, less storage space, much less

---

[2] "TruBulk®" is a trademark of Syngenta AG, Basel, Switzerland.

labor needed, ease of inoculating the legume, and no seed returns at the end of planting. Fear of losing more customers was the primary driver that switched competitors into replicating our efficient TruBulk® system. Although we had the trademark and could legally block our competitors from using the "TruBulk®" term or logo, the name and system quickly became institutionalized. Bulk seed handling systems in the United States were referred to as "true bulk" as an illegal maneuver to avoid our trademark.

I approved all manufacturer equipment specifications (e.g., tanks, conveyors, and scales) that met our seed handling and identity preservation standards. Since all competitors used the same bulk equipment from the same manufacturers, I thereby sustained quality standards for seed companies selling soybeans as bulk.

Ultimate success of a trademark is to have it become an industry homonym without it becoming a proprietary brandy eponym, or generic term. For example, someone may order a "coke" but mean a soft drink not a specific brand "COKE®"[3] that is a registered proprietary brand trademark of the Coca-Cola Company.

Bayer AG (Leverkusen, Federal Republic of Germany) introduced its drug Aspirin in 1897, six years after my grandfather was born. More than a hundred years later, through genericized trademark, someone may want modern brand-name head or muscle ache relief mediation and ask for an aspirin (a generic term).

A copying process, xerography, meaning "dry writing" in Greek, was popularized by the Haloid Photographic Company founded in 1906. By the late 1950s their copying process termed XEROX[4] became so popular they changed the company name to Xerox Corporation. When someone needed a copy of a document, they asked for a XEROX.

Searching for something on the Internet you may "Google" it no matter what search engine is used. With good marketing, "Google" web searching was institutionalized and trademarked by Google Inc.[5]

---

[3] COKE® A trademark of The Coca-Cola Company, Atlanta, Georgia USA
[4] XEROX service mark owned by Xerox Corporation, Norwalk, Connecticut USA
[5] © 2015 Google Inc. All rights reserved. Google and the Google Logo are registered trademarks of Google Inc.

When U.S. or Canadian farmers want soybeans delivered in bulk, they ask for "true bulk," actually meaning bulk seed handled with "Tru-Bulk®" standards.

Occasionally, an equipment manufacturer would convince a competitor of ours to purchase their conveyor, or other equipment. When seed dealers asked if the equipment met "true bulk," meaning TruBulk,® standards, the equipment manufacturer would call me to approve their system or ask me to advise on what needed to be changed.

Within a decade thousands of bulk soybean systems were installed in every soybean-producing state and Canadian province. Environmentally as bulk replaced packaging, millions of paper bags, wooden pallets, poly bags, and plastic boxes were not burned, not put in city dumps, not diverted to unauthorized uses, nor returned. Since bulk was only a one-way haul, millions of gallons of fuel were saved each year by not having to return unplanted seed, return used wooden pallets, or return packaging to the originating conditioning plant.

Ok, enough! What's the point?

Did I mention "team"? No. There wasn't one. Several responsible individuals were doing their job, just like business carried on for thousands of years without teams.

The TruBulk® program was developed and implemented in North America within months and within a few short years it was trademarked and institutionalized across the continent.

Over the years, I received a design and three utility patents for equipment and functions to increase bulk product handling efficiency. Hundreds of millions of acres were planted using our bulk system, and never once did we have a team to direct the project. The initial seed dealers kept selling seed; within a couple years of TruBulk® origination our soybean manager left the company, and our expert field sales representative retired. Until retirement, I kept the project going, but I was not the primary invigorator. Projects create a natural adoption cycle when efficiency is recognized and not regulated by teams.

By 2010 the TruBulk® program dominated the U.S. soybean industry. Although I never had an office in any of our company's headquarters, I was asked to fill out an electronic form to enter the TruBulk® system in our company's worldwide recognition and awards program. Like any computer-generated format, certain boxes had to be filled in before the form could be submitted. I could not fill in the blanks for "team members." There was not a team.

At the time, we had about 90,000 company employees, so I could choose any to submit the bulk project into the award program. A marketing expert in our Minneapolis area office worked with me on promotions and she agreed to be on the TruBulk® "team" as did a well-known agronomist from Des Moines, Iowa. A manager of one of our Minnesota soybean conditioning plants and someone from our seed treatment division also agreed to be on the "TruBulk® team" to finally complete the form.

Suffice it to say, we did not win the worldwide award. Heck, our so-called team never met, while bulk systems completely dominated the soybean industry by the time I retired in 2012 thanks to all the people I worked with that simply did their job. Teams therefore allow job avoidance by shirking responsibility. Businesses use teams when managers and workers are incompetent to do their assigned jobs.

My last project, a couple weeks before I retired, was to tour company colleagues from Argentina helping them identify keys to implementing a similar system in their country. Every person on our corporate soybean team refused repeated invites to join the Argentines on a TruBulk® tour. I hold no animosity toward them. Rather than learning how to expand our superior system, our company's soybean team was simply caught up in corporate team meetings.

Without traveling to dealers using the TruBulk® system, our soybean team did not envision it beyond a bulk versus bag system. With any product, to be effective teams must not only change systems, they must increase efficiency or competitors will. Teams spend so much time in meetings they do not realize how business activity changed; consequently, they are unable to anticipate and adapt to new trends.

Farmers were getting older and wanted to mechanically handle seed rather than throw bags. Young farmers always looked to do less time-consuming physical work. My goal as an equipment expert was to increase handling efficiency and as an agronomist to increase grain yield.

Our TruBulk® system handled seed fast and safely while it allowed minuscule amounts of micronutrients, fungicides, inoculants, and other natural biological agents combined with flowability products to increase plant stand with healthier seedlings, which equated to higher yields for each field. There was no way to pre-apply prescription seed treatments for each farmer's field when delivered in paper bags. Our corporate soybean team simply used data to evaluate costs of bulk steel bins, plastic boxes, and paper bags that were within their realm of analysis. Increasing yield was another team's responsibility.

With a career spanning over forty years, working in the military, government, and private business structures, I've never seen a team fully implement a project quickly, efficiently, or sustain it for a substantial period. Short term, as in hours, teams work; intermediate and long term, they are lacking.

Using my degree in Commercial Economics, I would say, administering a business using the "team concept" insures marked up budgets, promotes weak managers, limits innovation, slows decisions and output, provides adherence to mundane corporate dictates, and maintains full meeting rooms while covertly letting talent exit the back door.

Teams are an excuse to avoid personal decisions and responsibility.

Teams replace individual initiative. The dichotomy is stark. Individuals are becoming more narcissistic, especially with one- or two-children families, while responsibility lies hidden in teams.

My favorite narcissist joke: How many narcissists does it take to screw in a light bulb? One. The narcissist holds the light bulb and the world revolves around him.

How many team narcissists does it take to screw in a light bulb? None. Nobody will take responsibility to find a bulb.

Teams are a business method for dealing with institutionalized narcissists.

There were ten siblings in my wife's family and seven in mine. We were poor. Everybody shared. In big families like ours, if someone thought the world revolved around them, others would not share their bubblegum—no matter how many nights it dried on the bedpost.

Now everybody gets his or her own bubblegum.

Narcissistic behavior is therefore also driven by family economics. Businesses will have trouble moving away from team operations when their employees are self-centered. What are the underlying causes?

A society where people marry at a later age ensures fewer children per family. The older the parents, the more likely their children will be given more money from childhood into adulthood. Money is the alternative to child/parent time.

When I was young, it was automatically assumed you were on your own when you graduated from high school. You were an adult. Economic responsibility had automatically shifted away from parent to child at age eighteen. Now, many children think it is their parent's responsibility to pay for their college education. In the United States, it all ties in with the voting age issue (XXVI Amendment) giving those age eighteen the right to vote.

Want more proof that narcissism is getting worse? The other day I saw a teenager wearing a flashy t-shirt stating: "I'M PRETTY MUCH THE BEST PERSON I KNOW."

When child/parent time is inadequate during youth and the child is not given responsibilities around the home, parents try to keep their children from growing up. Parents with more years of formal education seem to be more likely to restrict their child's maturity. An example follows.

Maggie Mulqueen, a psychologist in Brookline, Massachusetts, wrote an excellent article about a family journal given as a surprise by her husband (a medical doctor) on their first anniversary.[6] Each year, a few days before their anniversary he would add his insight into how their family and relationship developed and changed during the year. As they aged, their annual discussion migrated one year to the question: What should they do with their journal upon death?

Mulqueen wrote:

> Our sons have heard me talk about how much I love the journal, but they have never seen it. And since they are just reaching young adulthood (they are 26, 24, and 21 years old), we have never discussed its fate with them.

Since the dawn of history, who has ever considered a twenty-six-year-old man "... just reaching young adulthood"?

---

[6] Mulqueen, Maggie, "The Book of Love, to Maggie Mulqueen a Tattered Old Journal Holds a Lifetime of Comfort," *AARP Magazine*, August/September, 2016, American Association of Retired People, Washington, D.C., pp. 74–75.

Writers try to bring attention to something they have written that will be remembered, and ultimately quoted, later. Mulqueen is a good writer using a small note in parenthesis to make her article memorable. Her husband's journal was the topic of the article although her adult sons received my attention. A mother referencing her sons' immaturity is not the boys' fault. Only God knows when she potty trained her twenty-six, twenty-four, and twenty-one-year-old sons (assuming she did).

As a licensed psychologist, Mulqueen has the legal right to manipulate the minds of her clients and children, but she fails to recognize what is considered a legal adult in Massachusetts and the remainder of the United States.

Since the article's author was from Massachusetts, I will review the adult status in that state and others:

- *Marriage:* Twelve-year-old girls can legally marry in Massachusetts with parent and/or judge's consent. Boys must be fourteen. Legal age to marry without consent is sixteen in Massachusetts. All states allow marriage without consent at eighteen and under. Thirty U.S. states plus Puerto Rico and the District of Columbia allow sixteen-year-olds to legally marry with no consent needed.
- *Birth control:* There is no established minimum age to obtain birth control products in most states although adult condom size may be inappropriate.
- *Abortion:* Massachusetts has no minimum age to get an abortion but a judge's consent is needed without parental consent. There is NO minimum age to get an abortion in some states with no parental or judge's consent needed (e.g., California).
- *Media:* Any age person could watch filthy, gory films until 1984 when the Motion Picture Association of America introduced the PG-13 rating system.
- *Crime:* At age fourteen in all U.S. states the law assumes you are responsible for your actions and can be charged for a crime and may be tried as an adult.
- *Driving:* Massachusetts requires the driver to be sixteen to drive and 18 to get an unrestricted license. In many states, fourteen to sixteen-year-olds can start driving a vehicle, but an unrestricted driver's license is issued at seventeen or under in thirty-seven of fifty states.

- **Firearms:** In Massachusetts, fifteen is the minimum age to get a Firearm Identification Card, although parental consent is required. Age fourteen is often considered the minimum age to legally possess a gun to hunt in most states, although eighteen is considered the legal age to purchase a firearm without consent.
- **Military:** With parental consent, a seventeen-year-old can enlist in the U.S. military. An eighteen-year-old can enlist in the U.S. military without parental consent.
- **Vote:** An eighteen-year-old can vote in all local, state, and U.S. national elections.
- **Alcohol:** Twenty-one is the legal alcohol drinking age in the United States, although in Massachusetts eighteen-year-olds can be bartenders and can serve, handle, transport, and sell beer, wine, and spirits. In non-alcohol selling establishments, forty-five states (including Massachusetts) allow parental and religious consumption of alcohol.
- **Tobacco:** For the first 200 years after the founding of the United States teenagers could legally purchase and consume tobacco. In 2005, Needham, Massachusetts, was the first city in that state to set the minimum age of twenty-one to legally purchase and consume tobacco. Although specific laws vary state-by-state and city-by-city, twenty-one is now considered the legal age for tobacco.
- **Drugs:** Although marijuana is currently an illegal drug in the United States, at age twenty-one it can be legally purchased for medicinal purposes in twenty-six states (e.g., Colorado and Washington).[7]

Do you see social dissimulation occurring?

As was the case with Genghis Khan 800 years ago, Massachusetts still allows twelve-year-old girls and fourteen-year-old boys to marry, but current culture forces them to be twenty-one before buying a beer.

With legal restrictions the last few decades on legal substances (i.e., tobacco, alcohol, guns, and films), the public must assume the age of maturity is getting older. Yet, condom use is getting earlier with growing demand for small ones.

---

[7] State Marijuana Laws in 2017, Governing the States and Localities, http://www.governing.com/gov-data/state-marijuana-laws-map-medical-recreational.html (sourced August 30, 2017)

Killing babies by abortion is getting younger with no parental consent needed for young teens in socially liberal places like Massachusetts and California. Adult killing: The historic legal age in the military to kill someone protecting the country is seventeen, but one must now be eighteen in most states and twenty-one in some states to purchase a firearm to protect family and property.

Some say marriage is a two-person team; rather it is a legalized partnership. Family status matters. Two teenage guys I know got married when their young brides were fourteen years-old. One guy has now been married fifty-six years and the other forty-four years to their original wife. Only anecdotal evidence, but it seems children from both couples are more economically independent than others. It seems like the younger couples marry, the more likely they are to teach independence and responsibility to their children.

Marital status changes as social and economic situations change. Depression, war, and economic independence influences marital status. The 1930s depression saw fewer marriages than the early 1940s when marriages peaked, but then fell during World War II. Although marriage popularity regained between 1950 and 1954, it has decreased since. With more economically satisfying jobs for women and more government social programs to support the unmarried between 1957 and 2009, postponing marriage became more common.

> While the proportion of all women who are never married at age 25 to 29 has increased substantially from 1986 to 2009 (27 percent to 47 percent), it did not differ statically for women aged 55 and over (5 percent to 6 percent).[8]

This 2011 U.S. Census Bureau data indicates a relatively stable 5–6 percent of the women fifty-five and over born before 1954 have not married. Whereas, those born between 1980 and 1984 were nearly twice as likely (47% vs. 27%) to have never married as those born between 1957 and 1961.

---

[8] Number, Timing, and Duration of Marriages, and Divorces: 2009, U.S. Census Bureau, U.S. Department of Commerce, May 2011 https://www.census.gov/prod/2011pubs/p70-125.pdf (Sourced November 12, 2016)

Reflecting the rise in the median age at first marriage, the percentages of men and women born in 1975 to 1979 who were married by age 20 (8 percent and 18 percent, respectively) were less than one-half the percentage of those born in 1935 to 1939 (21 percent and 51 percent, respectively).[9]

Unmarried people, no matter what age, have a different outlook on life. They are more self-centered, and more likely to change society through voting self-benefits than those married and supporting a family. It is likely a higher percentage of Americans will never marry. As population ages, societies throughout history have always adopted cultural changes, usually by slavery or immigration (similar labor systems) to maintain economic status.

THE TRANSITION

When did the transition to irresponsible children, spectator sports, team efforts, and narcissist bulb-holders occur?

If this is a recent phenomenon, did it entrench in the 1940s? 1950s? 1960s? 1970s? 1980s? Or 1990s? It is well established, so it could not have occurred after 2000. The system was in place by then. Likewise, those born before 1940 could be partially culpable as hosts but are not primary vectors.

Phenomenon! Confused on what is the "recent phenomenon" I am referring to? Probably!

The "phenomenon" is the combination of responsibility, sports, team, and narcissist. To keep it simple, I will fall back on my Air Force, Air National Guard, Department of Agriculture, and corporate background and invent the acronym ReSTN: "Re" (Responsibility), "S" (Sports), "T" (Team), and "N" (Narcissist).

I have assumed ReSTN is not used in FUFFUAA or as an established acronym.

What's FUFFUAA? Partially, it is an acronym joke because government and corporations tend to use hundreds of acronyms. FUFFUAA

---

[9] Number, Timing, and Duration of Marriages, and Divorces: 2001, U.S. Census Bureau, U.S. Department of Commerce, February 2005, https://www.census.gov/prod/2005pubs/p70-97.pdf (Sourced November 12, 2016)

was an actual book published by the Hawaii Department of Health in 1972: *FUFFUAA: Frequently Used and Fairly Frequently Used Abbreviations and Acronyms: a guide for consumers and providers of health services.* No wonder Hawaiians needed it—the government title was nineteen words long.

Did the ReSTN phenomenon occur in the 1970s? Yes.

Constitutional Amendment XXVI was ratified in 1971, which likely stimulated "Re" and "N" in ReSTN. Eighteen-year-olds, by national law, were "Re" (responsible) enough to vote.

Thirteen years later, July 1, 1984, the Motion Picture Association of America introduced the PG-13 rating system to minimize the violence, nudity, and language viewed by children who have not reached their teens. William Lincoln patented the first motion picture machine, the zoopraxiscope, in 1867 and until 1984 anyone could legally watch any published film. With increased production of sexuality, gore, and violence-themed movies, the public demanded more restricted ratings such as R, X, XX, and XXX.

Narcissists thrive on individual rights.

Because voting at eighteen was an individual's right since 1971, hence it established "N" (narcissism) as a national teenage standard. A hindsight backlash indicated that an individual was not "Re" (responsible) to watch filthy movies before age thirteen nor smoke or drink before they were eighteen. National moral standards have migrated. Over the last few years some have been lowered by allowing teens to purchase condoms and have abortions, but they cannot buy historically legal substances, alcohol or tobacco, until age twenty-one.

A maturity shift is taking place across America. What is happening to families over the last seventy years? Review some numbers.

Table 1 numerically indicates over a seventy-year period, there has been an inconsistent decrease in family size, but a consistent decrease in household size. As couples married and started households in the 1950s (after WWII), the Baby Boomers[10] peaked in the 1960s. With a significant increase in children, per household and family peaked in the 1960s; children demographics under eighteen resulted in a bell-curve with the tail still decreasing in 2010. It is interesting to note family and

---

[10] "Baby Boomer" is generally defined as a U.S. baby born between 1946 and 1964.

TABLE 1   Average population per family: 1940–2010*

Year	per Household				per Family				
	All ages	Under 18	Over 18	% Over 18	All ages	Under 18	Over 18	% Over 18	% Under 18 living with 2 parents**
1940	3.67	1.14	2.53	68.9	3.76	1.24	2.52	67.0	Na
1950	3.37	1.06	2.31	68.5	3.54	1.17	2.37	66.9	Na
1960	3.33	1.21	2.12	63.7	3.67	1.41	2.26	61.6	87.7
1970	3.14	1.09	2.05	65.3	3.58	1.34	2.25	62.8	85.2
1980	2.76	0.79	1.97	71.4	3.29	1.05	2.23	67.8	76.6
1990	2.63	0.69	1.94	73.8	3.17	0.96	2.21	69.7	72.5
2000	2.62	0.69	1.93	73.7	3.17	0.98	2.19	69.1	69.1
2010	2.59	0.64	1.95	75.3	3.16	0.93	2.23	70.1	69.4

* Average Population per Household and Family: 1940 to Present," Table HH-6, U.S. Bureau of the Census, September 15, 2004 https://www.census.gov/population/socdemo/hh-fam/hh6xls (Sourced October 6, 2015)

** "Living Arrangements with Children Under 18 Years Old." U.S. Census Bureau, http://www.google.com.mx/url?q=http://www.census.gov/population/socdemo/hh-fam/ch1.xls&sa=U&ved=0CB4QFjACahUKEwj6-N3ur67IAhVLmoAKHeaWBHI&usg=AFQjCNE4DfhfcR4MfVhwW2DLoBfkzEumwA (Sourced October 6, 2015)

Source: U.S. Bureau of Census with percent columns calculated. "na" Not Available

household members over eighteen have continued to decrease, but the numbers can be puzzling.

Children per family under eighteen indicate the traditional family size peaked in the 1960s. The percent of family over eighteen years of age reached its low point during that decade. Since 1980 the percent in households over eighteen exceeded the late depression demographics of 1940.

To further emphasize the zenith of America's traditional family, the percent of family and household over eighteen was at its lowest point in the 1960s. During that decade, only 12.3% of the children did not have two parents in the family. (Compute from the far right column of Table 1.) Since the beginning of the twenty-first century, over 30 percent of the children under eighteen are being raised without both parents.

When two parents do not raise children, the child then becomes the focus of attention when staying with either parent (or grandparent, other family or nonfamily member). The attention is often bribes–more toys, personal television, phones, cars, and allowances.

Children should not all be treated the same, as they are in classrooms. Give a toddler a box. Traditionally, the boy will make a truck or build something with it and a girl will make it into a table, set it, and prepare imaginary food. Boys and girls are just different. As they grow older, girls desire fancy panties and the boys want to remove them.

Biologically, it takes a male and female to produce a child, but nearly a third of "families" are raising children with one (or less) than one parent. Why are there more than two people in a "family" over eighteen? Families are not giving more care to their ageing live-in parents; instead, children are not leaving home.

What is the result of single or dual child families reared by separated parents and camped at grandparents? Narcissism.

Narcissism in children increases with fewer siblings.

They want something for nothing, which someone else should provide and as if by magic it appears.

A couple of years ago, my wife and I were bicycling around Portland, Oregon–a very bike-friendly city. We bike about a thousand miles per year and appreciate gas-guzzling drivers being courteous to cyclists. Many Portland streets have their own white-striped bike lane and separate (small) traffic and turning lights for bicyclists. Anyway, we biked from an RV park on the Columbia River into downtown Portland for a cup of coffee. Like any major city, the homeless (many by choice, usually drug addicts) were hanging out downtown holding out their hand or sign for a donation. The most clever handwritten sign on a piece of brown cardboard read, "*METH DOESN'T GROW ON TREES!*" That was proof enough to me that even stone heads know money doesn't appear by magic.

It is likely that many on illegal drugs were narcissistic youth. Everyone told them they were the most important person in the room. When on their own and with nobody to boost their ego, they self-absorb their mind with stimulants and hang with people that require an ego boost.

Kids know more about illicit drugs than parents. When an opportunity presents itself, talk to your kids about illicit drugs, learn what the current trends are, and be aware of what's happening in your area.

One time our teenage grandson was with me heading south of Omaha, Nebraska, on I-29. We passed a pharmacy billboard and he burst out laughing. "What is so funny Austin?" "That drug store advertisement in this town." I quickly pulled off the next exit and drove down Main Street past "Stoner Drug." I also found it humorous because I attended school with a family named Stoner.

Many probably still remember the story of Aladdin and his lamp popularized by the 1992 Disney movie *Aladdin*. The motion picture may not have covered the same details as in the print version. Antoine Galland wrote the first printed record of *Aladdin* in his March 25, 1709 A.D. diary noting that its source was a Syrian storyteller.[11] Fables and stories were often passed on for hundreds, if not thousands, of years without being written.

Nobody knows the origin of Aladdin. Likely, it and many other life-lesson stories were memorized in "schools of thought" well before any written language. I believe mankind has always been inquisitive, inventive, and sought self-preservation for succeeding generations. Before being able to write, it was unnecessary. Minds were trained to remember. Stories, songs, poems aided memory and allowed events,

---

[11] *Aladdin* by Antoine Galland, https://en.wikipedia.org/wiki/Aladdin (Sourced November 18, 2015)

genealogies, poisonous and medicinal plants, and other history, and life-sustaining information to be passed to future generations.

For example, in the late 1990s I traveled Turkey for a month. One stop was in Hisarilik where we toured the likely ancient city of Troy known for Homer's poems, the "Iliad" and the "Odyssey." They may have been delivered in rhythmic song as the Iliad is, on occasion, referred to as the "Song of Ilion." The poems are attributed to the ancient Greek poet, Homer who lived 751 to 651 B.C.

What is unusual about the battle of Troy as described by Homer? The Trojan War, which modern archeologists date from 1260 to 1180 B.C., occurred many generations before Homer was born. How could Homer write about a war that occurred at least 500 years before his birth? Memory. Many generations likely passed on the Trojan War story of Troy until it could be written by Homer.

Using only memory, the illiterate passed history from genera- tion-to-generation through poems, stories, songs, psalms, and facts on genealogy, kingdoms, and edible and inedible resources. The several hundred-year-old Arabian story of Aladdin told more about life than rubbing a lamp. Swab. Bam! A genie appears. Swoon the rest of your life.

Here are a few snippets from a grade-school English literature text- book first published in 1882 A.D.[12] The first sentences began:

> A poor tailor, who lived in a large city in China, had a careless, idle, lazy boy. This boy refused to do anything to render himself useful, and wasted his time running about the streets. When Aladdin … was about fifteen years old his father died. Having no one to control him, Aladdin became still more idle and worthless … playing in the street with some of his companions.

How many grade school teachers today require their class to read about a naughty young boy that becomes a ne'er-do-well teenager?

How many children are taught that the Aladdin story in British lit- erature originated in China untold years ago, and was carried to their country by memory of an illiterate Syrian?

---

[12] *Aladdin and his Lamp*, Sheldons' Modern School Fourth Reader, Sheldon & Com- pany, Copyright 1882, 1885, pp. 61–64.

Society's mental capacity has dwindled. The trend has been going on for hundreds of years and is escalating.

Since the Brits likely could not pass on the Aladdin story verbatim from memory, it was written down in 1709. Less than 300 years later, in 1992, an Aladdin movie was developed–likely the only way most children ever envisioned the Aladdin story. Quite likely parents born in the 1960s still remembered hearing or reading the story and wanted to take their children to the movie in the early 1990s because they no longer had the book and could not remember all the details.

If the parents had given proper background to Disney's *Aladdin*, how many children would beg to see a movie about a lazy kid that did not listen to his parents? It would have been a good time to repeat the Fourth Commandment: "Honor your father and your mother...."[13]

Do you remember why Aladdin was stuck in the cave with the lamp? He took off with a bad guy and got greedy. The cave was too small for the magician, a "... very cunning and a very deceitful and wicked man...." Aladdin was sent into the cave to bring the special lamp back to him, but Aladdin "... Could not take it from his bosom without pulling out the jewels which he had picked from the trees, and he did not wish the magician to see these."

What did Aladdin do as soon as the genie let him out of the cave?

"Aladdin hastened home and told his mother everything that had taken place, and gave her the lamp."

When a kid escapes trouble and needs consoling, what does he do? Cries, Mommy! Mommy! Aladdin went to his widowed mother. Famished for two months, "... his mother proposed to clean the lamp and sell it for money with which to buy food."

The story drags on about how magic made Aladdin rich and without magic he became poor and finally became rich and powerful after recovering the magic lamp. Is that how the 1880s school textbook ends the story? No. The final sentence ends with another lesson of morality: "I have known some boys who wished they could find a lamp like the one which Aladdin found in the garden (cave), but I do not believe they would enjoy themselves any more, or would be any happier than they are now."

---

[13] Exodus 20:12, NKJV, p. 108

By age fifteen many want to break out of school. Life will be so good when they happen upon a load of money and be happy ever after without an ounce of work. When not given everything, and taught early to be independent, children know life is not a magical rainbow leading to a pot of gold–meaning unsubstantiated credit becomes a vice.

Likewise, when government steps in to take care of children, as it did against free-range parents, parents have an excuse to shirk responsibility for parenting. Instead, a team is needed, as in the old African proverb "It takes a village to raise a child." There is a cultural difference in meaning. Historically, especially when the proverb originated, someone was a child until puberty. Now in the twenty-first century, underdeveloped and developed countries consider teens and young adults "children" and are defined as such on healthcare and other laws.

Structured teams seem to be modern culture's childrearing system, whereas, young children are bought off with more toys, gadgets, and fast food after daycare.

After finally achieving independence, the child's structured rearing teams are unaccountable. Dereliction becomes the parent's albatross.

Children learn quickly how to pull adult strings way before their teenage years. String pulling is a trained memory–remembered better than an Aladdin story. Parents must teach discipline early and give responsibilities (by age two) to pattern a child's disposition. It is not the responsibility of teachers, coaches, managers, or teams to correct them.

8

Free Range

Riddle: What spreads but has distinct
beginnings and ends?

Often, I hear people talking about how much things are changing. "I am
unable to keep up with all the changes" is a favorite saying of senior citizens. In reality, *learning has slowed*. Technological gadgets have replaced
intellect, and senior citizens are referencing their inability to operate
gadgets. Gadgets and intellect are not interchangeable. A well-designed
app cannot replace a well-educated brain. Students want to use gadgets
to look up an answer so they do not have to remember and thereby learn.

For several years I was an ex officio board member of South Dakota's Certified Crop Advisors (CCA) organization. As a senior agriculturalist, I was to advise the board members and volunteered to annually
rewrite the entrance examination for new members. Often two board
members, who represented two technical colleges, commented that students look up answers rather than learning and remembering details.
The educators lamented: "How can we get them to learn, if they can just
look up an answer?"

To become a certified member of our organization, applicants had
to pass a national and state agricultural examination on subjects ranging from pest identification and erosion control to nutrient and water
management. Every year far more applicants were passing the national
examination than our state examination. Things had to change if our
state testing standards did not allow enough new members to replace

attrition or those retiring. The board of directors considered options to lower entry standards or improve applicant evaluations. Our board chose the latter.

Our test rewriting group of three (a university professor, a senior agronomist from a company I competed against, and I) replaced 25 to 30 percent of the questions each year on the statewide test. Analyzing the entrance exam, we realized we had many poor questions. On many questions those scoring the highest had a lower "guess rate" than those with low scores. Those questions were either rewritten or dropped.

Second, we were asking too many technical questions that could be answered with gadgets. Instead, we focused on drafting questions to see if applicants understood the subject. The result: Over a period of three years (rewriting basically the whole exam), more applicants were passing our state examination, but proudly we still maintained a tougher standard of agricultural knowledge than was expected nationally.

It was frustrating for technical college instructors on our board who could not motivate students to learn a subject. Gadgets remained a learning excuse. Often it was easier to identify with personalities and lower course standards in order to allow students to graduate. When emotional connection and gadgets replace learning, standards are lowered. Perhaps that's why every year fewer applicants were passing our standard CCA exam. They enjoyed the outdoors and wanted a career in agriculture, but they were not motivated by test-taking or were graded by emotional acceptance.

By rewriting our CCA entrance exam, we sought to know if the tech-school students were learning at a slower pace, a different pace, or not learning.

Teacher evaluations are also changing.

To justify the lower IQ (Intelligence Quotient) of teachers, an EQ (Emotional Quotient) is increasingly being considered a better standard for teachers. For example, would you want a National Aeronautics and Space Administration (NASA) statistical mathematician teaching quantum physics to your five-year-old learning disabled child? No. However, technical ability of NASA mathematicians would certainly degrade over the years if graduates had been graded based on their emotional connection with teachers and classmates rather than by their mathematical potential. EQ is replacing IQ in what I refer to as educational depreciation. One should not replace the other.

Intellectual and emotional learning should take place jointly. Since the 1960s EQ seems to be the highest priority at the elementary level and gradually decreases through graduate school. Elementary teachers need more EQ but do not have as much IQ as summarized by Julie Mahfood in an interesting article "10 College Subjects with the Lowest Average IQs."[1]

Just like we should not expect NASA mathematicians to be the best teachers for kindergarten or students with learning disabilities, we should not expect future NASA employees to have the same first fifteen years of education as elementary teachers.

Rather than having average or below average teachers in math, science, and languages, children need to segregate based on their interests and compete with skills and ideas of others. Children hone their interests as they grow. In any culture in any country in any century until the last half of the twentieth century in developed countries, children had to hone interests as they grew into adulthood.

Wages are one result of the untrained. Now workers of all ages complain about inadequate government-established minimum wage. Introductory jobs were never meant to provide family sustenance at government-established minimum wage. What should be the pay of someone with no experience? Nothing? That is not fair; it should be something.

How can today's youth gain experience, or understand work responsibilities if they are prohibited from working by excessive minimum wage, insurance regulations, or child-labor laws? Unfortunately, without responsibility children are unable to thoughtfully organize, efficiently develop, or effectively complete projects. Consequently, modern young adults are worth less as they age.

Since ancient times, children segregated based on their interests, which developed over time but were generally contemplated by puberty and developed thereafter. Below is a 2000-year-old written example of a carpenter's son:

---

[1] Mahfood, Julie, "10 College Subjects with the Lowest Average IQs," March 10, 2014, The Biggest, http://www.therichest.com/rich-list/the-biggest/10-college-subjects-with-the-lowest-average-iqs/ (Sourced April 27, 2016)

And when he was twelve years old, they went up to Jerusalem according to the custom of the feast.... The Boy Jesus lingered behind in Jerusalem. And Joseph and His mother did not know it.... After three days they found Him in the temple, sitting in the midst of the teachers both listening to them and asking them questions. And he said to them "Why did you seek Me? Did you not know that I must be about My Father's business?"[2]

His parents had traveled three days with their group before realizing Jesus was not with the caravan. Twelve-year-old children back then were expected to be responsible and have independence. It would not have been unusual for him to be gone a night or two.

As I approached age sixty-four, I was invited to hike a mountain on a Mexican family's ranch. Grandsons, ages seventeen and eighteen, led the way on a six-hour roundtrip hike to the highest two peaks on their grandfather's ranch. Carlos was eighteen, married, and had a two-year-old daughter while his seventeen-year-old brother had just finished school. Both worked in the family retail business. On the way down, the youngest said, "This was our favorite spot to come when we were young." In their culture, at their age, they were mature, responsible adults. As working adults, hiking the mountains to the ranch brought them peace of mind reminiscent of youth.

There was no school in the mountains. Education was on the job. As a ten-year-old girl, their mother brought a burro to town weekly for supplies. Springs seeping from the mountainside provided water for herself and beast of burden—a donkey. A full-day's journey in the rainy season would have been slowed by heat, mud, and overflowing streams. So what? That did not change her responsibilities, or desire to be employed in town upon reaching adulthood.

Age of maturity has different expectations in different cultures. Often, parents underestimate maturity, responsibility, desires, and children's career interests.

Parents often do not know or understand their children. Parents are generally blocked from understanding. How? Public investment.

---

[2] Luke 2:42–43, 46, 49, NKJV, p. 1462

Investment in the school system is overhead cost—a cost justified by calling it "education." Does the public endure those costs to justify a child's education? Apparently. Or, are other factors involved? Yes.

In rural areas, once a school is closed, the town dies. High-paying jobs are lost. When grouped, teachers are often the highest paid business employees in the community. Yes, school is a business. Schools are not civil government. As a monopoly, public schools have established their role as a quasi-government organization servicing social desires.

Ask any American parent why they send their children to public schools rather than home school. I have done it many times. Never once has a parent said it was for providing their children the best education. What is the number one answer? "School offers social interaction."

Home-schooling has perceived negative connotations. In the twenty-first century, primary, secondary, public and private schools, universities, and businesses use the Internet for online learning. I have asked teachers the same question but modified it to online learning. Teachers oppose nonschool online learning. Why? The number one reason: "Online learning lacks social interaction that schools offer."

That means the public is paying thousands of dollars each year for each child with the primary goal to socialize. It is as if parents and teachers never heard of day care, playgrounds, dance class, swimming pools, 4-H, scouting, picnics, church, backyard ball games, or social media.

Schools are an identity for the community—good or bad. With public investment (overhead) comes standardization. The longer the school standardizes learning, the longer it takes a child to develop their interests. Unfortunately, some never do. Children have been denied that privilege with a generous society supporting them for at least the first couple of decades of life.

In other words, dependent students must be budgeted as lifetime public overhead costs. Independent students will eventually pay for the livelihood of formerly dependent students. School costs are not just annual budgets. Depreciation of dependent adults must be built into the modern school system.

Ancient societies developed metallurgy having only a thirty-year life expectancy. We are dumber than cavemen if we continue to keep kids in school caves for at least a decade after puberty and surveil them with teacher door guards that need two decades of prior institutionalization.

Stay-at-home parents have been offering music lessons to some of the most talented children for centuries. Sports camps, intramural teams, and summer leagues operate privately. Since man's beginning, parents have taken their children on hikes. Discussing nature does not require a degree in biology. Culture is learned.

Electronic learning toys will continue to be developed for all subjects. Those parents that read to their babies and toddlers teach their child to memorize and read. Young readers consistently outpace others in comprehension, school, and life. Parents wanting their children to appreciate music, sports, and outdoor learning certainly should not shackle free-form education and their child's exercise only to school buildings and facilities.

Math, social and applied sciences, nursing, languages, agriculture, aviation, and technology for all industries can be taught without entering a school classroom. If a child can use a computer, they will likely learn to read before setting foot in school. Reading is fundamental to any modern career and it does not have to be read like the cave art of our ancient ancestors.

Some technology has taken decades, even centuries to adopt. China was using toilet paper in the sixth century A.D. and they had commercial production by the fourteenth century. Five hundred years later, Joseph Gayetty is credited for introducing the first commercial toilet paper in the United States in 1857.[3] The material and purpose was the same, but for centuries the technology transfer system was crappy (pun intended).

Since the Industrial Revolution, the technology adoption rate has quickened. Although there is disagreement as to what was the beginning of a functional Internet, it was operational by 1969. Thirty years later, 1995–2000, the technology-dominated NASDAQ[4] stock index went from under 1000 in 1995 to over 4500 in the year 2000 before

---

[3] Toilet paper, https://en.wikipedia.org/wiki/Toilet_paper (Sourced October 12, 2015)

[4] NASD, National Association of Securities Dealers, headquartered in New York, originated February 8, 1971, regrouped as NASDAQ in 2006, is composed of 3000 global, electronically-traded company stocks known collectively as the

dropping 80 percent by late 2002. It was called the "dot-com" bubble. Stock buyers expected faster adoption and more profits than the companies delivered. Internet use did not peak then, but during the late 1990s, everyone that cared knew about the World Wide Web. All major companies used it.

In the western world, toilet paper took five centuries to adopt whereas the Internet took thirty years.

Instantaneous communication is adopted technology. We must learn to live with it or impede its use. Some refuse to use it. Isn't that clever? Heads up public school system: Will sustained ignorance ever win a war of ideas?

Technology will continue to unfold. Some will become established while others will be abandoned or postponed to a more appropriate adoption era. Even U.S. teachers finally found a substance to wipe their butt (paper) 1300 years after innovators and early adopters.

Social media is a social medium for all literate ages. The world is beyond the adoption stage of electronic social media. Struggles will ensue. What are acceptable manners? Appropriateness is being enforced. For example, at meetings, concerts, plays, and funerals, attendees are asked to switch their phones to silent mode. Such limitations are not yet defined during family time, at restaurants, or while going to the bathroom.

Pre-school through high school systems should not be the establisher of social norms, although they may adopt, reject, or modify what is acceptable. School systems do not invent technology; they sometimes use it.

Although Texas Instruments invented the handheld calculator in 1967, such tools, including adding machines were inappropriate when I departed high school in 1971. By the mid-1970s, at university, students were expected to use handheld calculators. That was very quick adoption considering chalk on blackboard, or pencil on paper was the standard means of ciphering for hundreds of years. Before that, individual minds calculated.

Currently, the Internet is allowed for research, but generally not allowed for tests. These examples are a part of the technology adoption cycle.

NASDAQ Global Market Composite (index) is a select group of 1450 companies meeting financial, liquidity, and corporate governance standards.

Families and society must establish social norms and technology adoption. It is wrong to assume the primary and secondary school system should be technology regulators.

My antagonists may argue the U.S. school system was established and developed over centuries and is not about to change. I agree.

The United States' first school was established nearly 400 years ago. A building (public overhead–fixed costs) for youth education was thought to be a necessary public investment. Boston had the first school established in 1635.[5]

Schools train and deliver information, but U.S. schools certainly are not the quickest adopters of technology. After commercial introduction, it took U.S. schools about fifty years to adopt toilet paper. Mr. Gayetty's commercial disaster in marketing toilet paper was because he focused its use on people with hemorrhoids. As a trained economist, I realized he failed to capitalize on liquidity of assets.

Since hemorrhoids are normally not a school-age problem, U.S. schools did not adopt toilet paper technology until the twentieth century. A technology designed for one set of demographics usually finds a much broader backside of initial use.

The public did not wait on the school system to adopt toilet paper, indoor running water, photography, typewriters, electricity, electronics, telegraphy, telephones, radio, television, cell phones, Internet, or social media.

Since we do not wait on the school system to adopt technology, why should we expect the school system to produce life-sustaining adults in a technology astute world?

On the other hand, in the last hundred years, the United States has implemented three monumental projects in less than a decade from concept to completion without reliance on the school system. Everything was accomplished by a trained labor pool educated before President Lyndon Johnson appeased labor unions with Head Start, preschool funding, college draft wavers, and highly subsidized education a decade into adulthood. Besides, who needs a job when someone else is paying for the schooling?

---

[5] "History of Education in the United States," https://en.wikipedia.org/wiki/History_of_education_in_the_United_States (Sourced October 12, 2015)

School skews timing. Innovation becomes an agenda item for later in life. After spending twenty years in school, where is the urgency to accomplish a project?

Let's review the three monumental projects, initiated, implemented, and completed in less than a decade by those educated during my grandfather's generation, before President Johnson took office. Remember, the school system of today did not exist.

Could people that have spent far more time in primary, secondary, and postsecondary schools complete the projects today? If not, why? Fundamentals of learning are deficient and the speed of learning has slowed.

1. France abandoned their 1881 attempt to place a canal across the Isthmus of Panama. Authorized by President Theodore Roosevelt in 1904, the Panama Canal opened on August 15, 1914.[6]

2. The United States initiated a small nuclear project in 1939, but its use as a potential weapon did not get fully underway until 1942 under the code name "Manhattan Project." Three years later, commanded by President Harry Truman, the United States bombed Hiroshima and Nagasaki to convince Japan to end the War in the Pacific theater.[7] Within a few short years, nuclear technology became a new means of generating electricity in Japan and around the world.

3. On May 25, 1961, President John F. Kennedy, before a joint session of Congress, announced that the United States intended to land a man on the moon in a decade. Keep in mind, the Russian, Yuri Gagarin, on April 12, 1961, was the only person at that time that had ever been in space. On July 20, 1969, the United States' Neil Armstrong exited Apollo 11's Lunar Module becoming the first person to ever step foot on the moon.

Although publicly directed, many private entities supported each project. One project that was privately directed with public support was the first transcontinental telegraph across the United States and the Pony Express. Operated only nineteen months between St. Louis,

---

[6] "Panama Canal," https://en.wikipedia.org/wiki/Panama_Canal (Sourced October 12, 2015)

[7] "Manhattan Project," https://en.wikipedia.org/wiki/Manhattan_Project (Sourced October 12, 2015)

Missouri, and Sacramento, California, the Pony Express was one of the shortest-lived public projects.

In 1860 the U.S. Post Office (contractor of the Pony Express) received permission and an annual federal allocation of $40,000 to build and maintain a telegraph line across the United States. Before telegraphs, ten-day Pony Express mail was the quickest means of getting messages from Washington, D.C., to California (the first state on the West Coast admitted to the union).

Gold was discovered in California in January of 1848; hundreds of thousands of gold seekers and their supporters headed to California by any means (ship, horse, wagon, and on foot)—generally known as the "forty-niners" for the massive arrivals of 1849. By September 1850, California became the thirty-first state.

Nine years earlier Los Angeles citizens did not find out newly elected President William Henry Harrison (1773–1841) died in office of pneumonia (April 4, 1841) until a month after his swearing-in ceremony. As wires were installed, telegraph communication was rapid between the Mississippi River and the Atlantic Ocean. Once the transcontinental telegraph was authorized in 1860, during the few months of construction 50,000 postholes were dug by hand every 200 feet for 2000 miles west of the Mississippi. California was connected by telegraph to Washington, D.C., with segmented starting points in California, Nevada, Nebraska, and Missouri.

Logistical issues (i.e., getting posts delivered by wagon, glass insulators off ships on the West Coast) and construction speed is hard for modern readers to fathom. Manually digging holes in native prairie, equally hostile Native Indians raids in treeless country, steep mountains, and flowing rivers compounded by labor shortages were constant obstacles. For example, free-range construction of the segment from Julesburg, Nebraska, under the direction of Edward Creighton (later founder of Creighton University in Omaha, Nebraska) planted their first post July 4, 1861 and was awarded $50 extra per man for completing the first transcontinental segment to Fort Bridger, Wyoming, by mid-October that same year.[8]

---

[8] Miller, Mark, "The Singing Wire, a Story of the Telegraph," 1953, The John C. Winston Company.

On the evening of October 24, 1861, the first telegraph message from the West was sent from California's Supreme Court Chief Justice, Stephen J. Field, to President Abraham Lincoln in Washington, D.C., pledging California's support of the Union. You see, not only was the country physically divided, it was in a Civil War that started April 12, 1861, only three months before the first telegraph posthole was dug on the western segment.

Buffalo rubbed their backs on telegraph posts, breaking many. Prairie fires burned uncontrolled. Hostile Indians cut telegraph wires with tomahawks. In June 1861, Missouri governor in exile, Claiborne Fox Jackson (a Confederate sympathizer), ordered the telegraph line West torn down. Yet, through constant menace and maintenance, telegraph communications connected the western half of the country to the East in less than a year.

To my knowledge, none of the telegraph line construction workers had a college degree.

The transcontinental telegraph system was amazing, considering now with highly educated teams and managers, it takes years, sometimes decades, to get a highway, pipeline, cell phone tower, wind and solar farms, and satellite communication projects approved and built. Progressive? Yes. Fast? No.

U.S. progress has slowed considerably with the public school system remaining a deteriorating constant. Schools train children into adulthood. They seem to be learning less about geography, history, project completion, and ability to cope with risk.

Could a 2000-mile project, like the first transcontinental telegraph, be completed today in a few months with modern diesel powered equipment, automated tools, and instantaneous communications? No.

Originally formed by telegraph mergers in 1856, Western Union Telegraph Company (better known as Western Union), the private transcontinental contractor, still operates today. Although their last telegrams were sent in 2006, they currently send money electronically around the world to 200 countries, 500,000 agents, and reach over a billion bank accounts. Companies, like Western Union, must selectively hire and train to their own standards in every country—a system developed with speed and risk without reliance on public schools.

In the last fifty years we created an educational default system where teachers lack flexibility to perform their duty. What is expected of those that teach a mixed class of underachievers and overachievers under government direction? Year after year in an institutional structure limited by warning bells at the beginning and end of each class, teaching drags on. Warning bells pace learning. It is no wonder teachers and students are stressed.

Projects used to get done quickly. Companies with vision survive.

One hundred years after the U.S. East Coast and West Coast was connected via telegraph, I was in the third grade in the fall of 1961 and our one-room school subscribed to only one magazine or newspaper— the *Weekly Reader*. We had no telegraph, no telephone, no radio or television, no typewriters, and certainly no calculators or computers.

As a young boy, I was baffled reading President Kennedy's (May 25, 1961) concept of sending a person to the moon. I had heard from a Mother Goose rhyme of the potential for sending a cow that far, but that had as much potential as a dish running.

> Hey, diddle, diddle,
> The cat and the fiddle,
> The cow jumped over the moon;
> The little dog laughed
> To see such sport,
> And the dish ran away with the spoon.[9]

Hey, diddle, diddle is a cute, perhaps 500-year-old, rhyme recited to the youngest children. Like many children's rhymes, riddles, and nighttime stories, each likely conveys adult concepts.

"The cat and the fiddle" are lazy. Neither does a darn thing in this rhyme like the cow, dog, and dish. "Diddle, diddle" is more like the American version of "diddle-daddle"—meaning to waste someone else's time. The dictionary describes "diddle"[10] as "to cheat, swindle, or victimize, or to waste (time) in trifling."

---

[9] "Hey, Diddle, Diddle," Mother Goose rhymes; first cited in print in 1569 in a play "A lamentable tragedy mixed ful of pleasant mirth, conteyning the life of Cambises King of Percia," by Thomas Preston. https://en.wikipedia.org/wiki/Hey_Diddle_Diddle, (Sourced October 14, 2015)
[10] "Diddle," *Webster's New World Dictionary*, p. 392.

School and students are like the cat and fiddle–they exist but what are they contributing to this six-line rhyme? Diddle, diddle?

With stealth, the cat had smarts and could entertain children. Likewise, the fiddle was mentioned but when not fiddled, it was nothing more than wood and strings (traditionally made of sheep intestines).

A child can diddle in school for a couple decades and may only daddle when they get out. Thereafter, an employer has to train them.

"The cow jumped over the moon" is certainly an aggressive vision. Both provide action in the mind as one turns and the other must aggressively jump. The cow is like a parent that will do anything for their precious child, as the mother jumps when the self-centered kid wants something.

"The little dog laughed to see such sport" is a great example of today's watchers. Our schools and universities do a good job of preparing adults to watch. Students, and former students, attend games, sit on the bleachers week after week, or watch television sports. The lazy dog just sits there and laughs while the cow, dish, and spoon(er) are providing the sport.

"And the dish ran away with the spoon" is like girls who can't wait to get out of school and will latch on to anything, even a dirty spooner,[11] just to get away. Times have changed somewhat. Some females may take offense to this statement, but up to the 1970s many girls went to college to find a husband. Some were cushioned children never given responsibility at home and never assigned the task of even washing tableware but often learned the "skill" of landing a husband. Those lost in the world, unemployed, unable to function independently are proof parents failed by allowing the school to be guardians rather than educating them for a job.

My point is not a joke, or kid's stuff. In the last century, using technology far inferior to what is available today, we built a canal from the Atlantic Ocean to the Pacific; built an atomic energy industry; and sent a man to the moon. All took less than a decade. No diddle-daddle.

Progress slows as we provide more formal education to our children. It can change.

---

[11] "Dirty spooner," in modern lingo, is a male friend capriciously making sexual advances.

Undeveloped and developing countries had quicker adoption of cell phones than did developed countries. Why? They did not have money to build infrastructure to build lines-on-poles systems.

Likewise, developed countries had the money to build school systems that have antiquated infrastructure not needed in today's communication-savvy world. Rather than quickly phasing out the monstrous monopoly, governments in developed countries are pouring more money into their school systems, thereby assuming that more money will improve the system.

If your car hits a bump in the road and oil starts running out of the oil pan, what do you do? 1. Ignore the dashboard's red light until the motor stops and the car is ruined; 2. Pull into the next fueling station and add engine oil; 3. Stop. Evaluate the situation and have your vehicle pulled into a repair station; or, 4. Pull into the nearest car dealership and trade for a new car.

Developed countries can borrow enough money to do any of the items above. Rather than stop, evaluate, and repair the quickly deteriorating school system, they ignore warning signals, pour more money in without repairing the system, or often build a new school all the while assuming student learning (necessary engine) will improve.

In less than a decade, student materials can be designed for remote learning any place in the world, and used by ages two to centenarians, without ever setting foot in a school or having a teacher physically in front of them. Cell phones connected the remotest parts of the world. Learning systems will, too.

Those administering the developed world's school system, including state and national government agencies, are either fools or are protecting their political turf. I think they are doing both. For a half-century, optimization of child learning for societal benefit has not been the school system's focus.

When I was in high school, more than one teacher told us how hard college was and that college was not for everyone. Perhaps only 10 percent of my classmates went directly from high school into college. After teacher warnings, I was not sure I was smart enough to go to college.

During the Vietnam War, many of the airmen I was working with had several years of college; some had degrees. Most joined the U.S. Air Force so they would not be drafted by the Army and sent to 'Nam. After a year in the Air Force, I realized that most of my high school teachers were not as smart as my average high school classmates. It is no wonder they told us college was hard. It likely still is for an average college student–many of whom are now average teachers. A higher percentage of young adults are entering college. To allow for graduation of the average student, standards have been lowered.

Many teachers today are likely not above average intelligence, but they are expected to teach all the students–half of whom are smarter than they are. That would be a challenge in any profession. Rather than work with the smartest, teachers spend more time with average or below average students–especially since the U.S. implemented No Child Left Behind in 2001 (detailed later).

While I was serving in the Air Force in Italy, we had an opportunity to take courses from the University of Maryland. Professors from the University of Maryland were taking a few months' or a few weeks' sabbatical to provide us classes. The Air Force offered the same program when I was stationed in northern Japan. Each class was like a summer course–condensed with the same expectations and final tests.

Over the course of three years, while stationed overseas, I took approximately twenty credits through the University of Maryland. Some of my best professors came to offer their talents. I learned and thoroughly enjoyed the opportunity to learn from professional teachers.

University of Maryland professors may have only taught one or two classes each week. In their off-days, they toured local historical sites, and probably took the opportunity to step back from teaching in a boxed-in campus to re-evaluate their life and profession. They were what I now call "free-range" educators.

With access to talented professional educators, a child can learn more at home or grouped with neighbor kids using computer technology and parental guidance as they can in school. The system would not be a whole lot different than ten or twelve airmen sitting in a military conference room, or a dozen of us kids grouped in a one-room school several decades ago.

One-room teachers in farming country during the 1950s and 1960s likely had little more training than my mother. We learned. I do not know of one of my country school classmates that failed in life. Children learn at home, with friends, and when doing school projects, but not all at the same pace.

My hunch is: Those opposed to "free-range" parenting as mentioned earlier will also fight "free-range" education. The concept of education as an individual and family responsibility is beyond the insight of many close-minded people. An educational system should not be designed to prepare students for school; it should prepare them to make a living.

A well-known publicist, author, and writing professor, Jane Friedman, wrote: "If you intend to earn a living from it (writing, editing, or publishing), most programs do not help students achieve that through their requirements or extra-curricular offerings alone."[12]

Think about it. Why would any student spend four to eight years in classes after high school "If you ... (can't) earn a living from it"?

Many teachers, school administrators, and government professionals vested in the current educational juggernaut are opposed to schooling at home or local groups sponsored by parents or other organizations. Of course they are! Their jobs are in jeopardy.

Educators argue home-schooled children do not have proper social interaction. It is an interesting dichotomy. Most parents who have taken children from public schools have done so because they do not want their children exposed to the school's social interaction.

I have absolutely nothing against any of the hard-working teachers, administrators, counselors, other support staff, and athletic and music directors. They do not know it yet, but they simply are not needed and can easily be replaced with an educational system not boxed into a school building. It will happen. The technology adoption rate will be faster than schools' adoption of toilet paper. New "free-range" education will be restrained by the current school system monopoly, but it could be implemented more quickly than the manned moon mission.

Twenty-first-century technology allows social interaction not available when current high schoolers were born. Electronic social media is proof. Unfortunately, they likely will be seniors (as in senior citizens) by the time the structural, inefficient education system changes substantially.

---

[12] Friedman, Jane, *Publishing 101: A First-time Author's Guide*, 2014, Amazon, p. 212.

Current established educational institutions are no different from English Luddites 200 years ago.

Luddites[13] were afraid of labor-saving weaving technology. They feared technology that replaced their jobs. Like current high-minded teachers, Luddites feared lower skilled people who had access to machines that did not require traditional weaving (or teaching) skills. The term "Luddite" was likely taken from a guy, Ned Ludd, who in 1779 supposedly wrecked stocking frames that replaced his job. Current Luddite educators are opposed to every method except the established school system.

Educators are not going to introduce or train students in a system that eliminates their job.

Luddite educators will try to perpetuate and expand their jobs to prove their value. One way is by getting lower-skilled teachers, day-care providers, assistants, and substitutes recruited as part of their Luddite community. Second, Luddites will educate their pupils as to their value by advertising their students as special and therefore the public should pay them more, not eliminate their job.

Four-year degree requirements of lower-grade teachers are a result of shrinking college enrollment, shrinking union members, and shrinking population as one- and two-children families approach adulthood. The system develops narcissists to think they are special so they should stay in school longer.

By the beginning of the 1970s, everybody depending on government's education program was special.

- Parents were so special they didn't have to take care of their children.
- Children were so special that they got a "Head Start" in school.
- Schoolteachers were so special they got paid to tell parents their children were special.
- Unions ensured that teachers were so special they needed a university degree—to teach youngsters before first grade.
- University professors were so special even teachers of preschool had to sit through their classes.

---

[13] "Luddite," https://en.wikipedia.org/wiki/Luddite (Sourced October 10, 2015)

Society should no longer wonder: How did so many people get to be so special?

World history documents that current society is full of "me-first" aboriginals. Narcissists can look in the mirror and see how original they are. Schools reinforce it. No society in history has been so self-centered.

Allowing children to have independent educational responsibilities will force them to gradually break free of parent praise and force them to proudly prove their worth. From the earliest ages, properly guided, age-appropriate training modules selected by parents will allow children to grow and learn at their own pace. That individual pace will be far faster than school learning because teachers instruct to the average. If teachers focused only on the bright or slow learners, the teacher would be more frustrated than the students.

Free enterprise and teachers with ability will develop computer-animated materials that far exceed the ability of one teacher. Currently, dividing time between a whole room full of students with different needs requires more teachers and slows the learning process, thereby fulfilling the purpose of the modern school system. The current system seems to be designed to maximize inefficiency.

Everyone my age watched "Popeye the Sailorman," a King Features Syndicated television animation. Only filmed for three years (1960–1962), Popeye lasted in our memories for decades. We all knew Popeye would overcome all odds in his love for Swee'Pee and Olive Oyl; he tolerated but detested Brutus, ate spinach for muscles, and empathized with Wimpy who always wanted a hamburger before Tuesday's paycheck.

Children also learn bad self-centered habits. The standard line for gluttonous Wimpy was, "I'll gladly pay you Tuesday for a hamburger today." I can never remember Wimpy ever returning to Popeye Tuesday, payment in hand. It was a lesson to the self-centered–you can be a fat slob and expect others to pay for your food without working for it. Oh, I guess I am referring to many in today's society that expect everybody else to pay for his or her needs and wants.

Educating children for fourteen or more years is too important to let some anonymous, bloated school system assign our children to teachers.

Today's children may identify with Popeye with his tattoos reminding them of their parents. Cartoons for the very young, and not so young, are absorbed by children from many sincere, but comic, themes. Immediate response got children to eat spinach.

Toronto Ontario's *The Globe and Mail* carried an article in 2010 about children's vegetable-eating habits and alternative training. After being exposed to other children's comments about peas, broccoli, and spinach their home consumption stopped. However, when shown "Popeye" cartoons, kids began consuming spinach again when bigger muscle implications were made.[14]

Even in cartoons since the early 1960s athletics was substituted for education. Some programs educated through cartoons using child humor.

Parents and teachers know cartoons influence children. Animated educational materials are also a way for parents and children to combine learning with parenting. Children and their parents can jointly enjoy age-appropriate educational materials. Market forces will ensure competitive program access. The bonus with "free-range" education is that the parent, or parent's assigned sitter, not the school, has control over content.

Many countries have the same problem with current-generation narcissists. China, for example, with its one-child program, initiated in 1979, reinforced the child's self-worth. Although the country began phasing out the program in 2015, extraneous exceptions bolstered the paternal society. For example, if the first child was a girl, the couple was allowed a second child; others are mentioned below.

In the mid-twentieth century, population control was the main reason the United Nations, member-nations, and China in particular, implemented government control of family structure. Narcissism blossoms when individual focus develops—especially in one-child families. Repercussions are evident in demographics, militarism, social structure (like U.S. single-parent public support), and even ethnicity. Why?

Although parents naturally decide privately how many children they want based on occupation, family needs, religion, personal choice, and surname longevity, government mandated programs provide

---

[14] Hewitt, Katie, "How to win the kid v. veggies battle," The Globe and Mail Inc., Toronto, ON, Canada, August 16, 2010, http://www.theglobeandmail.com/life/parenting/how-to-win-the-kid-v-veggies-battle/article4267723/ (Sourced October 13, 2015)

exceptions, especially locally and regionally when allowed. By some counts, before China's one-child policy began phase-out, over twenty additional exceptions were allowed including ethnicity, geography, foreign born, parental military service, disability, child loss from natural disasters, or simply by paying a "social maintenance fee." These are likely public backlash from government intervention in family, or unknowingly natural narcissism prevention.

In 2013, my wife and I stopped in Fiji for a few days to shorten our overseas flight to Australia. Our first night in Nadi, we stayed at a chain hotel that included breakfast with the room. When we arrived in the expansive dining room, one section was filled with Chinese tourists. They seemed to be excited and pleasant. However, the three or four children accompanying the group were out of control. The floor was covered with their uneaten food. Their table looked like a pig had rooted around on top of it. The children apparently finished eating and were seeing how many booths they could climb over, straddle, stand on, and mess up.

Our Fiji hostess, approximately age fifty, was so disgusted, she didn't know what to do. She told us that the group had been staying several days, and every day the Chinese children made the same kind of mess and appeared to be on stimulants. Over the several days, not one parent had disciplined their child.

Children learn quickly who is in control. Narcissism is taught.

Can the Chinese parents be blamed? They had a few days' break from a country totally controlled by the Communist Party. Living in spaces the size of a U.S. bathroom, the Chinese middle class is limited on how many children they can have and what stuff they could buy. They travel as an alternative.

Schools are not stand-alone institutions of the "me-first" society. They have international reinforcements. China, as a society, is more government structured than the United States. Consequently, the "free-range" education will likely be implemented in developing countries far faster than in China, Europe, the United States, or other so-called "developed" countries.

In developing countries, both parents seldom work outside the home. As a result, "free-range" education technology will likely be adopted faster than developed countries where parents find jobs rather than caring for and educating their children.

How can you put more focus on a self-centered child? Expose them to grow in knowledge and talent not bound by average teachers. Have them experience life with responsibilities as they are being educated for the real world. That is how the ancients did it. Give them "free-range" education.

9

Freebies

Riddle: I am contained, but free, yet cost more each year. What am I?

Children are taught to live off freebies.

Parents, many approaching retirement, are still providing for their adult children or paying off debt incurred sending their children to college. Most children, as they approach adulthood, realize if public schools are free, everything else should be free, too.

There is a difference between developed and developing countries. In developed countries people learn to live off the government. Developing countries have not figured out how the public can pay for that lifestyle. In both categories, it is not surprising that parents who live off the government teach their children to also live off the government.

Governments operate by taxing its people. Tax is a two-edged tool: One side is used to cut income; the other discourages it.

Personal income is taxed numerous ways. Countries with weak systems for collecting income from individuals apply a gross sales tax on virtually all retail items. The system is justified by reason that those with higher income purchase more and therefore pay more in taxes. Gross sales tax primarily targets the middle class. Rich and super rich do not personally consume annually a large proportion of their income. The middle-class pay the highest proportion of their income under a gross sales tax system, whereas the poor and very poor purchase little besides food and clothing that are often out of taxing authority's reach, or are often exempt or taxed at a lower rate.

For example, in the case of poverty, a thirty-year-old male or female has no dependents. Age, however, is not a poverty requirement. Assume also, he or she is physically and mentally capable of work, but prefers not to. Like anyone in the world, to survive they must eat, drink, be clothed, have shelter, and receive medical care to keep living. Formal education is not a need; it is a want. Wants are costly.

What is the cost of education per student?

U.S. estimates are higher now, about $12,000 per year. However, the latest available official data supplied by the U.S. Census Bureau indicated $10,705 was spent in 2013 per pupil for public elementary and secondary school systems compared to $5,001 in 1992.[1] Earlier data was not comparable. Costs per student have doubled in the last two decades. Not all is inflation. Do you think students received twice the education?

Based on the same Census report, $530,552,795,000 was spent nationally for public elementary and secondary school systems of which 60.6 percent was spent on "Instruction." Of that, only 6.7 percent was spent on "Instruction content" and 53.8 percent spent on Instructors' wages and benefits. That means the other four of ten U.S. tax dollars spent on public youth education was spent on "Other functions" and "Supportive services."

Not to get bogged down in data, but I think it is relevant to mention total school debt in the United States (mainly financed by public bonds) is $415,238,582,000 which means it would take nearly all education taxes for the nine-month school year just to pay school debt.

With today's communications and virtual technology, is public school debt to finance buildings really necessary? It is certainly out of line with historic education.

How do education costs compare to income? As of this writing, the national minimum wage in the U.S. set in 2009 was $7.25 per hour. Based on a forty-hour work-week, that equates to $15,080 per year. Obviously, at $10,705 spent in 2013 on each grade school and high school pupil, minimum wage earners are not paying for their children's education. On

---

[1] "Public Education Finances: 2013," June 2015, U.S. Census Bureau, Economics and Statistics Administration, U.S. Department of Commerce, pp. XVI, 6, http://www2 .census.gov/govs/school/13f33pub.pdf (Sourced January 28, 2016)

the other hand, minimum wage was not intended as a family income but as an introductory wage for those entering the labor market.

U.S. freebies are available with no education required to receive benefits. A logical question is: Why is the public now paying nearly $12,000 per year per student if that student is not going to work after graduation and contribute to society?

Historically, education was for those who needed it–those who physically and mentally worked.

Even with limited education, developing countries are supplying many of the world's manufactured goods.

Many so-called "developed countries" have developed enough productive workers or have enough exportable natural resources to supply those that do not work. In developed countries, supply of efficient workers is dwindling. As Baby Boomers age and young adults delay entering the workforce, there is increasing need to squeeze more from those that do work. The trend cannot continue.

At some point, productive workers retire. A dwindling supply of young workers with slack work ethics will not be able to supply the wants of the population. Eventually, service needs will not be met, or immigrants will fill the void.

Poverty in one country cannot be compared to poverty in another. There is no standard for comparison.

As government health programs expanded, there was less reason for families to work, pay health insurance, and care for their children. Medicaid, in the United States, is another government substitute for irresponsible parents. Need in severe cases is being consumed by the irresponsible. I am not familiar with free food programs in other countries, but the U.S. government is feeding an increasing number of families with Food Stamps (now called Supplemental Nutrition Assistance Program) along with housing assistance, home heating assistance, maid service (for some), and free health care for many parents and children. Grants were also given, especially for single mothers to go to college and pay for childcare.

Someone collecting all those benefits, tax-free, must be an important person. Typical of narcissists, free food, housing, medical care, and all other government benefits are deserved. Narcissists do not care how hard others must work to pay for their freebies.

Many no-income people, plus teachers and university professors, think someone else should pay for their livelihood. President Lyndon Johnson, as a career politician, knew the more people dependent on government, the more likely they were to vote for politicians that provided their income, or rather services in lieu of income.

Ancient Romans were familiar with the Latin term *quid pro quo* (meaning "this for that"), and it has been implemented as public policy in monarchies, dictatorships, theocracies, socialist, communist, and democratic societies ever since as a method to satisfy the populous. In modern socialist democracies it is standard operating procedure to secure votes with free or heavily subsidized goodies for free-giving politicians to remain in power.

Here is a personal example of how it works at the local level. In the mountains of Guatemala in 2015 our family raised enough donated funds to replace a family's dirt and corn stalk home with a concrete floor, block walls, concrete stove, and galvanized roof. When finished, they had no electricity, no bathroom, and no running water in the house, but at least the family of five had a dry, cozy (11-foot x 13-foot) one-story place to sleep and eat. However, the city had a water faucet and open sewage ditch (about a foot wide) just outside their front door. Families along that street had concrete steps or boards over the sewage ditch to get out of their houses.

We had enough extra galvanized roofing material to make a 2-foot by 4-foot shower over the sewer ditch. Before we could construct the family (and potentially a neighborhood) shower, the mother (landowner) had to get permission from the city mayor to build over city property (the sewage ditch). Within an hour she returned with good news, with one caveat—the mayor approved her request if she promised to vote for him in the upcoming election—a quid pro quo. We spent the morning using leftover materials for a concrete base, drain hole, metal surround, and showerhead over the city sewer ditch.

Back to narcissists, there is a difference between groups—some are freeloaders whereas narcissist teachers and university professors work for their pay. No-income people work to get more freebies from government, nonprofit organizations, or suckers willing to support their penniless, but ostentatious, lifestyle.

If someone dies without family means to be buried, for health reasons local government covers the immediate costs. Historically, when an elderly spouse passed away, the remaining grandparent lived as a part of the family with their children and grandchildren. Long-term care of the aged grandparent is still a major responsibility of families in developing countries. Citizens in wealthier countries have tended to shift the burden of burials to government, and senior care to nursing homes, home-health services, and dependent or independent living facilities.

My paternal grandfather Wietgrefe born in 1891 lived with us from 1959 (when my grandmother died) until 1976 when he passed away. Grandpa would have been counted as part of our "family of ten." The trend of family caring for an aging parent likely peaked in the 1960s, as nursing home and other care facilities shifted the burden from family to institutionalized care.

However, in the last couple decades there has been an increase in children staying at home even though they may be working full time, or attending technical schools or university. As expected, those enrolled in school were identified by the (U.S.) National Housing Survey as a reason for continuing to live with parents. Others did not have enough income. The twenty-three to thirty-four-year-old freeloading "children" claim ". . . unemployment and delayed marriages" as main reasons to not move out of their lifetime bedroom.[2] I almost gag in disbelief when a thirty-four-year-old adult is called a "child."

Unless mentally incapacitated, someone over thirty must be pretty dumb or lazy if they are still living with their parents and going to school or cannot get or hold a job that pays well enough to cover life's necessities of food, water, and shelter. Many expect parents to continue paying for their basic needs while their own income covers wants.

My guess is that many egotistic or egocentric live-at-home freeloaders have degrees with schooling paid for by the parents. Many may have

---

[2] Ritholzt, Barry, "Why Are Young Adults Living with Their Parents and When Will They Move Out?," The Big Picture, August 4, 2014, http://www.ritholtz.com/blog/2014/08/why-are-young-adults-living-with-their-parents-and-when-will-they-move-out/ (Sourced September 30, 2015)

never held a job (any paying job). It would be below their dignity to take a position below their education or pre-doc category.

Free food. Free house. Good television. Mom washes clothes. Why move out? Television is not a necessary item, but the parents may want to watch reruns of the 1970s fictional television show *All in the Family*[3] where Archie Bunker may have responded, "We've never figured out how to wean the meathead."

With Vice President Lyndon Johnson looking on, President John F. Kennedy (1917–1963) in his inaugural address January 20, 1961, with great oration said: "Ask not what your country can do for you–ask what you can do for your country."

Obviously, Johnson did not agree with Kennedy's statement. Within months of Kennedy's assassination in 1963, using the sympathy vote election victory in 1964, President Lyndon Johnson introduced "Great Society" programs (i.e., expanded education and medical care including urban freebies). Basically, he was telling Americans: "Ask not what you can do for your country–ask what your country can do for you."

During U.S. President Lyndon Johnson's term (1963–1969) when he was blowing budgets and Vietnam villages, Johnson escalated the Vietnam War while increasing spending on domestic programs under his banner, the "Great Society." "Guns versus butter" was debated economically and politically. The "Great Society" rhetoric was a domestic smokescreen from his failing Vietnam initiatives. To deflect his failed international policy of warmongering, Johnson shifted his attention domestically to get votes from minorities like nonworking (often college-student) rioters, hippies, and American Negros (as they were politely called then). Meanwhile, many working young black men were drafted into Johnson's military machine.

Children are taught discrimination by teachers, perhaps also by parents, pastors, parishioners, and professors.

The worst riots in American history were racial riots. They did not occur before the 1860s Civil War, but in the 1960s after President Johnson declared war on poverty.

---

[3] Archie Bunker, played by Carroll O'Connor, was a fictional character in a popular 1970s television sitcom, *All in the Family*. https://en.wikipedia.org/wiki/Archie_Bunker (Sourced September 30, 2015)

President Kennedy addressed discrimination with his push to enact the lengthy Civil Rights Act. He was assassinated before it was enacted.

Many of my readers may be too young to remember that the 1964 Civil Rights Act outlawed discrimination. The 1860s American Civil War was fought over the ownership of slaves. For a century thereafter, businesses, government offices, schools, voting booths, and every other enterprise could legally discriminate.

That one momentous Civil Rights Act outlawed:

> ... Discrimination or segregation on the ground of race, color, religion, or national origin. All persons shall be entitled to the full and equal enjoyment of the goods, services, facilities, and privileges, advantages, and accommodations of ... any inn, hotel, motel, ... restaurant, cafeteria, lunchroom, lunch counter, soda fountain, ... retail establishment, or any gasoline station ... motion picture house, theater, concert hall, sports arena, stadium, or other place.... No person shall withhold, deny, or attempt to withhold or deny, or deprive or attempt to deprive, any person of any right or privilege secured by (this Act) or coerce any person with the purpose of interfering with any right or privilege secured, ... or punish or attempt to punish any person for exercising or attempting to exercise any right or privilege secured....

Fifty years later, it is incomprehensible for younger generations to understand the radical shift in attitudes against blacks and whites, Indians or Jews, or any other segment of the population. Are there still bigots? Sure. There always will be. Protection from discrimination is now U.S. law.

World War II was primarily fought to protect the world from Adolf Hitler's (1889–1945) Jew-killing machine. In 1964, a congressional act provided a legislative solution to peaceful coexistence. It provided a grand example for conflict resolution.

However, some minorities think they should have more rights than others, but the Civil Rights Act of 1964 never identified reverse discrimination specifically, but deliberately. Wording addressed protection of minorities and majorities. It may take another fifty years, or wishful thinking, to iron out all discrimination without denying the religious and personal beliefs of others. In the meantime, courts and lawyers will be busy.

Johnson signed President Kennedy's pet legislation, Civil-Rights Act, finally to rectify a national travesty a hundred years after the Civil War. However, President Johnson also used Kennedy's assassination and the nation's mourning era for his "war on poverty" and war in Vietnam. Using his right hand to sign social legislation, his left hand was pulling the trigger in Vietnam.

Watch birds–they don't fly too well using only their left wing or their right wing. Likewise, governments lean too far when one party, for a decade, controls the executive and legislative branches of government as President Johnson did during the 1960s when he averaged 60 percent of the Senate and 61 percent of the U.S. House of Representatives to endorse his social and military policies and deficit budgets. The U.S. government system is a republic not a democracy. Geographic representation usually balances simple majorities.

Like any country, overwhelming support of one political movement is not good. Total control is disastrous.

China's 1960s infamous leader, Mao Zedong (1893–1976), killed tens of millions of his citizens during the early 1960s with the Communist Party of China's program "Great Leap Forward." By outlawing private farms and forcing citizens to work unproductive collective farms, Chairman Mao led his country into a period of mass starvation. Although Mao claimed support for education, schools were closed throughout China sometimes for months, but universities were closed for more than four years during Chairman Mao's radical "Cultural Revolution."[4] The learning system took a dramatic shift before and after Mao's reign.

Ancient Rome provided free food and entertainment to appease its social agitators with a series of programs which Roman Poet Juvenal (100 A.D.) unofficially termed "Bread and Circuses."[5]

Readers take note: Anytime you hear of a government initiative entitled the "Great Society," "War on Poverty," "Great Leap Forward,"

---

[4] Näth, Marie-Luise, *China After the Cultural Revolution: Politics Between Two Party Congresses*, University of California Press, 1977, p. 68. https://books.google .com.mx/books?id=YyT9pxmcmxgC&pg=PA77&source=gbs_toc_r&cad=3#v=one page&q&f=false (Sourced September 30, 2015)
[5] Bread and Circuses, https://en.wikipedia.org/wiki/Bread_and_circuses (Sourced September 28, 2015)

"Cultural Revolution," or similar terms, grab your checkbooks and don protection. The government will have a hand in your pocket and a knife to your throat while they "care" for your children through indoctrination. For decades thereafter, life will not be "Bread and Circuses."

Government policies of military conquest are designed to protect its expanded borders. Alternatively, central government policies of social conquest are designed to expand and protect its voters.

Public-controlled response to stimuli is not new. Rome's so-called "Bread and Circuses" program was not a studied science eighteen centuries ago, but Roman leaders knew they could control the general public with free food and entertainment.

Today's school system is an industry unto itself when students graduate and their employment is the system in which they were trained. Those confined to a training circle are stressed looking around for outside employment. Many students become teachers. Confined to a circle, like student-teacher-teaching students, leads to anxiety that progresses to the point of fearing those on the outside. Resisting change becomes the norm in order to protect their comfortable freebie system continually supported by an established political network.

There are political ramifications when a system is dependent on government. The more concentrated a population, the more likely an individual will conform to the norm and resist the desire to be independent.

Teachers support teachers, unions bond with other union members, those in cities are more dependent on services provided by the municipality. All highly integrated systems are more interdependent. It is a learned trait. Dependency creates dependency. Consequently, cities are more socialistic politically than rural areas. Throughout the world, populations in rural areas are more independent. They must be to survive.

Ranchers, rural businesspeople, fisherman, and hunters for example are considered consistently independent. Why? They have to rely on their own skills to be successful. They do not wait for a doctor to deliver a calf, or wait for a team to give direction when to harvest a crop. They do not attend school to learn how to order product, contact the city to supply water, or demand the city's animal control ward off a skunk. As independent operators, they develop a different mindset as to what is expected from public agencies.

City children grow dependent on government services, whereas rural children depend more on their parents and themselves.

Americans have always been more independent than dependent. Natives roamed the prairies surviving off their skills and abilities. Mountain men, fur traders, and pioneers chose to be independent of government support. A freebie then was a dying buffalo in a sinkhole that would support a hungry outdoorsman and his family.

Today's political conservatives would claim political bias in the school system. Obviously, it is true. On the other hand, liberals and socialists would proudly claim efficaciousness of their generational influence showing they care by passing their bias on to students.

Dependence is taught.

Children naturally seek independence. They want to investigate interesting things. They want to be older than they are, while seniors are more receptive of the status quo and wish years would pass more slowly. Why?

Think of it this way: A four-year-old child wants to be five so he or she can go to kindergarten. A five-year-old wants to be six to be in the numbered grades, but a year passes too slowly. By age fifty, nearly everybody claims the years are passing too fast—even though they desire retirement; they want the annual clock to slow. Why?

The thought process in children and adults relates to Albert Einstein's twentieth-century Theory of Relativity. To simplify, compare one car passing another car on a highway: If the passing car is going five miles-per-hour (mph) faster to pass, they are passing at the rate of 5 mph. If the passing car slows to 60 mph, the same speed as the car being passed, they are driving at relatively the same speed. Drivers viewing each other appear to not move, as if they are sitting still in a parking lot.

Back to the five-year-old; he or she wants to be one year older. To the child, it seems like they will never get to six. Why? It is because at five, one year is 20 percent of a child's life. Why then does a year seem to pass so quickly to a fifty-year-old? It is because one year is only 2 percent of their lifespan. A year to the fifty-year-old passes ten times faster relative to the five-year-old.

Now compare a five-year-old with a fifteen-year-old. The five-year-old wants to be six and in the numbered grades because he or she likely gets to learn more than is taught in kindergarten. On the other hand, the fifteen-year-old often wants to get out of school because he or she thinks they know everything (at least that is what parents often say).

There is a natural and historic learning transition that occurs between five and fifteen. Preschoolers thirst for knowledge and generally lose that desire—some immediately upon entering the school system. By age fifteen, feelings of adulthood emerge. Rather than provide an outlet for those natural learning instincts, the school system increasingly has tried to restrict students in their early to mid-teens.

Parents and schools should take advantage of the natural teenage desire for career freedom. Socialistic school systems, state truancy laws, and structure classes protected by police are not conducive to free learning. Students in their mid-teens are more like rural people who seek independence from an overbearing system.

As an example, a few years ago while spending some time in southwest Mexico, I befriended a local Mexican taxi driver who operated the business with his wife. They had two children; the oldest, a fifteen-year-old boy, showed very little interest in school while his sister excelled. Banana and pineapple fields surrounded the small farming and fishing village.

One weekend in the presence of his parents and grandparents the boy announced he wanted to be a pineapple farmer. "Why a pineapple farmer?" The father asked. His son explained everybody I see working on pineapple farms is singing; they are always happy. They are free. They get to work together; and are outside all day, not cooped up in a building, like school.

Assessing the situation, the grandfather presented an option. He knew a local pineapple farmer who needed help since it was summer, there was no school, and pineapples needed harvesting. The teenager jumped at the opportunity and was waiting at 7:00 a.m. Monday morning at the designated worker pickup point.

Upon returning home that evening, the boy announced at late dinner that he was exhausted from picking pineapples in the hot humid fields, filling 50-kilo (104-pound) harvest baskets, and getting poked and cut all day from pineapple leaves. It was his way to announce he no longer wanted to be a pineapple farmer.

Tuesday morning the fifteen-year-old was in bed when he should have been meeting the field workers. "Get up," the father pleaded. "I'm not working today," said the son, "I've decided I'm not going to be a pine-apple farmer." "That does not matter," added the stern but sympathetic father. "Your grandfather made a special attempt to get you a job with his friend (the pineapple farmer). I don't care how tired you are. Get up. You go immediately to the farmer and tell him you are no longer work-ing for him. Tell him why you do not want to be a pineapple farmer. It is common courtesy to your grandfather and his farmer friend."

The son saved face, met the farmer, explained his change of mind, and maintained the family reputation in their small, close-knit community.

Two years later we were back in that town in Mexico. I asked our friend what his children were doing. He announced proudly that his daughter was still doing very well in school and that his son was in a technical school training to be an auto mechanic. "He always showed an interest in mechanics, and that attempt at being a pineapple farmer was a good lesson for him," the father summarized.

Their daughter found school interesting and their son did not. Rather than ignore the son's teenage desire, the father, grandfather, and employer (the pineapple farmer) took action and presented an oppor-tunity. Absences of multigenerational family time and child-labor laws unfortunately restrict employers in developed countries from present-ing similar opportunities to teenagers.

What often happens is that teenagers graduate high school, attend college, switch majors a couple times, and graduate at twenty-three, twenty-four, or twenty-five years-old with a certificate but no interest in using their degree in their field of study. What a waste!

Learning, personal passion, and career development have often been forced, stymied, and left the formally educated adult unemployed with student loans and living with his or her parents. Free school can become a personal cost.

All can be traced back to a lack of responsibility and freebies given by the parents. If parents do not give responsibility at a very young age, they become frustrated with their irresponsible, often rebellious teenag-ers, and encourage them to get more education—an ignorant substitute for personal responsibility.

Responsible youth never lose their desire to learn even though they may not finish high school or attend college. Often the irresponsible, highly educated, want to use their education to influence others.

10

Feed the Chickens

Riddle: What is not a henhouse, but compensation is considered chicken feed?

Never in human history have so many lived so long off the efforts of so few.

After spending the most years in world history being formally educated, more young adults are living off older workers. Never in human history have young adults been structurally blocked from work and a decreasing part of the labor force. Never in recorded history, as explained in *Relating to Ancient Learning*, has life expectancy been so long. Never in recorded history have the so-called "educated" been the laggards in technology adoption. Never in recorded history have so many lived off government freebies. It will not last.

There's hope.

In 2015 after spending a month on the north shore of Lake Atitlan in the mountains of Guatemala, my wife and I were waiting for a boat taxi in Santa Cruz la Laguna. Having a few minutes to wait, we checked out a few shops near the small two-boat dock.

About the third shop up the cobblestone path a young Guatemalan girl greeted us in English. It was very unusual since most females only spoke one or two dialects of Mayan, and a few in their late teens spoke limited Spanish. She apparently noticed we were waiting for the boat taxi. As we completed greeting niceties, she invited us into her very small open-door shop draped appropriately with blouses and bags a tourist might want. However, since we travel lightly with only small backpacks, we were far more impressed with the girl, her presentation, her English, and sales demeanor than the contents of her quaint little shop.

"You speak English very well. How did you learn it?" I asked.

"Thank you," she politely replied. "I had to quit school because I could not afford it. My friends that are going to school stop by every afternoon and help me with English since it helps me run my shop."

Amazed, my wife, Patricia, holding a scarf asked, "How old are you?"

"Fourteen" was her reply.

We could hear the boat approaching the dock and had to board within a minute. Patricia quickly purchased the colored scarf that the girl selected. We departed heaping compliments on the young girl and wished we would have had time to buy something else in her shop. Since then, whenever we have very good or very poor customer service, we still use the fourteen-year-old Guatemalan girl as our example of superior, self-educated, individual customer service and brag of her tenacity.

For a month we helped replace dirt floors with concrete, dirt walls with block, and built efficient cooking stoves to replace open pit fires in the poorest communities we have ever seen. In less than five minutes a 14-year-old girl renewed our hope for Guatemala's future.

A year later we disembarked in Venice, Italy, in late March after a three-week transition cruise from the Caribbean. After spending four years on continuous summer, it was chilly and Patricia needed more clothes. We strolled the narrow walking paths in the San Marcos district of Venice looking at various clothing shops with doors open (as if it was warm). Patricia was looking for a plain black dress—one that would complement her fully beaded, multicolored Guatemalan belt our daughter Charmion had gifted.

Half-exposed in the doorway was a black dress. We walked into the shop greeted by a young perhaps eighteen- or nineteen-year-old girl who spoke perfect English. After Patricia explained her desired dress, the girl sifted efficiently through her four racks of dresses. It was a small shop no bigger than the one described earlier in Santa Cruz, Guatemala. Four dresses were pulled as the girl very quickly sorted through colors and sizes. It was obvious she knew her inventory. Patricia was impressed but scared of the price.

"Thirty-nine Euros," the girl said. "All our dresses are 39 Euros, except these over here are 29 Euros."

Cautious, Patricia said, "What's the catch. This is Venice and these dresses are too cheap."

"See all those boutique shops?" Pointing out the door, the girl explained, "All those dresses are made in the same workshop. We go to the same market and buy from the same venders as they do. They pay to have their boutique label attached to their dresses and charge 100 Euros or more. We have a different marketing plan."

As I stood by the door looking around I realized this shop marketed to ladies who were in Venice only a few nights and needed a dress or two for evening dining. These dresses, priced from 29–39 Euro (less than the cost of an evening meal) may never be taken home. The same boutique dresses in the other numerous shops were likely prized at dinner parties in home countries promoted as being purchased in Venice.

As Patricia was trying on dresses, I asked the young girl, "Do you own this shop?"

"No," she said. "I just work here after classes."

Assuming she was at university, and since her English was perfect I asked, "What are you studying, English?"

"No," she replied. "German and Russian."

Impressed, I followed with questions about her other languages besides Italian. Like many Europeans, they included French, Spanish, and English with Latin studies. Not many schools teach German any more she explained, but Russian was of increasing importance as affluent Russians were traveling more (as we had noted on the trans-Atlantic cruise).

"How come you are working in the middle of the afternoon, rather than being in class?" I asked.

She replied that her boss, the shop's owner, was sick. As the only employee, she was called to work. The owner obviously knew her shop would be in good hands. Fortunately, the girl had no classes that afternoon but had to self-study for hours that evening. The young girl went on to explain that she normally worked the 4:00 p.m. to 8:00 p.m. shift after classes. This was simply a longer workday. "I have to work." She explained that full-time classes were barely affordable; her family could not offer financial support; and that she wanted to pursue a career in international business. After complimenting her on work ethics and efficient use of time, she explained: "The less free time I have, the more efficient I am at studying."

How true. Many adults never learn that reality. Schools do not teach it. Some people sit at work or home all day and wonder why they never accomplished their intended tasks. When not actively pressured to complete a job, less gets done when all day is available to complete what could have taken an hour or less.

We travel with two small carry-on backpacks and sometimes a small suitcase, but we left the shop with two dresses, a blouse, and a hefty tip in the girl's hand. Wherever we travel, what a pleasure it is for us to see young people happily serve others with a smile and drive to please as they go about their life's goal.

Work ethic is not hereditary—it is learned. Success is apparent when parents are industrious, give independence, teach responsibility to their very young children (age two, no later than three), and expect each task to be successfully completed. Their children will succeed. Failing is also apparent. If parents live off the welfare of others or are always complaining about work, children learn that work is a bitch and welfare is a career. Parents provide the choice—it is not genes.

If someone reaches twenty years old and has never worked, never had home chores, and had someone else always pay for their welfare and schooling, when do parents expect them to become independent? They should not. It is a false expectation. It is too late. Youth is learning. Unfortunately, many have learned the indolent life.

Since the 1970s, upward spiraling business resources are spent finding good employees. It is far more expensive now. Poor quality employees, training expenses, regulations to protect the slothful, drug testing, and unemployment taxes force businesses to be ever-diligent when hiring. To sort through the riffraff of college/university graduates, businesses spend profits on human resource departments sorting résumés, hiring outside venders to verify credentials, and spend hour upon hour in interviews to select a new hire.

Why? Businesses question applicant ethics. Will they be responsible employees? Is the information correct on applications? Are résumés inflated? Have they worked? If so, when, where, how long, and why did they quit? Do they have a criminal record? Are they on drugs?

Throughout history, learning was different. Even up to the mid-twentieth century, employers simply asked about work experience and education. Individual responsibility was assumed. Résumés inferred accuracy. Employers presumed applicants were ethical. Hiring hand-shakes were a contract. Team and independent work was expected. If not, they were fired for cause.

How do children learn to be independent along with being service- and goal-oriented young adults? I thought back to our guide, Alex, raising his boys in the mountains of Guatemala.

"Rather than doing everything for your son, maybe it would be better to teach him to feed the chickens—even if he is two years old," was advice I gave our hiking guide.

Over the years, I have told my children and grandchildren that a child is never too young to give them responsibilities.

Two is old enough. Give them by three.

On our second visit to the mountains of Guatemala, our daughter, granddaughter, a couple friends, my wife, and I hired a local twenty-some-year-old guide, Alex, to lead us on a strenuous hike up San Pedro Mountain in central Guatemala. As we crossed switchbacks through the jungle, corn, and coffee fields from 5000 feet elevation to the top at about 10,000 feet, we exchanged cultural stories.

He spoke good English, Spanish, and two dialects of Mayan. With-out formal education, and no apparent employment opportunities in his home country, like many young men, Alex sought change. Greener pas-tures led him from central Guatemala across Mexico and illegally into the United States.

Having no documented skills, he simply said, "Mayans can do any-thing" when a job opportunity appeared. Like many undocumented ille-gal aliens, no matter which country they cross into, he found work as a construction laborer. After seven years of sending money home to sup-port his parents, the system was catching up with him. Alex wanted to return to Guatemala, marry, and raise a family. His last construction job was building a five-million-dollar home in the United States. Com-pared to many Guatemalan homes, often one room, less than a hundred square feet and no running water or electricity, this American home was huge—unbelievable to Alex. He told us, "They even had their own computer room."

Alex returned with a little money in his pocket and married shortly after arriving home. Immediately, his wife was pregnant. He had no home. As is customary, he moved to his wife's village where they spoke a different dialect of Mayan. He looked different. Alex was an outsider in her village. Nobody had a job for him.

One day he heard that a gravel maker needed rock crushers. After a thirty-minute walk each way to work, for six months he smashed one rock against another to create road and construction gravel. Hard work. No gloves. Dirty.

Women in this adopted village, feeding their family mainly corn, kept asking their husbands, "Why don't you get a job?" The answer was always, "No jobs. No jobs."

After several months in the village, trying to learn the local dialect of Mayan, Alex's wife told him what the village women were saying to their husbands. "If that outsider, Alex, could get a job, why can't you?"

Alex had created change in the village—an expectation that there were jobs and that men should work to feed their families.

Alex changed work expectations.

In a couple years, Alex became father to a second son. It is customary for the women to carry their children in a pouch wrapped over a shoulder. It was also a woman's job to go to the market to get necessities.

Alex was a proud father though he regretted being away from home working in other villages. Leaving before his children woke and often not returning until after they had gone to bed, Alex worked. To spend more time with his sons, after their second son was born, every market day (when not working) Alex would walk to the market, oldest son hand in hand, with his new baby son in the shoulder pouch. The trio would wander the market, pick up supplies, and head home.

Not knowing exactly what the village men were saying, he knew they were mocking him. "Look at Alex the fagot. Carrying a baby like a fagot of wood. Doing women's work." Alex didn't care; he had a job and was proud of his young family. After several months, Alex noticed several other men his age carrying or walking their young children to the market.

Alex changed local social norms.

Since the Spanish invasion in the sixteenth century, Guatemalan men taught their sons Spanish, the common working language no matter which of many dialects of Mayan were spoken. Traditionally, women could only speak their local dialect of Mayan. Because Alex had worked illegally in the United States, he picked up a skill not common in the mountains of Guatemala. He spoke English.

Being conversational in English, Spanish, and Mayan allowed Alex to get a job as a hiking guide for North Americans, Europeans, and Australians to villages seldom visited by tourists. There are no tourists some months. No income. Alex found work wherever he could.

As Alex would walk around his wife's village, young boys would walk with him. "I want to be like you when I grow up." They would question him, "How can I get a job like you have?"

Youth were emulating Alex. He had created change in his village. Alex dressed nicer and appeared to have more money than other families in his adopted village.

The only regular work in the mountains of central Guatemala is cutting sticks and hauling them down to the villages and selling cooking wood. Often not making more than a dollar per day, money always seemed to be scarce, but corn (sometimes the only food) had to be cooked, creating a constant need for more wood. Every day families from age four to aged grandfathers and grandmothers could be seen scouring the mountains, machete in hand searching for wood, hoping to sell enough to buy a bag of corn for the month. If they sold enough, they could buy a bag of beans or rice. An extravagant month would allow the family to enjoy a squash. Chickens produced eggs–a valuable protein supplement. Spent hens boiled into a mouth-watering soup once or twice a year were a special treat.

Alex asked about our children. My wife, then sixty-four, was hiking ahead of the others. He had seen how our daughter, Charmion, in her mid-forties, was climbing Mount San Pedro like a trained athlete. Our granddaughter was not far behind. We obviously had money to fly to Guatemala and hire Alex as our guide. He viewed us as successful.

Like any father, Alex wanted to raise his sons to have good jobs, to be successful. "What should I encourage them to do? Be a lawyer?" he asked.

"Alex," I said, "teach your kids to be independent, and they will figure out how to be successful."

"My boys will only be two and four, I realize that they are too young for me to worry about their life," he said.

"No, they are not," I replied as we continued to climb.

"I have to be away all day when I take guided hikes." Alex continued, "My oldest son is now going to preschool. I sometimes walk him there and he says 'Daddy, I don't want to go to school today. I don't want you to go to work'." Alex asked, "What should I do?"

"OK," I said. "Some day when you do not have work, walk your son to school. When he finishes school, meet him. He will be surprised to see you. Like most kids after school, he will be hungry and ask for a snack."

"He always does," Alex replied.

"Tell him, 'Your daddy had no work today. We have nothing to eat. I have no money to buy food.'

"'But, daddy, I'm hungry,' will be his reply. Wait an hour and just let him complain about being hungry and repeat, 'Daddy did not have work today. We have no food.' He must learn the connection between being hungry, and having to work."

Note that Mayans have been living in the Guatemalan highlands for thousands of years. Many live above 5000 feet elevation where the season is too short to grow corn, squash, beans, and vegetables year-round. The dry season runs from November through June so little grows then.

What had been dried and stored must sustain the family until a new crop matures the following summer. Bananas, coffee, and wild mountain fruit may supplement their diet through the lean months.

After the Spanish invasion in the early 1500s, Mayans were driven to the mountains putting pressure on scarce food supplies and livable valleys. In modern times, from 1960 to 1996 during the Guatemalan Civil War, Mayans fighting the central government concentrated even more heavily into the limited-access mountains without late twentieth century resources.

Many Mayans still live that way today. No electricity. No running water. Dirt floors. Dirt walls. The only cooking fuel is sticks gathered from the mountains. Lung disease kills as a result of ingesting fumes from cooking in smoke-filled adobe huts. For those with enough food, or malnourished, life goes on as it has century after century after century.

"Your children seem so successful," Alex commented.

"Yes. Our three children have different jobs; took different educational routes, and are successful adults," I said proudly.

"How did you do it?" he asked.

"I really cannot take the credit," I said. "These are all my step-children. They were six to thirteen when we met. My wife was a single mother raising three children on a very, very limited income, raising a garden, and taking jobs wherever she could. Milking cows, laboring in a garden shop, and opening a café as cook, waitress, coffee pourer, and clerk until the owners would come in mid-morning. Life was hard for my wonderful wife who had to quit school, married, and had a daughter at seventeen.

"Even before they were school age, our kids had to get themselves dressed in the morning. When school started, they had to get there, and make toast as a snack when they got home from school. My wife kept a good home and cooked, cleaned, and washed clothes. It required each of the kids to help with household responsibilities. We married after dating three and half years. Our children knew the routine. Their responsibility developed well before I came along.

"Even after we got married we both worked. I had a sales job and was gone from early morning until late at night. 'What does your dad do?' I overheard my stepson's school friend ask one evening. 'Well, he leaves in the morning. Talks on the phone all day, and comes home late for supper'. That is when I knew I was not the father I wanted to be, but I knew our kids grew up having independence, with responsibilities. After over thirty years of marriage," I said, "look ahead. There she is hiking this mountain. Give credit to my wife that our children are independent responsible adults."

"How do I teach my sons to be like your children?" Alex asked.

"Do you give them chores?" I asked.

"They will be only two and four." He repeated.

"They are plenty old enough to do chores." I continued questioning as we walked. "Do they have pets?"

"Not really. We only have four chickens."

"Do you have your boys feed the chickens?" I asked.

"No."

"OK. I'd suggest that your oldest boy should be responsible for feeding the chickens." I continued, "Your youngest, will soon be two. While the older one is in preschool, the younger is responsible for gathering the eggs. They are certainly old enough to feed four chickens and pick up a few eggs each day."

The following year, we hired Alex again to hike Mount San Pedro with all our children. My wife's two sisters, then age sixty-four and seventy-three, were with us. Hour after hour we hiked up the mountain. Our son was leading and daughters behind us. One segment, when Alex and I were hiking together, I asked, "Are your boys doing the chicken chores?"

"One is now two and the other four. After our discussion last year, my wife and I talked about how we want to raise our boys. They are now feeding our four chickens and gathering the eggs." He replied matter of factly.

In my grandfatherly voice, I continued, "At that age, children want to take on more responsibility. It is a learned behavior. They want to help their parents. It is not hard to teach them." I asked, "Are they responsible?"

Alex smiled proudly.

When given responsibility at two, three, and four years old, children grow and live as responsible people. Those that graduate from college at twenty-two or twenty-five, and have never had chores at home or responsibility at a job, are the losers.

Parents may think that paying for college is a parental responsibility. Where is that written? Historically, that was not the case. As modern society became economically successful, parents had fewer children. They gave their children fewer chores, and negligently shifted responsibilities onto themselves.

A child given responsibility early develops to be independent and caring by helping others, just as they did at two or three. Character is built, not reached at a certain age. When are we giving college-educated adults responsibility? Graduation day!

After opening congratulation cards, real life emerges.

A job-hunt is the graduate's responsibility as is finding an apartment, paying the utilities, fueling the car that is wearing out as college years progressed. What? Teeth cleaning costs? Just a couple weeks earlier, parents' allowance covered the graduation haircut. As student loan payments begin six months after graduation, reality sets in. Life's realization emerges.

Competing in the job market is different than competing in class where a "B" is good enough. An "A," "B," or "C" does not mean squat to an employer—they want a responsible worker. College graduates look around and ask themselves, why are some of my high school classmates that went to tech school making more after two or three years on the job than beginning salaries for college graduates? Why are they taking vacations? Why are they living in a better neighborhood, and driving a better car?

Disgusted by a lack of interviews, rejection letters or rejection emails (if they come) are a daily fear. Job search pressures mount. Graduation money is spent. A Master's degree seems more inviting–student loan payments can be delayed. Getting more student loans is easier in the United States than finding a job. Graduate statistics are checked: Graduate degrees pay more than undergraduates. Life's responsibilities are again delayed as college life is renewed.

Many in their mid-twenties are stressed out. Marriage and families are delayed. Often college graduates cannot take care of themselves and become a societal burden until they do. Those are the ones that never learned responsibility as a child. As an adult, they do not know how to take responsibility. Once they get a job, take-home pay is much lower than expected. They are inexperienced. Training is sought from employers.

Surprise! School system monopolies do not prepare graduates to work. Team mentality on the job becomes an excuse to share work and shirk responsibility.

The deepest lake in Central America, Lake Atitlan, laid majestically blue several thousand feet below our hiking group. Three in their forties, three of us in our sixties, and one in her seventies, up, up, as our daylong climb of Mount San Pedro continued, I asked Alex, "Would you know how to raise seven children?"

FARM SYSTEM

To put it in perspective, I told Alex how my parents raised seven children on our South Dakota farm. My sister was eleven months older than me. Five brothers followed.

My sister, Susan, was always doing house chores. When we were toddlers we would follow grandma to gather eggs. When I was five, we had moved to the Manful ranch near Gettysburg, South Dakota, before my grandmother died. I would have been two, three, and four when I tagged behind her to the chicken coop. She would reach under the chickens and fill her kitchen apron with eggs. I'd get some eggs and put them in grandma's apron. When I reached into the nest of an old cluck, she would always peck my hand. "Ouch! Ouch!" I would say. Grandma would reach under the old clucks, young pullets, and continue gathering eggs. Old hens, pullets, and grandchildren respected her authority. Pecking order. No pecking her! Those that respect authority learn when young.

As my brother, Mark (one year younger than me), got old enough– probably before he was two, he would also get to come with grandma, my sister, and me to the hen house. Over time, my next brother, Wayne (two years younger than me), would come along.

Occasionally, a hen would lay eggs near the woodpile or under bushes. Before we knew it, the hen would be leading her nestlings around the farmyard, one-after-another, sometimes twelve total, searching for bugs and worms. Thinking back, grandma was just like an old hen with us kids: One, two, three, and four followed her to the chicken coop. Grandma was the leader, and taught leadership skills.

At six, Harry Manful taught me how to milk cows, by hand, of course. At that age, I was old enough to feed pail calves. Mark was old enough to throw ears of corn to the pigs. Wayne took over feeding the chickens about the time he started school. The following year Wesley took over feeding chickens; Wayne moved to feeding pigs; Mark moved to feeding pail calves, and I started feeding our milk cows and horses.

Of course, Wesley, Neal, and Kent attended kindergarten–so they are obviously smarter and learned more in school than us older four. Otherwise, why would children attend preschool and kindergarten rather than just start in the first grade?

Before and after grade school, us two oldest boys' job was milking cows. The older we got, the more milk cows dad bought. Wayne was feeding calves and hogs; Wesley's job was feeding chickens and gathering eggs until Neal and Kent were old enough to do outside chores. That did not mean we left Susan alone cleaning house.

Mom and dad worked in town, to support our family of ten (including grandpa who was living with us); otherwise they were doing fieldwork. How did our farmhouse get cleaned? All seven of us had a room to clean. The following week all changed to a different room. Rooms bigger and harder to clean were rotated among the oldest.

The worst room to clean was our seven-by-ten entryway. With muddy shoes or dusty jackets, there never was a day that the rugs did not get shook nor the floor swept. If someone did not clean their shoes to standards before entering, they were reminded what would happen when it was their turn to clean the entryway. Other rooms, a light sweep or dusting was enough until the big cleaning day–Saturday.

How was that entry rule enforced? Everyone knew if the entryway was not swept, mopped, and cleaned to expected standards, then us siblings forced responsibility onto each other. Without a clean entry, dirt was tracked into the rest of our farmhouse. Those entering with muddy boots only needed to be reminded that when the entryway was their turn to clean, expect muddy boots. It worked.

Entering is the way into any school, job, or home. Control the entry in a responsible manner and internal rules are respected. For example, my sister-in-law is a Japanese farmer's daughter. Japanese always remove their shoes before entering anybody's house. Shoes are always removed before entering her home. As in other cultures, responsibilities were established in our farmhouse.

Questions about standards were easily referred to our parents. We avoided that alternative. Many parents do not establish house rules when children are very young. As a result, they fail to use an ancient lesson of responsibility training.

Chores had to be done before and after school. We separated the cream from the milk in our house basement; then, in return, buckets of skim milk were hauled back down the (small) hill to the calves and hogs. Heavy snow, frozen pipes, tossing extra bedding and feed, and mending a fence always meant nearly every school morning we were often running late.

Since we could not miss the morning school bus, while my sister Susan was doing house chores, my two youngest brothers, Neal and Kent, both under seven, would set the table, make toast, and fry our eggs. Our intercom from the basement was a loud voice. "Mark wants three eggs all fried hard this morning; six toast. Wayne wants two soft eggs; four toast. Make my three eggs crispy on the sides and six toast. I think Wesley is done with the chickens and already in the house. Are we out of ketchup? I think Mom's getting six more bottles today."

Saturday morning our folks usually made the twenty-five-mile drive into Aberdeen to pick up machinery parts, farm supplies, and groceries.

Saturday morning was for thorough farmhouse cleaning, during cartoon commercials. By 11:30 a.m. the rush was on as our parents would be home soon. Seven kids can do a lot of sweeping, vacuuming, mopping, and dusting in a half hour.

One Saturday, we thought we had done a decent job before they returned. Looking around as she hauled in cases of cereal and bags of bread, mom could find no obvious misses. She walked up to the doorway separating the dining and living room, brushed her finger across the top woodwork and said, "Filth! Absolute FILTH!" Out came the dust rags. (I like to tell that story, because it is the only one I remember of us not cleaning to standards.) Mother was just keeping us aware; when she said "clean," we cleaned!

In those days, bread at the day-old bakery outlet was five loaves for a dollar. Bread was cheap enough that mom could not afford to buy flour, yeast, and sugar and fill the propane tank to bake. She somehow would find time to make or do anything else if it was more economical than buying something.

Did we learn? Yes. Did we eat? Six growing boys doing farm chores ate a lot more than kids do now, and we did not have beer bellies at ten.

School athletes do eat a lot. A few years ago, my youngest brother, Kent, stopped at his local grocery store one day after work and picked up four boxes of cereal, three loaves of bread, three gallons of milk, and two bottles of maple syrup. Casually, as she was running the cash register, the clerk asked, "Running a bed and breakfast?" "No," my brother said, "We have two teenage boys."

Back to the farm: A typical morning on the farm was awake at 6:00 a.m., milking cows by 6:30, done feeding all the animals by 7:30, and on the school bus by 7:55. (We were only five miles from town, so the bus driver usually only had to make one more stop before we arrive at school by 8:10.) Everybody had jobs. Everybody knew the schedule. It was our individual responsibility to meet the schedule. It sure could not be anybody else's fault.

With seven kids to feed and clothe, and my disabled grandfather living with us, income from a 960-acre, semi-arid farm was not enough. Our mother and father usually had jobs in town. Mom often cooked at a café. Dad found work servicing cars at the local gas station, drilling wells, or assembling machinery for an implement dealer until he was able to get steady work on a building crew for a lumberyard. Dad was paid more, so mother basically took over most of the farm tractor work in her late thirties, before I graduated high school.

Often, my thoughts have wandered back to how our parents taught responsibility and taught us young. There was no question in the morning of what time we were getting up, what chores we had to do, or who had to do what. It was automatic. Evenings and weekends were the same. That is how our farm ran: a well-managed organization. Everyone had responsibilities. Did we work hard at times? Yes. Were we overworked? Never.

Over the years, I have had many jobs in construction, Air Force, Air National Guard, South Dakota Department of Agriculture, Governor's Office of Economic Development, wholesaling, retailing, seed conditioning, research, and marketing. I have never worked in an organization that was as well managed as our farm.

Did our farm operate any different from farms 4000 years ago? 2000 years ago? A hundred years ago? Perhaps we were a bit more efficient, but had no less responsibility than any youngsters over the centuries.

How many parents today give responsibility to their children? What age do parents give responsibility? If it is at college graduation, they are two decades too late.

From age two on, can parents assume the child will clean their room, make their bed, put their toys away, feed the cat or dog, and take the trash out? Are grade schoolers today required to sweep and dust the house and school (as we were in the one-room country school)?

Are parents of high schoolers expecting the house to be cleaned, laundry finished, table set, vegetables prepared, and sometimes dinner in the oven when they return home from work? If not, what are children doing the few hours between school and dinner? One thing is for certain, they are not milking cows by hand.

Are children watching cartoons? Playing electronic games? Phoning friends? Completing homework? Where is the responsibility? Who cleans the table after dinner? Who does dishes?

In many households today both parents work. My folks usually did not have a chance to talk all day. Before leaving in the morning, they seldom said more than a few words to each other. They were exhausted after dinner. (We called it supper.) Off to our living room our parents would go, while all of us children cleared the table, did dishes, and cleaned the kitchen. We certainly had not worked as hard as they did. We knew it. Our biggest complaint was that mom seemed to be able to use every bowl in the cupboard and pot in the pantry to make a meal. With our stomachs full, to whom were we going to complain? We only griped under our breath if it was our turn to wash the pots and pans.

It also was automatically assumed that once we graduated from high school we were to support ourselves. No college fund. No cash send-off. We could vote. We were adults. Adults should be able to support themselves. For many (those who were never taught responsibility at home), independence is a huge learning curve.

After getting out of the Air Force, I found it astounding that the mother of one of my college roommates had to work until her only son graduated from college. He started two years before I arrived, and had at least two years left to get his degree in wildlife management when I graduated with two majors. He had no incentive to take a full course load. His mommy and daddy were providing tuition, books, room, board, a car, gas, and more beer money than any of my friends. My guess is that he had no chores at home and was given no responsibility as a child.

Failure to give responsibilities leads to a failed society.

For thousands of years, most people lived off the land. What their plot would produce fed their multigenerational family. They traded for the rest. Everyone worked. Everyone had responsibilities. Life expectancy was often less than forty. Teenagers had to learn how to feed themselves. With rare exceptions (e.g., ancient Rome city dwellers), people worked to eat.

As populations grew, governments were created to protect and regulate their people. Farmers gained efficiencies. Agriculture, as in the United States, has become so successful that less than 1 percent of the population can feed the other 99 percent with surpluses exported.

Currently, about half the U.S. population lives off government subsidies including free food. "Children" can stay on their parents' healthcare until age twenty-six. For thousands of years, a person of twenty-six was considered middle aged—tipping the scale toward being a senior citizen of their society.

When children are not taught responsibilities as a very young child, by two or three, they learn to demand freebies. Is a high school graduate today like a toddler never wanting to give up a milk bottle? Are they suckers, or are their parents?

Eventually becoming needy adults, they expect the government to not only feed, clothe, and house them but they also expect free health care, forgiveness of school loans, free or subsidized childcare, government regulated (if not subsidized) phones and cable television, and other luxuries that historically only came from hard work or inheritance. Large inheritances ruined many lives because heirs never learned personal responsibility.

Maybe that is why many shun the Bible. In a letter written about 51 A.D (about 2000 years ago), besides traveling, preaching, and being in prison, the Apostle Paul stated they worked and expected others to do the same, not simply live off the welfare of others. He wrote:

> ... Nor did we eat anyone's bread free of charge, but worked with labor and toil night and day ... (therefore) we command you this: If anyone will not work, neither shall he eat. For we hear that there are some who walk among you in a disorderly manner, not working at all, but are busybodies.[1]

When is the last time a politician, community leader, or manager of a homeless shelter said that? Many church leaders are deceiving their donors by providing free meals to those who choose not to work.

Work, like food, is a necessity.

---

[1] 2nd Thessalonians, 3:8-11, NKJV, p. 1683

11

I'm a State.

Riddle: It is not an airport, but it is the most common place to check bags.

Early cultural awareness starts at home.

Over the years, especially as a grandparent, I have learned never to underestimate the knowledge of a child. Fundamental concepts are instilled in them before they reach age three.

Our first grandchild was born in Colorado. It was a long drive from Colorado Springs to Sioux Falls, South Dakota, where we were living. Patricia had our house decorated for Christmas. I had white lights glistening in the snow around the house. Our grandson, Austin, and his mom and dad were coming for Christmas.

I think our daughter, Charmion, was the most excited. It had been seven years since she lived at home; but that year she lived over 700 miles from our place. Nearly every day she would tell one-year-old (twenty-two months) Austin, "Only ten more days before we go to South Dakota." The next day, "Only nine more days until South Dakota." The countdown was on. I think Austin knew the numbers concept before he was two. He had memorized story books by then.

Patricia and I were both working. We could only get to Colorado every few months to see our only grandson. Their arrival for Christmas was the best gift we could have received.

Christmas Eve: The wood stove in our living room was cranked up. Our house smelled of burning pine and holiday goodies. Outside lights lit the snow as we were sitting with our Colorado family around us. All eyes were always on Austin as he found plenty of things for play. Once he toddled over to me, tapped me on the arm, and said something like "Sow akota, Sow akota" in the language of a one-year-old.

I picked him up, he squirmed around after telling me something I did not understand, and jumped from my knees back to the floor to find something else he had not noticed thirty seconds earlier.

A few minutes later he came back to my side of the room. Tapped me on the arm. "Sow akota. Sow akota." I picked him up again. We chatted. Hugged him and he was off my lap again venturing to a new corner of the room.

I looked at Charmion and asked, "Did he call me South Dakota?" Since Austin was the center of attention, everybody chimed in, "Yeah. He called you South Dakota."

Charmion said, "Every day we would count down the days to come to South Dakota. Apparently, to Austin you are South Dakota. He was coming for you."

Two decades later, I tear up thinking about that moment. He spent days counting down to see me.

To a one-year-old, South Dakota was someone he loved at some distant destination. Austin understood the concept that they were leaving home. The trip was long—fifteen hours on snowy roads. When he arrived, just as his mom promised, there was *South Dakota*.

When Austin's sister, Emily, was born a few months later, he would tell her about South Dakota.

Each summer we would host our grandchildren for a week or two. When Emily and Austin were about eleven and thirteen, Austin asked me, "Why do we always call you South Dakota?"

"Austin," I replied, "I was wondering when you were going to ask me that question." I explained the story to them of how I became a state. Now they call me "Grandpa South Dakota."

WHERE'S THE CHECK?

As an agriculturalist, if there was any one crop for which I was most noted, it was millet. Knowing my interest in the crop, my son-in-law,

Clayton, planted a four-acre patch of millet by their house. That was grandson Willie's crop.

Willie would ride in the tractor, combine, pickup, or grain truck for hours and hours. He never seemed bored–that was life of a farmer's son.

My job at that time required me to check fields throughout central South Dakota. In the spring of 1996, when Willie was two, he rode with me from 8:00 in the morning until late afternoon, checking wheat and corn fields for bugs. Usually Willie would get out and try to find them too, other times he dozed in his car seat.

I had a newer pickup. After starting the engine, an alarm would notify me if someone was in the passenger seat. Before the warning ding, Willie would buckle himself into his car-seat.

Without fail, every time we would get in the pickup he would ask, "Grandpa, do you have the airbag turned off?" (Safety airbags explode from the dash quickly in an accident. Airbag impact could kill a child. Upon starting the vehicle, there was a manual switch to disengage the passenger airbag.) At two, Willie could relate a dashboard switch, the danger of an unseen airbag, and the requirement before driving that his seat belt must be fastened.

Was he a two-year-old that really liked riding in the cab of farm equipment or a truck? Yes! What did Willie know about farming? He was two. Adults expect two-year-olds to know nothing.

Willie would stay in Blunt, South Dakota, at a babysitter most days when Clayton could not take him to the field, while our daughter, Michelle, worked in a local office.

When Clayton would pick Willie up, they would drive by his millet field on the way home. Clayton would say, "Willie, that is your college fund."

Does a two-year-old understand college? Neither Clayton nor Michelle had gone to college. How would Willie know the concept of college?

As the millet field was nearing harvest, Clayton commented to Willie, "You can ride with me when we swath your millet." As harvest neared, every day Clayton would say the same thing. Several days went by waiting for the right time to swath the millet.[1]

---

[1] If left to dry standing, millet will shatter from wind whipping the stem. It had to be laid in a windrow (swath) to dry a few days before combining (threshing) the grain from the straw.

One day, Clayton noticed the field as they were heading home. He said, "Willie, your Uncle Carl must have swathed your millet on the way to a bigger field." Cautious to keep Willie from being disappointed and since he did not get to ride to swath his own field, Clayton said, "Willie, you can ride in the combine with me when we harvest your field." That satisfied Willie.

A few days later, September 1996, they were heading home and to Clayton's astonishment, the small millet field had been combined. Willie liked riding in any farm machinery, but oh no. Somewhat disappointed was Willie after the missed swather ride. Now he could not even get to ride in the combine to harvest his own field.

Clayton turned to Willie and in a sincere voice said, "Willie, your Uncle Carl must have combined your millet field on the way to the bigger field."

After seeing the field, Willie looked at his dad unfazed, and asked, "Where's my check?"

Willie was not even thirty months old, but he could conceptualize two missed opportunities (swathing and combining), a college, a millet field, harvested millet grain equaling money, and a piece of paper (the check) was money saved for a fund he had never seen.

Whether you are a parent, grandparent, aunt, uncle, friend of the family, or babysitter, NEVER, NEVER underestimate the ability of a two-year-old child to understand concepts. Responsibility is well understood before a college fund.

THE GOOSE HOUSE

A couple weeks before I wrote this, I was visiting with my older sister–eleven months older than me. (We basically grew up together, but since we have both retired, I enjoy calling her my older sister.) I asked her if she remembered playing in the goose house at "The Little Place." She did.

We went on to discuss how both of us were able to play in the small, approximately 2-foot x 2-foot "A" frame goose house. The door opening could not have been bigger than 10 inches. It was built for a mother goose to sit on her eggs in a protected area. The hen goose could sit on her down-covered nest, look out the door, and hiss or bite anything that came near.

Yes, a mother goose will bite a curious boy, or anybody that threatens her goslings.

After the mother goose would leave with her goslings, Susan and I would play in the goose house. The worst thing about it was the last time we both played in there I kept hitting my head on the roofing nails. I remember I did not have that problem the year before. Susan had more hair. Perhaps the nails could not penetrate it.

To confirm the timeframe, I called our mother and asked her, "Mom, when did you and dad tear down the goose houses at 'The Little Place' where Susan and I used to play?"

"1954," she said.

(Here I should note that our mother had the best memory of anybody I had ever met. Names, genealogy, places, and events were her specialty with us kids, and especially extended family calling her when they had a question. Until she passed at age eighty-five, she was the source of when someone was born, died, married, how many kids from the first and second marriage, their names, where they lived, how long, when the last time she had seen them, who was at the event, what table they sat at, what dishes were used, and what cover was on the potato pot.)

"Mom," I replied. "I would have been only one in 1954 and Susan two. I remember hitting my head on those nails the year before."

Mother came back and said, "I never did like you kids playing in those old goose houses with the rusty nails and old wooden shingles. Well then, I think the last you would have played in them would have been 1955. I didn't like that yard. To keep you from the road, the goose house was about the only place I could let you play and still keep an eye on you."

I never remembered my brother, Mark (born in 1954), ever playing with me in the goose houses. He was too young. It is still hard for me to believe two of us kids could get through a goose opening and both play inside a one-goose nesting area. Mom and my sister confirmed my 1955 memory at two. Remember playing in the goose house the year before confirms my earliest memory (1954)–at one. I did not have my cap on which would have protected my head from roofing nails making it a warm day, likely May, when I was fourteen or fifteen months old.

In northern South Dakota, considering geese hatch their eggs only once per year, the goslings would have been out of the nest by the end of April. The second time it must have also been spring because we were excited to play in the goose house again. Likely May 1955, when I was about age twenty-six or twenty-seven months, is a memory confirmed by my head nailed at two.

Some say that it is very unusual to remember things at that early age. However, I think most adults have the ability to recall very early memories; they are likely unable to specify a date and location.

If adults, like me, can remember things that happened at age one or two, certainly the human brain is building a learning structure (e.g., language) and conceptual understanding that will be used the rest of our life.

Placing a child into a public structure at age three, four, or five modifies early learning and establishes lifelong patterns of thought. Grouped with mean children, others learn to be mean. Playing with the naughty teaches naughtiness. Grouped with children that think mashed peas are poop, peas are avoided. Grouped with average children, to avoid ridicule, children learn average is okay. Combining under- and overachievers, the school system trains for the average.

THE LITTLE PLACE

The Little Place was where our parents moved when they got married June 3, 1951, until the fall of 1958. We always called it *The Little Place* to differentiate it from our other farmstead—the big house and barn where my dad's parents lived a half-mile away.

How little was *The Little Place*?

When I got out of the Air Force in 1975, I noticed that our old house was burned down. I asked my mother for the dimensions of *The Little Place*. She said she did not know. It was a four-room house (entry, kitchen, living-room, bedroom) with no upstairs and only a small dirt cellar.

In the fall of 1958 even Wayne, at two years old, remembers playing at *The Little Place* as do us other three siblings then ages three to six. One incident, he remembers mom was cleaning the house as we were preparing to move to the other farm. She had the screen door locked to keep us kids from tracking onto her clean floors as a skunk in midafternoon came walking down our driveway. Since skunks are nocturnal, the fear was that it had rabies. As a group of children, we ran to the house in fear.

Mother, when in her mid-eighties, recalled things about staying with her grandmother at age two while her mother was teaching school. I always thought Wayne had the best memory in our family, but we all remember details at a very young age, like living at *The Little Place*.

Our cousin, Roger, used to come out from Minneapolis and stay with us for the summer. Roger was about ten years older than me. One of dad's youngest cousins, Clifford, would stay with us for months on end. My great uncle said his son, Clifford, stayed to help dad with the farming, but as a teenager, mother later realized he was having school troubles.

Mom would also babysit children of a rural schoolteacher, Brian and Betsy Lou, who stayed with us many nights during the 1956–1958 school years. We really liked it when those two kids our age could stay overnight.

I remember brother Wesley's baptism in that house around Christmas 1957. I was four. Our dining table was set up in the living room in the northeast corner and a large kitchen bowl was used for the baptism. Though I do not remember the winter weather, apparently it was too bad to take our family of seven to church five miles away; so, the minister came to *The Little Place* for the ceremony.

Why mention such details? My point is that I believe most people remember things when they were one to five years of age, they simply cannot put a date on the memory. It is important to establish a memory timeline as caretakers in early childhood affect a person's learning and cultural understanding.

Even if places and events of early years are not remembered, that is when life's actions, language, accent, independence, responsibility, and work ethics are learned.

Moving from one farmhouse to another in the fall of 1958 was a big deal. That spring I recall dad holding the two handles of a metal scraper (called a tumble-bug) pulled by our old tractor operated by mother as they dug the basement of grandpa and grandma's addition.

Farmers seldom move. Rarely do they build homes. Memories like that stick, and dates can be confirmed. March 1, 1959, we moved from our second farmhouse to an even bigger ranch house between Gettysburg and Hoven, South Dakota.

As a five-year-old child, simply watching dirt moved by horse-drawn equipment modified to be pulled by a tractor, was a learning experience. I remember driving our workhorses, Lady and Bab, from the field pulling a hay rack. Dad used our horses one spring to plant because it was too wet for the tractor. I followed, but lost a shoe. It seemed I searched for hours, but never found it. Potential danger from a rabid skunk, picking prairie crocus (pasque–the first blooming native-sod flowers in spring), and keeping grain in a wooden triple-box wagon as it rolled out of a threshing machine were all learning experiences for me before I started school.

Like all others, those early childhood memories are the basis for life-long knowledge indirectly contributing to how a person processes feelings, thoughts, smells, sights, and sounds. Likewise, children institutionalized in day care, preschool, kindergarten, and early grades adapt their learning to function at a non-home environment with four walls, standardized schedules, and institutional materials.

Never in history were any civilizations' children institutionalized in mass and retained for their first two decades of life. As long as children can function properly in a classroom environment, they may do well in school, but miss the opportunities of real life outside the school system. Hence, school systems are forced to measure school achievement rather than potential life challenges for children who have not been trained to operate independently.

Are city parks busy? No. Children have not been taught how to play independently in them. Instead, they are far more comfortable within four walls playing their electronic toys.

My childhood home was too small to be confined to it with three to eight other children. Since my mother did not know the dimensions of *The Little Place*, I took a tape measure and ran it back and forth several times to confirm the outside dimensions of the house. There were no attachments. One level. One bedroom. No second floor. No bathroom. No basement—only a crawl space where mom would keep canned goods until it got too cold in the winter. Our fuel oil stove barely kept the inside of the tarpaper siding, 2 × 4 frame house heated. The foundation was 18 × 20 feet. Yes, the outside house dimensions made it a 360-square-foot, one-story house. Tiny living was our life before tiny houses became popular.

No wonder; mom did not like *The Little Place*. Today, teachers would complain if they had only a dozen children in small desks for a few hours in that small space. The one bedroom held a crib and my parents' bed. The rest of us four siblings, Roger, Clifford, Brian, and Betsy Lou all slept in the living room. The kitchen with a sink, cupboard, and table connected with the living room. That was it, except for the entryway, which had a floor trapdoor to get into the basement.

Many people live in 3600-square-foot homes—ten times the size of *The Little Place*. Does growing up in a bigger house make them any happier than we were? I doubt it. Do they learn more about socializing in a bigger home? Doubtful.

For the past couple years, our daughter Charmion has organized a project in the mountains of Guatemala to replace dirt floors with concrete, rusty tin roofs with new ones, dirt walls with concrete blocks or bamboo. Are Americans happier in their big houses compared to the 90 square feet (8.4 square meter), or even the bigger 168 square feet (15.6 square meter), one-room Guatemalan mountain homes? Perhaps Americans are healthier, but not happier.

Home size does not extrapolate into happy families and smarter people.

For thousands of years, before the 1960s A.D., most children, like those in our family, grew up in a structured parent-organized environment. The structure was repeated generation after generation. Culture continued. Learning passed from parent to the oldest children, and younger ones learned from both parents and siblings. The government-structured school system has modified traditional structured learning.

Engineers will attest, unless a project is structurally and functionally sound, it will prematurely fail. Early construction stages are critical—the life of the project is based on the initial structure. The best government structure, educational system, sports team, or business organization will fail without participants' respect for its anatomy. Family, as a body, disintegrates without knowledge and capabilities to perform during the natural biological process.

Four thousand B.C. is the same as now. Animals procreate and nurture young through education to adapt to their environment for water, sustenance, and hygiene before weaning. From youth to biological maturity, they learn survival habits before procreation restarts the cycle.

Animals like the wild ass can wean offspring. Why is it now so difficult for some parents?

Perhaps from birth to adulthood, many parents let institutions raise their child. It is not even a requirement that the institution instructors have biological experience in raising young.

Would you fly on a jet, knowing few, if any, assembly workers had experience in jet production? That is a mechanical process—part "A" connects to part "B." Why then do parents turn over their biological process to the inexperienced?

Is it selfishness? Ignorance? A learned habit? Government intervention? Economic or personal satisfaction?

Is someone who has never made their bed, cleaned the bathroom, or cooked a meal, even in their twenties biologically competent to raise a child? Are they an independent adult? Apparently not. At eighteen, someone that cannot feed and shelter himself may be biologically mature but psychologically immature.

Why, you may ask, tell stories of two- and three-year-olds and why make a point about those in their mid-twenties being immature?

The point at which someone is mature has varied. It has little or nothing to do with the biological function of procreation. If the Stone Age population had a life expectancy of thirty, and the current life expectancy is eighty, that means that we now have roughly four times the average adult life of the Stone Age person living 5000 years ago.

When do most inventions occur? Seldom before someone is twenty. Ideas occur then, but few inventions. Implemented innovations occur in mid to late careers. Today, those in their forties to fifties have the most experience, connections, and enough ambition left to use their creative mind and accumulated knowledge to invent. Society should utilize old resources and it should be structured to stimulate the young.

Average minds conditioned in average schools with average teachers producing average results with average teams are not where inventions originate. We must stop building nations of mediocre minds of average ambition without inventiveness.

Many young people have good, even great ideas. Perhaps they have not been taught the impossible, so they try. Having never worked, many young adults simply do not have the ambition and determination to initiate, investigate, implement, and complete the process of turning a novel idea into a potential product.

Our generation has the life expectancy to capitalize on creative minds, but we have a school system that has stymied creativity, encumbered efficiency, and conditioned a population to be average. Our future has educated citizens expecting to live beyond eighty but with shallower minds than cavemen.

12

Change or Punt

Riddle: Where is change expected, but has uniform standards?

Artificial culture influences life's natural inclinations. It starts when exposed to artificial structures like day care and schools, but is modified by surroundings like music trends or parental abandonment. Expect deviance.

The term "deviance" may rile some readers, especially those already riled by previous chapters. However, consider "deviance" as in statistical analysis. A complete model when analyzed has no deviance—it is complete. Statistics are used to analyze with sample data. Although there are minimum data sets employed to minimize standard deviation, there will always be differences between subsets and the original whole. Let us explore historic international subsets.

British singers (generally beginning in the 1960s with the Beatles) found immediate and broad acceptance in the United States. For more than five decades the trans-Atlantic trend continued. On the other hand, television shows in Britain find limited viewers in the United States. Why? British humor is different from American humor. Australian humor is different from British humor. Irish humor is different from Mexican humor. Why? Cultural differences. Each country has a different learning environment.

Music transcends cultures but seldom do consecutive generations appreciate the music of the past. Lyrics may not transcend time.

Rhythm is internationally copacetic. Humor, on the other hand, is often cross-culturally intolerable. What I think is funny, you may find unsettling or not understandable.

Canada and the United States received a lot of Irish emigrants originally during and after the mid-nineteenth century Irish Potato Famine (1845–1852). More than 150 years later, one winter in Mexico I was visiting with an Irishman who had emigrated to Canada in the 1980s.

Here's a bit of cultural background: The Irish like to drink and so do Mexicans. However, Mexicans can find it hard to relate to the Irish or their jokes.

For example, several of us were having a beer under an outdoor Mexican palapa and the Irishman had a joke for us. He deadpanned: "I saw an Irishman walk out of a pub."

I thought it was hilarious. A Mexican frowned. Why?

Climate affects jokes.

Mexico is hot and they like to drink outside. There are no pubs. Drinking inside a bar would be hot and stuffy. Irish people go to a pub for warmth. Smelling peat smoke, sipping dark Guinness®,[1] and storytelling while listening to an off-key ballad is legendary. The Irish are also generalized (whether accurately or unfairly) as being heavy or regular drinkers; so Irish jokes are often about an Irish person in a bar—not coming out. Example: A priest, a rabbi, and an Irishman walk into a bar. The bartender asks, "Is this some kind of joke?"

If the Irishman would have started a joke: "I saw an Irishman stumble out of a bar ...," the Mexican would have been listening intently, but the joke would need more. The art of delivering humor is to know when to stop.

Humor is generational. My grandfather and grandchildren may not laugh at a joke from my generation.

Medicine provides a good example. Body temperature used to be taken with an inserted thermometer. Now, my grandchildren have their temperature taken with a small instrument swiped across their forehead.

---

[1] Guinness® Copyright Agent: Norwalk Office, Diageo North America, Inc., 801 Main Street Norwalk, CT 06851

In my grandfather's generation after examination, the doctor would go to his office medicine cabinet, pull out a bottle, and give it to my grandfather telling him how much to take and when. In my generation, the doctor handwrote a prescription and told me to go to the pharmacy to fill it. In my grandchildren's generation, young doctors cannot write cursive. If they could, the pharmacist would not be able to read it. Instead, the doctor sends an order for a prescription electronically from his office to the pharmacy. Subsequently, my grandchild's medication would only be issued by a pharmacist with secured label and lengthy instruction.

Technology affects jokes.

The joke:

A doctor reaches to his pocket to write a prescription, pulls out a rectal thermometer, and says: "Some assholes got my pen." That joke could only be understood by someone from my generation.

Location affects jokes.

When I set foot on the continent of Australia for the first time in 2012, friends recommended that I read Bill Bryson's travel book about Australia, *In a Sunburned Country*. When I got to Australia, I looked at the airport and the local well-stocked library for his book. It was nowhere to be found. I considered since it was published in 2000, perhaps it was no longer available.

One day while searching for more reading material at Port Macquarie (a larger coastal town in northern New South Wales) I asked the librarian for books written by Bill Bryson. At that time, I could not remember the specific title. Immediately, the helpful librarian directed me to *Down Under* by Bill Bryson. It was a hilarious Australian travelogue covering many walks of life, places, and customs.

Later, I was told the two books were identical. *In a Sunburned Country* was the title of Bryson's book published in the United States and Canada; *Down Under* was the published title for Britain and Australia. Even though the American title came from an Australian poem "My Country," the title was too offensive for Brits and Aussies. While I enjoyed reading *Down Under*. Australians indicated that the American,

Bryson, did not shine a good light on many Australian actions, customs, and places.

That interesting title shift indicated a cultural difference. The more time we spent in Australia (eight months over three years), the more humor we found coming naturally from the isolated island. They are generally a happy people with a great sense of humor.

Culture affects language.

Australians use a different version of English than Americans. It is laced with humor, camouflaged vulgarity, pronunciation caveats, and spelling changes.

I traveled: they "travelled."

We said hello; they said "G-Day."

We are retired so had the day off; they took a "sickie" from work.

I parked my car in the parking lot; they parked in the "car park."

We wanted to leave after breakfast; they had already completed "brekke."

We went for a hike; they went for a "walkabout."

We left right away; they left "straight away."

I was certain I had seen a baby kangaroo; "London to a brick" it was a "Joey" "roo."

Everything was dry from drought; "Nun's nasty" as a "dead dingo's donger."

He told a good joke; it was a "corker."

We walked by a university; they walked by a "uni."

I wanted black coffee while my wife wanted it with cream; "whilst" they wanted a "long black" and "flat white."

We wanted a cup; they wanted a "cuppa."

My wife likes chocolate; they like "chokkie."

We wanted French fries; they wanted "chips."

We ordered ketchup; they ordered "tomato sauce."

We ordered sandwiches; one ordered "cut lunch," the other a "sanger."

We wanted take-out; they wanted "take away."

The guy on the café's television was obnoxious; "no worries," the "Ozzie" "bloat's" "up oneself." Ignore the "rubbish" on the "telle."

I took my swim trunks; they took their "swimmers."

We took flip-flops; they took "thongs."

I took a big beer; he packed a "tallie."

We went through the trees; they went through the "bush."

We thought the hike was easy; it was a "piece of piss."

I said the mosquitoes were bad; they said "mossies" were a "ripper."

We lost a prescription; "scripts" "gone walkabout."

I greeted someone with "How are you?" They asked, "How you goin'?"

School children were outside for physical education; they were doing "physie."

We were going to host a hot dog cookout on the grill; they didn't want "snags" and "bangers" on the "barbie."

Later at dinner I used a napkin; they used a "serviette." I was told a napkin is a female personal item. "Pardon me," I said. "I didn't want to put it in the wrong place."

Each culture is different.

What is innocently said in one culture is inappropriate in another. Translating words to different languages is touchy. International companies spend countless hours ensuring a product or brand introduction that is acceptable in one country is not offensive in another. Consequently, it is not uncommon to name the same product differently in various countries depending on how a brand word translates.

Motions, hand signs, phrases, tone of voice, emphasis, and even plainly spoken words of the same language can be offensive within communities in the same country. Furthermore, familiar words or phrases used by a grandfather can have another meaning to his grandchildren. For example, my grandfather contemplating an interesting thought would say, "So," meaning he was thinking about a noncontroversial statement. At times, I wondered if he questioned my phrase. I could take offense to that simple word, but my generation would simply utter, "Hmmm" with the same meaning.

Correctness gets even more complicated within a country, especially when trying to appropriately address ethnic groups and races. For example, in the U.S. during the 1800s "the Black Race" was more appropriate than saying "Negro." Later, "Negro" was a polite term, whereas in some areas, "Coloreds" was acceptable. "African," "African American,"

"Blacks," "blacks," and "black people" were all terms pleasantly appropriate at one time but out of favor at other times.

Culture varies locally.

Words used within a race or ethnic group can be different than if the same word is used by outsiders. Writing for multiple generations becomes difficult when word use, especially inflection, changes over time. However, daily work and interaction for pleasure with different races, ethnicities, and religions encourages befitting motions, signs, phrases, and terms with appropriateness pleasantly corrected when needed.

To blend in, my wife and I get involved in communities wherever we stay. In Australia, I helped at a historic farm and vineyard operated totally by volunteers. From 9:30 to 10:00 the men took "smoke-R"; the women took "tea time"; and I took a coffee break. Before starting to work there, we stopped in for a wine tasting. It was free. We bought a couple bottles of wine.

One day while raking bamboo leaves around the tasting area I noticed backpackers were leaving. They were charged $2.00 each for tasting wines. After they left, I asked why they were charged and earlier I was not. "Backpackers don't buy anything, so we charge them." Was it economics, or a cultural cost?

As pointed out above, words of the same language are used differently. Some words are spelled the same but can have a very positive or negative context depending on the tone of use. In Australia, "mate" for example can be good or bad. Good: "You want to go fishing, mate?" Bad: "You owe me 30 bucks, mate!" It's hard to differentiate between the two versions in writing but, when spoken, the difference is clear.

Term and voice inflection are taught in a social environment that is different from school. Learning, especially that taught by parents, relatives, and neighbors, is different in each culture. Each country has a different system of learning and each culture has different codes of social acceptance.

What is acceptable to an American may not be acceptable behavior to a Native American. What may be acceptable to an Australian Aboriginal may not meet social norms of other Australians. European formality would be awkward to a Texas rancher.

Unlike the school system, learning at home can be as it was historically. Parents and children pass through trends and different technology.

Some parents have always been overprotective and spoiled their children. The difference historically is they did not have the school systems' support in pampering. Throughout the centuries, teenage exposure to the working world helped correct to social norms. Whole cultures are effected by changing learning systems.

The British system changed America and Australia. Those that failed to change, if given the option, returned to Britain. When possible, people migrate to a system where they feel most comfortable.

Loss of American colonies after the Revolutionary War (1775–1783) limited Britain's economic opportunities from the late 1700s through the 1800s. After sending about 60,000 prisoners to North America, an empire in search of sustainability sent thieves, rogues, and more accurately "poor" people and sailors to Australia. (Some say to free jails.) The change created a different learning environment.

FIRST FLEET

A short four years after the American Revolution, May 13, 1787, a group known as "The First Fleet" with about 1530 people set sail from Britain for Australia. There were 736 convicts (men and women) and their seventeen children. The other half was 211 marines, their twenty-seven wives, fourteen children, 300 officers, and an assortment of miscellaneous staff. Chance for a shortened prison sentence, free land, and economic opportunity drove the selection of convicts, marines, and a few businesspeople half way around the world.

The more legitimate goal for establishing colonies in Australia was to establish a source of raw materials in the southern hemisphere with reciprocal climates. For eighty years, about 162,000 British prisoners were shipped to Australia between 1788 and 1868.

It is peaceful but a bit melancholy to look at the first cemetery in Port Macquarie, Australia of the first woman prisoner who was buried there. The woebegone prisoner was convicted to seven years. Eventually, she was freed, and married, or at least had a common-law husband, Andrew Callaghan. He was a tailor by trade and also had a penal colony conviction of seven years for stealing linen cloth.

No wonder British jails were full.

After getting to Australia, justice was not sparingly parsed. Court records of August 9, 1865, reported Julia Lawless was found guilty, although pleading innocent, for the dastardly deed of stealing a teapot.[2] Was it her surname that tipped the judge's hand to rule guilty, or was it her family's occupation?

What caused such high unemployment? Why was Great Britain having labor and crime problems in the eighteenth and nineteenth centuries?

Family separation, introduction of technology, geographic movement, government policy, and prematurely moving children from home all change cultures. Australia was certainly different after British prisoners arrived than Aboriginal Australia the previous 10,000 years.

Regarding technology, since the 1960s innovation has slowed while adoption of technology has quickened. Truly novel concepts developed during the nineteenth century were refined during my grandfather's generation (1891–1976).

For example, electromagnetism, the precursor to radio, was a novel concept originating from Danish physicist, Hans Christian Oersted (1777–1851). During a lecture April 21, 1820, he noticed compass direction north was changed by turning an electrical battery on and off. Papers published in 1887 and 1890 by German physicist Heinrich Rudolf Hertz (1857–1894) first described electromagnetic wave transmission–a system we now call radio.

Many subsequent radios using electromagnetism have developed in the last century, but transmission novelty has not been surpassed. Today's generation listen to the radio, watch television, and may change cell phones every year without realizing the source of their pleasure. Pleasure occupies their minds and time, which could be used to develop a better system of transmission. Radio is an example of generations living off past novel ideas and failing to develop other innovations because of it.

Today's adoption rate of technology can be credited to work on nineteenth-century radio electromagnetism–not today's school system.

Coming out of the European Dark Ages, it could take centuries for technology to be adopted.

It took 2000 years for radio to replace paper communications.

---

[2] *South Australian Advertiser*, August 10, 1985, p. 139, http://trove.nla.gov.au/ndp/del/article/31852449 (Sourced July 20, 2015)

The Chinese had invented paper around 200 B.C. They were using it as toilet paper by 600 A.D., although it took 1200 years for Chinese paper-making technology to reach Europe. Papyrus, a type of unprocessed paper, was used by Greek and Egyptians well before the Chinese processed commercial paper. Muslims trading with the East are credited with bringing commercial paper-making technology (a Chinese trade secret) to what is now Spain around 1000 A.D.

Although Great Britain was the originator of the Industrial Revolution around the 1760s, well before then, printing presses were kicking out fliers, newspapers, and books. In 1450, Johannes Gutenberg of Mainz (Germany) received credit for making what is now called the Gutenberg Bible—the first major book printed with moveable type.

To summarize, it took processed paper about 1200 years to reach Europe; 800 years for it to be in volumes usable as toilet paper, and about 450 years to produce the first major book using moveable type.

The adoption rate of paper was slow, but the technology of moveable typing letters was adopted rather quickly. Radio was faster. It would be like today's adoption of genetically engineered food compared to new cell phones. Models (phones) change much faster than concepts (genetic modifications). Radio replaced paper. Concepts take more thought to comprehend than a thingamajig.

Concept utility takes longer to develop than a product. It took a century for radio to move from primordial concept to wide public use. Paper and radio communications is not new; neither is plant breeding. However, genetically engineering plants and medical techniques will take time for the public to understand and accept the concept. Consequently, it is not a matter of if concepts are adopted; it is a matter of when they will be fully accepted.

With an ever-growing world population, human health and sustenance depend on adoption of genetic engineering. People can live without paper and radio, but they cannot live without food and health. Hopefully, it will not take a plague or famine to enlighten.

The spontaneous adoption of mechanical technology is what put the unskilled out of work for the last three centuries. Europe suffered, especially Britain. America at the time did not have excess labor.

Once printing became easier and cheaper, more people became literate, which resulted in societies more capable of sharing ideas. Likewise, availability of electricity in the last century had more do with learning than schools.

By the late 1700s Great Britain's Industrial Revolution and its elimination of jobs was in full swing while her American colonies were seeking independence.

For a thousand years, peat provided local fuel and jobs in the British Isles.

Mechanical mining of coal replaced wood and peat. Water and steam power employed more iron and tools. Machines and tools replaced people. Peat cutters, woodcutters, punters,[3] to name a few, were being forced out of work by machines.

Imagine your great-grandfather, grandfather, father, and now you in your thirties having never thought of any work besides pushing a boat through the Thames. So was the life of a punter. Then one day, a boat with a diesel motor passed you as the operator sat on a chair giving you thumbs down at your ridiculous waste of labor.

How could Great Britain respond? No previous time in history had technology replaced labor at such a rapid pace. A mechanical revolution was causing a societal revolution. Likewise, today's cell phone and Internet access have more social and educational assets than the school system.

What one learns in a week on computer can take a year in school. Is it any wonder students are going rogue? Things will change–there is no more "First Fleet" to the land of "Oz."

Yes, cutting in peat quagmires or pick-axing coal from pits all day was drudgery, especially in cold dreary weather. Hauling bundles (faggots) of sticks all day was not only tiresome but also boring. Punting a boat upstream was back-wrenching work.

Since Roman times the wealthy used fossil fuels to heat hypocausts to warm their baths. Did the common people want easier work? Sure.

When working ten to twelve hours per day, it is hard to recall Aesop's fable "The Old Man and Death." The moral: "We'd often be sorry if our wishes came true."

---

[3] Punt: (noun) a flat-bottomed boat with broad, square ends, usually propelled by a single long pole; (verb) to propel (a boat) by pushing with a pole against the bottom of a shallow river or lake. Punter: a person who punts (the boat). *Webster's*, p. 1153

Aesop, the ancient Greek storyteller lived 620 to 564 B.C. When our grandchildren came to visit, I would read Aesop's fables before bedtime. They had to listen closely because it was their job each night to interpret the moral of the story.

Our oldest grandson, Austin, was a great reader even at a very young age, thanks to the patience of his mother, Charmion. She taught her children to read (at least memorize books) before they were out of diapers. As our grandchildren began school, each one year apart, it was their responsibility to read the nightly fable when at our house. During a two-week stay one summer, when Austin was between the third and fourth grade, he read the whole Aesop's fables book by himself in one day.

That further reinforced my notion that it is never too young to train youth and give them opportunity to control a situation–like nightly reading to others. Austin, being the oldest, put pressure on the younger two, Willie and Emily, to be prepared to read the following years. Reading was important; contemplating Aesop's morals was priceless.

Back to Aesop. "The Old Man and Death" fable goes something like this:

> An old guy, bent from age, exhausted from cutting, stacking and carrying sticks in from the mountains one day decided to give up. As he was struggling up another, seemingly everlasting, hill with nobody to help him, he dropped the load from his back and sat on an old log forlorn. "I can't take it any longer. I'm better off dead."
>
> Suddenly, a skeleton appeared carrying the scythe of death. "You called poor mortal?"
>
> "Yes! Would you please help lift this load of sticks to my back?" asked the old woodsman.

The moral of the story: Be careful what you wish for.

Old or young, acclimate to change. Laugh about it. Enjoy it. Adjust. Otherwise, all your children may look forward to is spending their life pushing a boat up a river with a stick.

13

Learning Race

Riddle: This has outwardly fair complexion, but includes many races.

Cultural awareness starts at home, and modified once exposed to artificial systems, but it is expressed as an adult. How often have you seen young children playing with others of different races or ethnic backgrounds? What happened? Years later, after staring school, they segregated.

San Vito dei Normanni Air Station, Italy, spring 1973: I walked down the hall, through two sets of doors into a six-table snack bar. Four of us organized the privately operated snack bar as a respite after wearing earphones hour-upon-hour. Two blocks away, the mess hall closed at 7:00 p.m. and reopened at 5:30 a.m. Between those hours there was no place to eat, get a soda, or take a break in the massive block building where over a hundred servicemen were harbored with no windows and one steel front door twenty feet beyond a wire-mesh security gate guarded 24/7/365 by military police.

San Vito had operated since the mid-sixties as a U.S. Air Force COMMIT[1] station. Sitting for eight hours, pushing headsets into our ears to better identify a signal was our excuse to take a short break every few hours.

One day I had just gotten off swing (a 4:00 p.m. to midnight shift). It was my turn to open the snack bar by 12:15 a.m. Dan, finalizing his sixteen hours of work, had just finished mopping the floor. Four chairs,

---

[1] COMMIT: Communications Intelligence

seats down, were on the tables. Dan was stocking the soda cooler. "I carried nine cases through the door today."

"Nine," I exclaimed. "Now I'll have to try ten."

That night I set the record of carrying eleven cases of canned sodas from our small storage closet through the doorway to the soda cooler. If I had stopped at ten, Dan would have the record because only eleven cases fit through the door with enough room for my fingers to suspend the cases above the floor.

Debbie was already there. Her husband, Joe, always worked the shift after me. With Debbie working in the snack bar, both her and Joe could ride to base together and she would not have to be alone in San Vito during the night shift.

Within days of opening, our snack bar became popular offering sodas, cigarettes, candy bars, chips, and grilled sandwiches. Hamburgers were the most popular, but my favorite was grilled SPAM®[2], egg, and cheese on buttered, grill-toasted bread with a shot of hot sauce.

We bit off a little too much. Four Air Force guys working eight-hour shifts after our regular job became too much. Debbie and a couple other wives were the first nonclearance people to get into the building—although not into the secure area.

It had only been a few months earlier that Air Force women were allowed to do our job. Before 1973, they were considered a security risk. Blackmail, I suppose. We were always getting training on how top-secret guys, like us, could be blackmailed after intimate relationships. Considering the Air Force majority was male, for some reason females were thought to be higher risk.

"Clarence is going to work with you the next shift," said Dan.

(Clarence's name has been changed to protect his identity, although he would be over ninety now.)

"Who's Clarence?" I asked.

"He's an older guy that will be getting out soon and needs to save up a little money before he does."

---

[2] SPAM® is a registered trademark of Hormel Foods Corporation, Austin, Minnesota, USA.

"Good, we need more people trained to work our shifts so we can get a day off," I said. Sixteen-hour days, every other day, in a fourteen-day consecutive shift cycle can even get to an insomniac.

Sure enough, Clarence, a security policeman, was waiting at midnight before I was relieved from my shift two days later.

"Ready to learn the snack-bar business?" I asked.

"Sure am!" He said as we began putting the chairs down.

Clarence was the kind of guy that would help wherever needed—grill, form burgers, cut tomatoes, fill the cooler, or run the cash register. Unfortunately, I did not get to work with him too many days as the shifts of military police did not often match the fourteen-day cycle of ditty-bops (the nickname for those of us that could transcribe Morse code).

Clarence was a black staff sergeant. He had lost more stripes over the years than I ever achieved. Clarence had been in the U.S. Army Military Police before he joined the Air Force. He served in Germany during World War II. After the war, he became a civilian for a while. In post-war American in the late 1940s, it was tough for a black guy in his early twenties, to get work—especially in a police force. He joined the Air Force before he was too old.

I had never seen someone in the Air Force as old as Clarence. We got along great. He was several years older than my dad. I loved his stories.

We sometimes talked about discrimination.

One such story: Clarence was in Germany guarding German prisoners of war. Military police had to escort the German prisoners to the chow hall. The Army's white military police would eat scattered among the prisoners. After the prisoners were through the chow line, the black military police could go through the line and get what was left. Clarence was one of those. While the prisoners and U.S. Army's white military police were inside, Clarence and his fellow black soldiers had to eat outside. Their place was sitting on the chow hall steps—cold, snowing, rain, or shine. Black police, like Clarence, had to eat fast and be finished eating before the prisoners, so they could escort the German prisoners back to their barracks.

Seventy years after the Civil War, Clarence was still isolated and eating outside.

I do not know when Clarence got out of the Air Force. Based on his rank and age, it was likely late in 1973, or 1974. Clarence was apprehensive about getting out of the Air Force. Military police was all he knew. That was his career. Maybe, with experience, if not police work he could get a job in a snack bar. Sure, he had a military retirement check each month, but that was barely enough. He needed to work another ten to fifteen years before he could collect full Social Security, which was something he worked for and paid into his whole life.

I say to this day, may the Lord continue to look after Clarence and all the people treated like him. Our skin did not match, but our souls did.

CIVIL RIGHTS

Civil Rights leader Martin Luther King, Jr. was quoted as saying "Intelligence plus character—that is the goal of true education."

It bothers me that those who consider themselves educated seem to assume that education equals intelligence. Dr. King did not.

The Negro race, brought to the Americas as slaves (due to a lack of local agricultural labor), survived. The survivors had not only physical stamina, but also mental agility to deal with the day-to-day whims and whips of their masters.

Negotiating often cruel, wealthy, educated, elitist, narcissistic, egocentric owners took spontaneous wit with agile mind and body. Not all owners were that way. Underclassed slaves, segregated by color, with less than a balanced ration while maintaining cogitative dexterity was a stealth sort.

As slaves were freed, opportunities opened for other minorities. American society benefited despite a century of university professors pushing their tarnished version of humanity. Professors were the experts; they wrote and taught history that twenty-first-century Americans will find hard to fathom.

Coming out of the Civil War, to imply black slaves were less intelligent (as scholars taught) because they lacked formal education is not only demeaning but also disgusting. Shortly, I will expose post-Civil War second-generation educators that attempted to continue segregation by belittling those of color. American Blacks were not the only category disparaged. The final years of the nineteenth century and first few decades of the twentieth century, Asians in general, Chinese in particular, and certainly Native Americans were placed by scholars in a category beyond advancement.

Consequently, even today if one is to believe some United Nations (UN) theories, underdeveloped countries must lack intelligence if the population in general lacks education, which causes increased fertility and thereby lowers income.

UN scholarly studies using statistical surveys confirmed fertility and IQ were diverging. Parents with more children had lower IQ than those with fewer children. How was their data supposedly confirmed? Now that statistical gathering internationally has become easier, years of education were used as a surrogate for intelligence. The UN–proposed solution: Females in underdeveloped countries should attend more years in the school system to increase their education (and supposedly their IQ) and ergo, fewer children.

Would a logical person imply parents that had more children were less intelligent then parents that had fewer children? Are parents that completed high school and had no college unknowingly less intelligent than their children they sent to college? Are American girls (for the last century) more intelligent than boys because they had more formal education?

Personally, I take offense to scholarly implications that my parents who had seven children and my wife's parents who had ten children had lower IQs than our friend's parents who had one to six children. Furthermore, as a result of scholarly studies, does that mean U.S. citizens must be more intelligent than citizens of nearly every other country in the world simply because Americans spent more years in school? Garbage! Absolute scholastic garbage!

This has been implied in scholarly studies by the United Nations, World Bank, and other international organizations funding university research and it is disturbing. The United Nations Development Program gives countries an Education Index (EI), which is the average "years education completed" age 25 and older, and "expected years of education" at school entrance age.[3]

In 2013, the last year EI data were available, the United States (89.0) ranked fourth behind Australia (92.7), New Zealand (91.7), and Norway

---

[3] Education Index, Human Development Reports, United Nations Development Programs, November 15, 2013, http://hdr.undp.org/en/content/education-index (Sourced January 3, 2017)

(91.0). Comparatively, the same UN Education Index in 1980 ranked Australia first (87.0) followed by the United States (79.0), New Zealand (76.0), and Canada (74.9). The number of years in school, before age twenty-five, has certainly increased (e.g., seventy-nine in U.S. in 1980 compared to eighty-nine in 2013; seventy-six for New Zealand in 1980 compared to an Educational Index of 91.7 in 2013).

Only three countries' EI has gone down since 1980 (or upon entering the study); the other countries' EI has risen in twenty-three years. University researchers interpret UN data to direct national policy. To researchers, older less educated, less intelligent people who had more children died off and being replaced with offspring having more years of education, raised the world's EI and thereby the country's intelligence.

EI should not equate to IQ. IQs are arbitrary and not uniformly measured. IQ studies place the United States at just below the world's median score,[4] whereas Hong Kong, South Korea, and Japan rank the highest. Why would a study of intelligence correlate to economic prosperity?

Gross Domestic Product (GDP) parallels a country's IQ ratings with African countries with low economic output ranking lowest on intelligence. Consequently, do not use years of education, economic status, or geographic location to determine a population's intelligence. As mentioned in the previous chapter, this is an example of how statistical measurements can artificially segregate and rile. To me, it is racist to rank countries by intelligence or years spent in school.

Why did I say the UN education report above was disturbing?

Rather than regurgitating information already covered in this book about how the school system has deteriorated learning, consider why UN member countries want to rank higher in education. Is it to decrease childbirth rates, increase member country's tax base, or control the population through youth indoctrination? Likely, it is all three. There are other reasons.

An "Education First" program was initiated in 2012 under the leadership of UN Director-General from 2007 through 2016, Ben Ki-moon.

---

[4] National IQ Scores Country Ratings, based on studies by Richard Lynn, Tatu Vanhanen, and Jelte Wicherts, http://www.photius.com/rankings/national_iq_scores_country_ranks.html (Sourced January 3, 2017)

The university-educated, South Korean career diplomat said: "When you ask parents what they want for their children–even in war zones and disaster areas–they seek the same thing: education. Parents want their children in school."[5]

Not to overstate the obvious, but "education" and "school" are two different things. Education is the process of accumulating knowledge; the latter is a building.

It is highly unlikely that the United Nations, the United States, or for that matter, any school system would recommend or develop a learning system outside the school system. Why? Those that were educated in a system automatically assume that school system is best.

Nearly everybody in the world has, or will have, access to the Internet. Programs to learn a new language, for example, are much more efficient, not blocked by teacher work-hours and include accurate voice and written methods. With limited, and expensive, staff secondary school systems and universities only offer a few foreign languages, whereas, the Internet has courses in most languages.

It seems logical that the multilingual United Nations would endorse such a free-access learning system. It does not and likely will not as long as the university-educated run funding programs that focus on school attendance rather than maximizing learning opportunities.

It is unfathomable, in an interconnected world where the Internet and cell phones are more accessible than transportation, the United Nations would imply school attendance satisfies parents' desire to educate their children.

If education was truly the UN's goal, why were the five primary objectives not learning focused? (They were eliminating cost barriers to attend school, completing school, nutrition, health, and social support.) That is a mid-twentieth century model in a twenty-first-century world.

In countries where girls are blocked from attending school, told what they must wear, who they must marry, and when, if, and who must be in their automobile, it appears the UN's school objectives go beyond education. It appears the UN wants universal school attendance to issue

---

[5] Global Education First Initiative 2012–2016, United Nations Secretary General, Ben Ki-moon, http://gefidr160719.businesscatalyst.com/index.html (Sourced January 3, 2017)

edicts that interfere with local and national customs, traditions, social norms, and religious doctrine.

Countries have followed similar indoctrination programs for two centuries. Ask Australian Aboriginals, Native Americans, Canada's First Nation groups, those in Germany's Hitler Youth initiative, and those forced into China's Mao-era reeducation camps.

Schools are a system of youth indoctrination. Population control, for example, is logically done with those of, or approaching, child-bearing age.

At what point do child birth rates become a macro-scale disadvantage? When young replacements are not available to provide for the aged or protect their country, they have a social and defense dilemma. On the other hand, continuing education of potential workers (taxpayers), with delayed labor force entry, magnifies economic and taxation woes.

Throughout history, civilizations collapsed with one or two of those predicaments. Civil and international conflicts are unavoidable when two predicaments cause four. As is the case now in many countries, surely others will be forced to rely on immigration causing potential racial and ethnic conflict.

What is the Education Index crux where too much for too many results in diminishing returns?

Based on a review of national Education Index scores since 1980, it appears as countries approach an index of 75 to 80, the country's education exceeded the demand for literacy and competency. Innovation slowed (e.g., Australia) and socialist political leverage exceeded economic realities (e.g., northern Europe) resulting in high unemployment, uncontrollable illegal immigration, and a situation where the school system replaces student education with pay and benefits for the employed.

In many cases (e.g., Latin America) where parents pay for students' secondary school, children of higher-income parents attend schools where, using an old cliché, prisoners run the prison or patients run the asylum.

In the last few years, I have been in classrooms as a guest teacher. Upon entry, teachers simply leave because there is no control over spoiled kids who think their parents' income gives them privilege to attend school. (Meaning: They cannot be thrown out no matter how poorly they do or disruptive they are.)

Many parents cannot afford uniforms or school supplies for their children. In those cases, "public education" is not public, but really a publicly subsidized private education system with all the pitfalls of children from mid- to upper-income families disrupting those who want to learn.

Middle class in some villages may have family income a tenth the poverty line in the United States or developed countries. Those with public privileged education attend post-secondary schools and (because of their parents' money and influence) become leaders subject to bribes and shenanigans to get or maintain influential government jobs. The lower class, with limited formal education, labor.

In many ways, developing countries have educational systems similar to the U.S. system of public and parochial schools a century ago. One of the main differences, at least in rural areas, was that more U.S. girls were given the opportunity to attend high school than boys.

Adults with more formal education in underdeveloped or developing countries get international jobs and represent their country in leading or supporting roles. Make note that the "educated" are the only ones employed by the United Nations where discrimination is ripe within and between nations. As scholars accumulate years of education they segregate and develop a mentality where they are of a higher order and have authority to describe, influence, and perpetuate their contrivances. Examples follow.

Over the years as my wife searched antique shops for furniture, I rummaged through old books and read some. I became increasingly astonished at the gross misrepresentation, bias, and discrimination in old history and school textbooks.

Read U.S. state history books of the early twentieth century and see if they come across more fitting as promotional literature than history. Railroads especially used promotions and historical bias to recruit coastal and European farmers and businesspeople to settle the vast American Plains. Textbook writers joined the railroad bandwagon. For economic reasons, state historians incorporated such promotions with the desire to populate their state.

Most troubling were high school and college history textbooks where "savage," "semi-savage races," "primitive," "slaves," "laggard races," with "physical and mental differences," and "racial badge of color and physiognomy" like "African negroes" and "North American Indians" were compared to "all the higher cultures," "heirs of a great legacy," "stronger races," "noble heritage," and "more favored brethren." These terms I pulled only from the first few pages of an 1888 history book revised in 1904 and 1916. For at least three decades it was one of few comprehensive ancient history books used by American schools in that era.

With each succeeding revision, the history book grew to over 500 pages. The author and supporters were notable. Written by a history professor, Philip Van Ness Myers of the University of Cincinnati (Ohio), the school history textbook was reviewed and proofread by notable historians including:

- Dr. W. Max Müller of the University of Pennsylvania,
- Dr. Joseph Edward Harry, University of Cincinnati (Ohio),
- Stillman Percy Roberts Chadwick of The Phillips Exeter Academy (New Hampshire, U.S.),
- Professor Nathaniel Schmidt and Professor George L. Burr of Cornell University (Ithaca, New York),
- Dr. Rufus B. Richardson of the American School of Classical Studies at Athens (Greece),
- Distinguished German history professor Dr. Eduard Meyer of the University of Halle (Germany),
- English scholar and history professor Henry F. Pelham of the University of Oxford (United Kingdom),
- Mabel E. Hodder of Radcliffe College (Cambridge, Massachusetts), and others.

Considering those in the South actively referred to the Mason-Dixon Line,[6] especially two decades after the Civil War, it is relevant that not one author on the list above was from a Southern university. Now, over a hundred years later, they still have universities that are primarily segregated by racial color. The history book is more damning because it was written by professors in an area that fought to free slaves while they stood in classrooms teaching discrimination.

---

[6] The Mason-Dixon Line established Colonial American borders by 1767 between colonies that eventually became the separation line extended westward between free and slave states in the U.S. Civil War (1861–1865).

The entire professor list above had a hand in teaching American children white races were superior in mentality and heritage than the more primitive races of color. As you will read below, it is very unfortunate those of color were placed at extreme disadvantage in school by white professors, textbook writers, and teachers who perpetuated scholastic bias. The lower classes supported the war to free slaves. Meanwhile, it was blatant scholastic garbage by white professors that perpetuated racial discrimination into the next century.

Today, educated elites at the United Nations appear to be interfering in countries through education initiatives—just like professors did a century ago.

Textbook authors and teachers were biased then and remain so today, although the subject matter and approach may not be evident to the public for a century.

If you have the stomach, please read a few quotes from *Ancient History*, by history professor Philip Van Ness Myers, whose racial slurs change somewhat between his first edition in 1888, 1904, and finally in 1916, but instruction remains the same.

> But how, in the absence of written records, are we to find out anything about prehistoric man? First, by studying the life of present-day backward races; for what they now are, the great races of history, we have reason to believe, were in their prehistoric age.[7]

Surprisingly, talent and abilities of "savage" people bewildered the author.

> But most prophetic of the great future of this savage or semi savage cave man of the Old Stone Age was the fine artistic talent that some tribes or races of the period possessed; for strange as it may seem, among the men of this epoch there were some amazingly good artists. (He) ... had a keener eye for animal forms and movements than the artists of more advanced races ... in some respects the art of these hunter painters has never been surpassed or even equaled.[8]

---

[7] Myers, Philip Van Ness, *Ancient History*, first edition 1888, first revised edition 1904, second revised edition 1916, all quotes taken from the 1916 second revised edition unless otherwise noted, Ginn and Company, p. 1.
[8] Ibid., Second revised edition, pp. 4–5

Unfortunately, Professor Myers goes on page-after-page to further degrade and segregate by race.

> The Old Stone Age was followed by the New. Chipped or hammered stone implements still continued to be used.... The North American Indians were in this stage of culture at the time of the discovery of the New World. The old Egyptians and Babylonians seem to have been just emerging from it when they first appeared in the dawn of the historic day.[9]

Mesoamerican's grand pyramids, processing of precious metals, art, writing, and pottery were well known centuries before Myers's history book was written. Conveniently showing scholarly bias, the history professors in advising and proofreading did not correct Myers when deriding Native Americans.

> All the higher cultures of the ancient world with which history begins were based on the knowledge and use of metals. Fire ... no people has ever been found so low in the scale of culture as to be without it.[10]

> In Egypt, in Babylonia, in Greece, in Italy, and in other lands the historic development ... thus formed the basis of the civilizations of all the great peoples of the ancient world. Some peoples, like the African negroes, passed directly from the use of stone to the use of iron, but in most of the countries of the Orient and of Europe the three metals came into use one after the other.... Speaking broadly, we may say that the Age of Metals began for the more advanced peoples of the ancient world between 3000 and 4000 B.C." (Note Myers did not capitalize Negroes, as is proper English.)[11]

> We of this twentieth century esteem ourselves fortunate in being the heirs of a noble heritage—the inheritors of the precious accumulations of all the past centuries of history.[12]

---

[9] Ibid., First revised edition, p. 5
[10] Ibid., First revised edition, p. 6
[11] Ibid., Second revised edition, pp. 7–8
[12] Myers, Philip Van Ness, *Ancient History*, second revised edition 1916, Ginn and Company, p. 15.

Talent of the uneducated was acknowledged but brushed off as irrelevant. The same holds true today. Professors elevate their ego above that of the uneducated, who they refer to as having "mental differences."

> It is probably that the physical and mental differences of existing races arose through their ancestors having been subject to different climatic influences and to different conditions of life.... The paintings upon the oldest Egyptian monuments show us that at the dawn of history the principal races were as distinctly marked as now each bearing its racial badge of color and physiognomy.
>
> The Black Race. Africa south of the Sahara is the true home of the typical folk (the negroes) of the Black Race, but we find them on all the other continents and on many of the islands of the seas, whither they have migrated or been carried as slaves by the stronger races; for since time immemorial they have been "hewers of wood and drawers of water" for their more favored brethren.
>
> The Yellow or Mongolian Race: But the most important peoples of this type are the Japanese and the Chinese. Already in times very remote this people had developed a civilization quite advanced on various lines, but having reached a certain state in culture they did not continue to make so marked a progress.
>
> The Indo-European family began to break up and to push themselves among older and more civilized peoples. They subjugated the aboriginals of these lands ... and the Europeanizing of the world is merely the continuation in the light of history....[13]

Professors used race to socially engineer Western society through textbooks. More customary is to socially engineer through political realignment, as did China's Communist Party Chairman Mao Zedong (1893–1976). Mao, a founder of the Peoples Republic of China in 1949 administered autocratically while ruling peasants communistically. As that system developed and food resources became scarce, rulers decided to limit their population with a One Child Policy.

Surgical implants, forced sterilization, and abortions were common. Being a patriarchal society, boys were preferred. Girls, if not aborted, were abandoned.

---

[13] Ibid., Second revised edition, pp. 18–20

China in 2015 finally began changing the disastrous One Child Policy, as there were not enough females to satisfy societal demand. Those born in the 1980s and 1990s came into childbearing age without opportunity to marry. An unnatural demographic developed.

Skewing natural demographics creates unexpected issues later. By 2015, China could recruit a hundred-million-man army, over five times more soldiers than all the other countries combined,[14] and could have all been killed in battle without one Chinese soldier losing a brother, sister, child, or wife. This is an example of how an old man's political policy could impact a commercial economy and populate a military one.

Chinese youth, like all societies, learn to eat, drink, walk, talk, fight or be at peace. It is natural, yet choices are made by political whims. Societies must occupy young adults through study, work, marriage, raising a family, or arming them until they get beyond fighting age. The best choice is when they do not have to fight.

Communist China had options to import food, develop a capitalist society, and put men to work, or go to war. Fortunately for the world, they chose capitalism over militarism. Questions remain whether their society will phase into a normal male/female society before excess testosterone of young men begin fighting internationally. Signs exist.

Leaders often create external conflicts to limit internal ones. Young educated stir the brew while politicians or professors supplement their thoughts. That is why race superiority foments as it has since the U.S. was established. Scholars manufacture reasons to segregate as did late nineteenth- and early twentieth-century American history professors, as does the United Nations today.

Please do not think one late nineteenth-century author (Myers) and his scholarly supporters were the only teachers of historical discrimination. Some were quite neutral and presented what appears to be accurate history; *Readings in Ancient History*, copyright 1912 by William Stearns Davis, Professor of Ancient History, University of Minnesota seemed well balanced (although I did not read the complete book).

---

[14] Global Fire Power in an article, "Active Military Manpower by Country," reported 125 top armed countries had just over 21 million military active duty personnel with China having the largest force at 2,335,000. See http://www.globalfirepower.com/active-military-manpower.asp (Sourced January 12, 2017)

Others had brutally accurate descriptions (e.g., King Honno's voyage). Others, like Myers, had a racially biased tone.

Throughout history, groups coalesced into kingdoms and nations by comparing outsiders as animal-like barbarians and ignorant. Their scholars perpetuated divergence. An ancient historic "Voyage of King Hanno of Carthage" is recorded taking place about 650 B.C. with 30,000 of his people in well-supplied ships. As Hanno's massive fleet left the Mediterranean Sea and followed the west coast of Africa south to the Equator, records describe native encounters. Not all friendly. In equatorial waters and running low on supplies the final native group reported to be:

> . . . full of savage men. There were women, too, in even greater num-
> ber. They had hairy bodies, and the interpreters called them Goril-
> lae. When we pursued them we were unable to take any of the
> men . . . but we took three of the women, who bit and scratched . . .
> and would not follow us. So we killed them and flayed them, and
> brought their skins to Carthage.[15]

Recorded over 2500 years ago, King Hanno's historical account appears accurate. Not all history scholars are that brutal or honest, but their intent is the same—disparage others not like themselves. Obvious in the exploits of King Hanno, some ancients were savage—his own navy. Professors and teachers of history perpetuated savage psychological brutality as their history books were used well into the twentieth century.

About the same time as King Hanno of Carthage was making his African exploratory journey, Greece was in turmoil. That was not unusual, as world history records good and bad leaders. Often historians inappropriately color their descriptions of history. For well over a century high school and college administrators made choices on books to order and use in their schools. *Ancient History* by Philip Myers, mentioned above, had competition. In a comprehensive history book, *Essentials in Ancient History*, Dr. Arthur Mayer Wolfson, copyright 1902, described leaders with demeaning, unnecessary superlatives. For example, when describing an ancient Greek tyrannical leader, Dr. Wolfson wrote:

---

15 "The Voyage of Hanno," http://www.metrum.org/mapping/hanno.htm (Sourced May 20, 2016)

... In 655 B.C. Cypselus (of Greece) succeeded in overthrowing the oligarchy and setting himself up as tyrant. Grateful to the gods for all the favors ... he was not niggardly with his gifts.[16]

In a nineteenth-century attempt to historically segregate and combine races by languages, the term Aryan (originally meaning "noble ones") resulted in a composite of Indo-European and Indo-Iranians (generally including those from India, Iran, and Europe who may have had the same ancient ancestry). Those that studied and developed the linguistic and historical ties were not common people; they were university-educated linguists, anthropologists, archeologists, and historians, among other educated elite who developed and spread their racial Aryan theories.

Superiority of the made-up name "Aryan race" easily made its way into high school and college textbooks. One such pro-Aryan history book, copyright 1899, that competed with Myers and Wolfson for classroom time was a 400-plus-page volume, *Six Thousand Years of History* by Edgar Sanderson, et al. (Please note that belief in superiority of the "Aryan race" should not be confused with "Arianism" which was a third-century heresy denying the divinity of Jesus Christ as the Son of God.)

Sanderson took the omnipotent approach that:

History is the written record of the past. ... The great pyramid is not history, and until Herodotus wrote and Champollion deciphered, it was but an artificial mountain.[17]

His enthusiastic historical theories were to influence his followers–young students studying history. Talking of himself and his nine professors that co-author the book, he finalized the book's introduction by stating:

It is the duty of those who have lived many years to guide the footsteps of those who with glad countenances are eagerly pressing upon the scene. At the portal we should stand, offering, as our most precious possession, the History. ...[18]

---

[16] Wolfson, pp. 95–96
[17] Sanderson, Edgar, et al., *Six Thousand Years of History*, Volume 1 (of ten volumes), 1899, E.R. DuMont Publisher, Philadelphia, Chicago, and St. Louis, p. i.
[18] Ibid., pp. iv–v

One can get a sinister sense of their biased approach to history from chapter 1, page 1 with the first sentence:

History deals with the life only of political communities, or nations, and not with races of men who have made little advance from a primitive state.[19]

He continued in the first few pages by reaffirming their superior Aryan position:

For European civilization...improved himself and all around him and all that came after him; the man conquered and governed the world.[20]

It gets worse:

It is the Aryans that have been the parents of new nations, and that have reached the highest point of intellectual development, as shown in their political freedom, and in their science, literature, and art....The Aryan branch of the Caucasian family presents us with the noblest pattern of the highest type. The study of these Aryan tongues has also told what progress had been made by this, the king of races....[21]

Then their version of history started in earnest to put down other races and raise Aryan as superior.

China is one of the oldest and strangest of nations...with an apparent incapacity for vital progress. The Chinese tongue has never attained to the possession of an alphabet, which, with nations of the higher development, has always been the first step....It is clear enough that Europe and true civilization had nothing to gain, and have gained nothing, in culture, from a country where 400 millions of people are treated like children....[22]

It is an interesting fact that China has gained, fed, and educated more people than any other country in just over a century (a billion plus). I am certain the late Aryan historian Edgar Sanderson would be

---

[19] Ibid., p. 1
[20] Ibid., p. 3
[21] Ibid., pp. 7–9
[22] Sanderson, Edgar, Ibid., pp. 10–15

greatly surprised that in the last four decades entrepreneurial (though communist governed) China has moved its populace from famine-to-full, invaded and dominated by the Japanese (WWII era) returned to an independent military might, and the world's manufacturing leader with exports supplying the world.

Likewise, Sanderson went on to state India was not any better than China.

> Indian civilization, like that of China, has contributed little or nothing to the culture of the Western world ... through the absence of energy and of true human dignity ... [23]

What is the result of university professors skewing reality, linguistically demeaning other races as they instruct young minds? At minimum, multiple generations of educated people were taught to discriminate. Uneducated peasants went about their life.

For example, for two centuries Mexico and the United States have shared a border. Mexican immigrants for decades have illegally entered the United States for economic reasons drawn by employers looking for cheaper labor. Currently, African Americans are the largest racial minority (~13%) in the United States but Hispanic or Latino Americans (at ~17%) are the largest ethnic minority.

It took a century and a half after the Civil War for African Americans to fully engage in American society. As they were developing full participatory citizenship, American university professors (e.g., Dr. Arthur Mayer Wolfson) and textbook authors (e.g., Englishman Edgar Sanderson) led racial discrimination in schools.

Once adopted as university dogma, professors are free to espouse and teachers are trained to indoctrinate youth.

Why, in the twenty-first century are Americans more accepting of African American racial diversity than Latino ethnicity? Discrimination of Mexicans was taught in school. A high school textbook published in 1898 and republished in 1910, *The History of the United States from 1492 to 1910*, was written by Harvard University-trained Julian Hawthorne who also wrote articles for *Cosmopolitan* magazine and *New York Journal*. What did Hawthorne instruct under the chapter on Mexico?

---

[23] Ibid., p. 16

(U.S. President James Polk) … believed in his country, especially in the Democratic aspect of it. When Texas revolted, she claimed the Rio Grande River as her Mexican boundary … (and) when Texas was annexed to us (United States), her boundaries became ours. … The Mexicans were a semi-barbarous people, with whom no civilized association was possible; they conducted negotiations by massacre and murder, and in war mutilated the bodies of the slain. They were a cross between Spaniards and Aztec Indians, combining the least attractive features of both.[24]

How can children become nondiscriminating adults with schools teaching such overt blasphemy?

I bring to the attention of my readers that school materials contain bias, like the history lessons presented above. Teachers, professors, and textbook authors have great leeway in guiding the student. Parents may seldom, if ever, read their children's schoolbooks. Teachers and authors, beyond parents' knowledge and beyond parental control, are influencing student thoughts, beliefs, and racial bias.

My grandfather, born in 1891, never attended high school. His sister did. Likely, she used some of the history textbooks described above. In 2016 I pulled some of the same books from the shelves of the Marcus P. Beebe Memorial Library in Ipswich, South Dakota. Ruby Bosanko, the librarian for twenty-five years, was not aware of the volumes I uncovered on her shelves.

One of the ancient history books had not been checked out since 1953 (the year I was born); another saw much use in the 1920s and 1930s, then not checked out until 1951 and one other time in 1965.

Would you want your high school children studying biased history, biased geography, biased social studies, or biased environmental studies as those presented in the quotes above or in textbooks today?

It would be foolish for me to anticipate, by parents' standards, what may be censurable textbook bias now or in the future. As a crosscheck, parents should regularly scan schoolbooks, web sites, and homework materials. Children are taught to defend their thoughts and materials.

---

[24] Hawthorne, Julian, "Mexico," *The History of the United States from 1492–1910*, Volume III, 1898, 1910, P.F. Collier & Son, pp. 836–838.

If children respond that information is personal, then it should not be used in school.

Standardized by school systems, discrimination and bias perpetuate through society. Independent learning diminishes the slant of professional educators.

Is it any wonder why President Kennedy and Dr. Martin Luther King's drive for racial equality during the 1960s caused riots before schools, busses, cafes, bathrooms, and all public facilities were desegregated?

Many adults in their thirties, forties, fifties, sixties, and seventies believed what they were taught in school. Their parents, especially if they went to high school, were taught segregation through history.

Scholars originated and perpetuated claims of backward races. Would authoritative textbooks be wrong? Of course! They were opinionated then and now. By today's standards history books of 1900 seem extremely racial and radical.

When they become grandparents, my great-grandchildren will likely be disgusted by biased textbooks (if they exist) and literature of this current era. My fear is there is no balance with practical experience. Instead, children are indoctrinated by the school system from age three to twenty-three. Independent peasants struggle to counterbalance scholastic extremism.

As textbook use decreases due to more online courses, parents have more reason to screen their children's study materials. Based on the current trend away from textbooks, it is quite likely my future adult great-grandchildren will not have access to textbooks as schools and libraries clear old inventories.

Perhaps having cousins that were half African American taught me lessons. Doing building construction and wholesaling agricultural products as a young adult on Indian Reservations, working beside U.S. Air Force colleagues of all colors, and having traveled thirty or so countries on six continents has given me a perspective that helps identify bias. I learned. We are all the same.

Many years ago, I had an experience that overwhelmed, yet irritated me. I wrote the poem below November 5, 2005, which is based on a true story that happened to me around 1990. While wholesaling products in western South Dakota, we lived on a small acreage on Dry Run Creek, east of the capitol city of Pierre. Product deliveries and sales calls allowed me to be home most nights, but to do so I averaged 65,000 miles per year driving. Driving. Driving.

Many things happened during that span of years. My wife was promoted to editor of a statewide newsletter; both daughters were married; one daughter joined the U.S. Army and was in Germany; our son graduated high school and I had written a couple of books and started a business. However, there are few things I remember as well as what happened at dusk one evening while driving home. This is a memory I wanted to write down, but I was always perplexed by it until I wrote the last sentence of this poem over a decade after it occurred.

Half Hour Lifetime Friend

Driving the road
From Bison to Pierre
Three hours long
And nothing appears.
Trip after trip
South and north
Nothing but normal
Back and forth.
I see the sky
It's dark in the west.
I better get home.
My wife knows best.
When clouds start rollin'
Better get past
Front ridge tornadoes
Or it may be my last.
I see a shadow.
It appears from nowhere.
Is it a bison? Cow?
Horse or a deer?
I get frightened.
It looks like a man
Middle the road
Waving his hands.
I'm past Faith

Before Cherry Creek.
Storm clouds rollin'
But this is unique.
Deep in my mind
I rehearse the verse
Never stop for strangers!
Hitch-hikers are worst.
Prairie Reservations:
Indian vision or ghost?
Waving his hands
Disturbs me the most.
I'm afraid of the storm,
But what if that's me?
Lightning will strike
That waving tree.
Hail and wind
Dirt blowin' past
The ghost in the road
This may be his last.
I lay on the brakes
Not knowing what's next.
Gun in the head?
Stab in the neck?
My heart knows
I need to stop

For this lonely young ghost
Like it or not.
My eyes were opened.
Easy to decide
The lonely young Native
Needed a ride.
If it was me,
He'd stop again
To pick up a white
Like next of kin.
Yes, my eyes were opened
Easy to decide
The lonely young ghost
Needed a ride.
"What are you doin'
On this lonely road?"
"My legs are weary.
I need to get home.
I walked twelve hours,
Maybe more today.
My girlfriend is pregnant
And I need pay.
I finished plumbing school
Yesterday at Fort Yates.
Tomorrow, heading to Pierre
To open employment gates.
I'm an Indian and afraid
They're not gonna hire me
To practice my trade
And raise my baby.
Do you know of a job?
What should I do?
I'm lonely and broke
And nearly twenty-two."
"My daughter's in the Army.
She's about your age;
Engaged to be married,

And not much pay.
I spent over seven years
Serving our Land
With many, many faces
Working hand-in-hand.
If Pierre doesn't treat
you right,
Remember this:
You're an Indian man
And should be proud of it.
Army, Air Force,
Navy, Marines
Are respectable ways
To raise a family.
The pay isn't much
But the benefits great;
Pride, dignity, and honor
For you and your mate."
Twenty miles past.
It's dark as can be,
But clouds were lifting
For this new family.
"Watch for a gate
Over the next hill.
Take a right
Down the narrow trail."
The gate came fast—
Grassy path seldom worn,
We wove through the hills
Before the storm.
I saw a lonely light
And nothing around,
But a small little place
And a dog unbound.
I shook his proud hand
And said, "*Goodbye.*
May God in Heaven

Always be by your side."
The storm clouds lifted
As I drove home,
Feeling my new friend
Was now not alone.
He's going to be happy.
That I am sure.
Many years later
As I remember his words.

I traveled that highway
Many times since
And never found the gate
Of the friend I miss.
Yes, I traveled that highway
Many times since
And never found the gate
Of the ghost I miss.

Race has a place in each of our lives, but intolerance should not. We are all tempted.

Since we retired, Patricia and I travel, staying places that allow us continuous summer. We have met wonderful people, and some pricks. You can learn a lot about people in poor communities where (often wealthy) outsiders vacation for a few weeks or months. We spent several months in La Penita de Jaltemba on the Pacific coast of Mexico in the winter of 2013–2014–the same place I began writing this book. Near the end of our first stay, February 1, 2014, I wrote this poem on what I learned over that winter.

Mexico Beach Town

People are of three types:
Those that give;
Those that take;
Those that live.
Those that give
Look to help more.
Those that take
Will cheat the poor.
Those that live passive
Have few expectations
Carry on if by missive
And don't seek representation.
Those that take
Are foreign in this land;
Reap but didn't make;

One full, stretch the empty hand.
Envy as a victim
Is a disease of the heart.
They look for a symptom
From those that impart.
Resorts, hotels, villas,
Squat in a palm covered dome,
Casa, cabana, casita
Are those with a home.
Roof is a luxury
For a dog on the beach
Not a necessity
For those that seek.
Parents give their all.
Children learn that fact.

For those lucky to walk the hall
They should learn how to act.
It is wonderful to relive

What I learned as a child.
My parents knew how to give.
Now retired, I get to smile.

—

14

Marbles

Riddle: Some are hard, but do not move even though they bump up to each other.

Walking Friday, August 21, 2015, on a cobblestone street, I noticed four boys playing. Strolling a small Mexican beach town, forty-five miles from the nearest resort, many things are like they were when I was young. As I got closer, I noticed four- and-five-year-olds grouped together watching one marble. A couple steps closer, I could see what they were focused on–to see how close the marble would land to a small green leaf that had fallen from the shade tree above.

Bounce and roll. The marble was flipped from about two arm's length away. Playgrounds are small in rural Mexico–from the front door to a few feet into the street. Ricocheted from the side of a four-inch rock, it bounced over the next into the grit. The marble stopped, a small rock away from the leaf. All four boys looked closely to see how close the marble landed.

The next boy to the left picked up the marble as it was his turn. About the same distance, he positioned for his toss. Focus. Not too hard and it would bounce off the uneven rocks. Too soft and the other boys would laugh at his weak toss.

The game: One marble, four preschool boys, a green leaf, and a cobblestone street. What were they learning? Counting? Measuring? Coordination? Sharing? Socializing? Supervising? Competing? Challenges? Rules? Strategy? Photosynthesis? Physics? Kinetics? Gravity? Solar radiation? Earth's rotation? Thermodynamics? Inventiveness? Doing with little? Everything are ingredients to being a respected employee, managing a business or office, and succeeding as an adult. With proper teaching, a simple invented game can provide a lifetime of practical knowledge. Self-teaching is culture. It's lifelong.

September 1963: All the fifth grade boys took their bag of marbles to the playground for recess. Mom and dad found me about ten marbles in an old one-pound coffee can that had rusty nails, screws, and a few arrowheads. Dad found those arrowheads as a kid (age six to ten) walking the two and half miles between his two grandparents' farms in the dirty 1930s. Nothing grew. Things appear interesting viewed through the lens of a child. Walking by himself, the windswept tilled fields exposed things he would not have otherwise found. Interestingly, when I was an agronomist checking a sunflower field nearly seven decades later about fifty miles south of our farm, I found a flint arrowhead exposed in the dust between cultivated sunflower rows.

Arrowheads were interesting, but I received usable marbles. Not only did I have marbles, I got to use the marbles my father had used when he went to the same school two decades earlier. New marbles would have been a foolish waste of money when the old ones could be used.

My marbles were different from those of the other boys. Theirs were mostly shiny. Mine were rather dull, multicolored but chipped from banging against each other and rocks many, many times. My friends maybe exceeded twenty marbles in their drawstring bag. I took mine to school in a sock. A couple of my classmates even had a big one, a shooter.

They had practiced–probably the year before, in the fourth grade, while I was still in country school. In fact, in grades one through four, I was the only one in my class. We just did not play marbles in country school–the grass stubble was probably too tall, even though Oliver Hoffman cut our school ground (an acre) for hay each fall.

Marbles: A simple game that has been played for several thousand years. It is a game of culture.

Marbles have been found in Egyptian tombs. Five-thousand-year-old ancient ruins in Pakistan revealed marbles. Romans played with them as was discovered under 2000-year-old volcanic ash of Pompeii. Although not glass or baked clay, American Natives played marbles; actually, they were rounded pebbles likely collected from streams.

Fifty-nine years after we got our first television, I walked through a Mexican farming and fishing village watching four little boys playing a street game–boys' fun. Just like boys playing the last five thousand years, the sun was moving–they moved to play marbles in the shade.

Anytown U.S.A. Summer 2015: No reason for marbles. No reason to go outside. Modern fun: Sitting in an air-conditioned bedroom with thumbs punching an electronic game. No need for friends. No need for TV–that is for old people searching for the marbles they lost.

"Mom," came a shout through the closed door, "would you bring me some pop and chips?"

The mother, just home from work, shouted: "I'll be right up. Do you want some cookies, too?"

That is now the life of a single-child family in twenty-first-century America.

Formal education should develop what has been previously learned. Interpreting, implementing, and modifying new and previous knowledge is learning.

Copies of wooden Chinese books (called "xunzi") are over a thousand years old and contain writings from a *"Hundred Schools of Thought,"* a period running from about 600 to 221 B.C. One quote of Xun Kuang (312–230 B.C.) is often attributed falsely to Benjamin Franklin (1706–1790 A.D.), but it preceded him by two thousand years.

It is common for people to attribute quotes, novel ideas or inventions to nearby generations. It helps them better relate to their culture. That is why I use my grandfather's generation in comparison to older periods because it helps *Relating to Ancient Culture.*

Xun Kuang was paraphrased as saying: "Tell me and I forget. Teach me and I remember. Involve me and I learn."

Preschool marble players in Mexico with nothing but a marble develop their own game, rules, and goals without a teacher guiding them. Their simple system indicated they were taught the basics of culture: respect, physical activity, individual responsibility, and involvement.

Children who reach school age and need a teacher to direct every activity have not learned preschool basics from their parents. Schools full of marbles do not mean children graduate knowing how to use them.

15

Servants

Riddle: What service with different names rewards accomplishments, but does not accept responsibility when they remain untrained servants?

While in high school, several of my teachers mentioned that college was hard. College difficulty came up several times when I was a senior. Such teacher statements likely kept many of my classmates from going into college after high school. Some did. More should have. Many would have benefited from a year or so of technical school training. Some did. Many went to work and picked up some formal education later.

After high school, while in the Air Force, I had met and worked with several people that had attended college. One roommate had three years of college, but before getting drafted into the Army, because of the Vietnam War, he joined the Air Force.

That is when I realized that college was tough for teachers in the 1940s, 1950s, and 1960s for those of mediocre intelligence. Primary school teachers seemed to be those who wanted to settle down in a smaller community and raise children. My high school teachers stressed the difficulty of college. Perhaps they could not find another field that sparked their interest, so they focused on educational classes. Is that wrong?

Throughout history, most young adults came of age and took up the profession they were most familiar with—usually following their parents. Many people have last names based on their family's trade. For example, I went to high school with Taylor, Baker, Kraft, Schaub (meaning a sheaf of grain or beer brewer symbol), Schumacher (shoe maker), Steen (stone castle), and Walker. Family culture and occupation were captured in their name.

Many surnames indicated not necessarily the family business, but the relationship to the father like Johnson, Peterson, Swanson, Olson, Walter, Williams, Davis, Simon, Halvorson, and Henderson. All those were surnames of Ipswich, South Dakota, families who attended school with me. Throughout history, first names often became family names, like "Johnson" rather than saying "John's son" the second, third, or fourth.

With a name like Hodson (interpreted as the son of the hooded man) perhaps it was a good reason to emigrate and find a new home in a new country where your name was not indicative of your family trade. Welcome to America!

Given the historical family name of Hodson, I thought there could have been a few on the First Fleet of prisoners departing British jails May 13, 1787, destined for the Australian wilderness. Many of the names on those first prisoner boats could have easily related to their actual crime or punishment including: *Samuel* Lightfoot, *Elizabeth* Lock, *Humphry* Lynch, *Samuel* Mobbs, *William* Pane, *Charles* Repeat, *Anthony* Rope, *John* Trace, *Ann and John* Ward, and *James* Underwood.

Occupations have migrated away from family surnames. Children are sent to school to learn an occupation. Many youths in today's developed world have attended school for at least a dozen years and yet have no skills. They are only qualified for unskilled jobs, but expect others, like immigrants, to do those jobs. However, a school skill is not always transferable to an unskilled immigrant.

The world seems to be developing a culture that failed three centuries ago. For example, in the twenty-first century, typing is a personal skill usually taught in school. It is not transferable to an unskilled immigrant. Many "educated" young adults never learned to type efficiently—a skill useful in nearly every job in today's computerized world.

In the eighteenth century, British jails were overflowing from the layoffs caused by the Industrial Revolution's shift to machinery rather than unskilled labor. Many British detainees were sent to Australia for violating at least one of more than 200 crimes, mostly petty, punishable by transportation, whipping, and/or hard labor. Stealing a teapot cost one woman prisoner a trip to Australia. One of the crimes popularized by a brand of Australian wine was "impersonating an Egyptian."

Once given a surname, the name (whether a nickname, incorrect spelling, or a crude mock) often stuck and carried on to following generations. Granted, it did not take much of a crime to be booted out of British prisons onto Australian-bound inmate ships. A few of the First Fleet prisoners had names that may have indicated their improper parley: *John* Cuss, *Richard* Dick, *Peter* Woodcock, and *Caroline* Laycock.

Although Wietgrefe does not mean "farmer" (more like "selling pastures"), I was interested in agriculture, like my forefathers, but did not have the money to get into farming. Even though I was a veteran, known as a "non-trad" (nontraditional) student, I had not determined a career my first year of college. Although the pay was poor, I thought that maybe teaching high school vocational agriculture would be good.

Four years earlier, in 1971, we had the top vo-ag (vocational agriculture) program in South Dakota, taking top honors at the state FFA (Future Farmers of America) convention that year. Our teacher, Don Tumbleson, was let go. Even though we were a small town, with most of the kids coming from the farm, our high school dropped vo-ag before the 1972 school year. It never was added later. Hundreds of farm students went through high school since then without any focus on the major industry in that community.

As the Danish Karen Blixen, the author of *Out of Africa*, wrote in 1937: "Perhaps he knew, as I did not, that the Earth was made round so that we would not see too far down the road."[1]

Education has moved family culture away from family names. Often teachers and local school boards do not foresee the impact of their instruction, or lack of it. Foresight eventually becomes apparent as communities stagnate and even teachers move for opportunities.

Although all of us look to the future, it is hard for students since little is remembered but much is learned before starting school. Children see the years roll by without learning to live the longest segment. Schools run on time; learning does not.

While attending pre-education classes, I realized many classmates were no more than average students who could see down the road only

---

[1] Blixen, Karen, 1937, *Out of Africa*, no current copyright found.

to the next test. That is when I decided I did not want to spend a career working with average people. I felt no personal challenge. Many apparently are satisfied with what they see, not what may develop.

A person certainly does not have to be smart to be a good teacher. Passion, enthusiasm, and the ability to motivate students to study and learn does not take a genius. Dim wit can be effective. On the other hand, very intelligent professors I had at the University of Denver, University of Maryland, and South Dakota State University were questionable teachers. That is when I concluded: Teachers do not have to be the brightest bulb in the room to enlighten. On the other hand, bright professors often have trouble getting students to understand.

Inability to plainly explain a topic is frustrating to learners. Perhaps the best teachers are those who have struggled themselves to learn their subject of expertise.

Who was to blame when one of my high school teachers told my classmate: "*If you cannot explain it with your own words, you don't understand it.*" Contrary to scholarly babble, workers must understand.

Historically, people had to be flexible. There was no nationalized fallback or economic support for the general public. World War II forced many women into the work force. Throughout the world, husbands and boyfriends were sent to war. It was an unfortunate opportunity that allowed many women with limited education to develop skills and professional careers.

War enabled females to seek jobs outside their home and hometown—not only as teachers and nurses, but also in manufacturing and management. When the war ended, men and women returned home, married, and started the Baby Boomer society. Tough experiences added to their economic stability and family discipline. Economies around the world grew with Baby Boomers.

Now decades later, economists, especially those associated with the United Nations, imply a society advances economically as the rate of childbirth decreases, which is often associated with increased education level. Because of social engineering, fewer young adults entering the workforce have skills to create demand for laborers. However, a culture can only develop as its educated are gainfully employed. Schooling without experience is not functional.

American females over the last century were more educated than males, but were not in positions to develop job-creating enterprises. Many were skilled office-type clerical staff that may have had great impact on much research and many products but their male bosses took credit for their work.

More women in the workforce in the twentieth century resulted in more economically measurable output. National, state, and local governments allowed or promoted enterprise development to tax it. Is that the current goal of formal education? It seems so. For decades, our youth and their parents have been continually told those with college degrees make more money.

More workers equate to more money floating through a local, state and national economy. More restaurants create more meal servants with more meals eaten outside the home. Retailers sell more apparel, shoes, and associated items purchased to wear to work.

As more automobiles were used to commute to work it required more vehicle dealerships and service stations, insurance agents, more repairs, and finally salvage and disposal shops. More bankers and their support staff were needed to handle the money of more wage earners. A service economy developed. Entrepreneurs built service businesses and hired servants. It created more garbage—more service staff was needed.

Service industries create efficiencies within their sector, but research and innovation is not their forte.

How many servants need college training? For service industries, what is a reasonable percentage that should attend college? What percent of young adults should get student loans for service industry jobs? What percent of those entering the workforce can get on-the-job training without college?

Are student education loans and public educational support focused correctly?

In the developed and developing economies, more service workers are needed than in the 1950s, or in today's undeveloped countries. Increased education level creates more service workers. Service workers are a higher percentage of the workforce now than in the late 1950s when the U.S. federal government started subsidizing college student loans.

Did those loans develop an innovative or a service economy? Obviously, the answer is a service economy. If student loans were subsidized for an innovative economy, to develop a space program for example, why are many of today's college graduates underemployed? Lacking skills and mental processes to be innovative, they migrate to service industries.

If federal student loans were to develop a service economy, are educated servants taught how to service customers? No. Service around the world seems to be poorer than it has ever been. The school system has taught them to be served, not serve others.

Only fools would suggest that most of today's service industry workers need a college education. Consider the entertainment business, like sports and tourism; they are service industries. What percent require a college degree? Less than 5 percent? Do more than 5 percent of mechanics, janitors, gardeners, welders, plumbers, carpenters, clerks, homemakers, and the like need college degrees?

Five percent provides for an interesting analogy between the school system and agriculture. Historically, saved seed was a major portion of crop production. The best seed was selected and planted the following year. The rest was eaten or fed to animals that were also eaten. About 5 percent of a crop harvested in the 1800s was used for seed. (One bushel of wheat was planted to produce twenty bushels.) Today, in the United States a planted bushel of wheat produces about fifty bushels–2 percent used for seed. Likewise, one teacher in a rural school in the 1800s taught perhaps twenty students with no support staff.

All functional systems will naturally migrate to more efficient production. Agriculture has. Corn (maize), for example in the 1800s yielded about the same as wheat, but used only 2 percent for seed. Today, corn has replaced much of America's oats, barley, rye, flax, wheat, and soybeans, because one kernel of corn planted for seed produces about 200 kernels. Half of 1 percent is used for seed.

Likewise, the school system, if it is truly an efficient educational system, should produce more skilled workers with fewer school staff. As the developed world has, through efficiencies, migrated to service economies, schools should need fewer staff and a lower percentage of the populations should need college degrees. Why? Servants should take less time to train than technical experts and managers. Available resources will only cover inefficiencies until more efficient systems develop. Those resources, like communications and computers, are available for education.

Retail clerks used to make change out of a cash box; now a machine indicates how much change is to be given–some machines dispense change simplifying the servants' job. Trade schools, not colleges, functionally serve the technical aspects of the service industry. Very few service industries rely on universities for trade services. Nurses and doctors are one of the rare exceptions, although they make up a small percentage of the total health care industry. Whether trained in a technical school or university, practical and technical training leads immediately to a profession.

A competitive service industry sets wages, if not artificially manipulated by regulations and illegal immigration. Consequently, countries, states, and municipalities that build their economy primarily on service industries should have low demand for college graduates.

In the late twentieth and early twenty-first century, as average years of education increased in developed countries, manufacturing shifted to developing countries while demand for services increased. If the trend continues, developed countries have three choices: Decrease services, increase immigration of low-skilled workers, or decrease years spent in the school system.

An economic and educational plateau is reached when the birth-rate does not support an aging economically affluent, service-oriented society. A college degree does not change the function of servants. The degree, however, does add economic, social, and psychological stress for decades on the debt-laden graduates working service jobs. Those degree-burdened with economic and mental stress create more service jobs for treating stress disorders, counseling, credit, insurance, and law enforcement services.

"Baby Boomers" in the United States are an example of a demographic subset borne (no, not "born") through a post-war economic era by affluence not seen in the history of man. All Baby Boomers were born from parents who did not have federally subsidized student loans. However, more two-income families created a need for more servants. Societal innovation slowed while mechanical, electronic, and digital efficiencies developed from prior novel ideas.

Today, many Baby Boomers are forced to delay retirement because they used savings to send their children to college. The children borrowed more money while in college to live at the parents' standards only to graduate incapable of supporting themselves. Unfortunately, the economic affluent in the most educated, service-oriented societies did not learn to give their children responsibility, which delayed marriage, encouraged abortions, and lowered birthrates. A true cultural shift has occurred.

Normal demographics are skewed to the point that there are not enough trained servants to serve the affluent-aged. Educated young adult minds were artificially puffed up beyond their ability. College debt became the sucker stick when the candy was gone. School debt became worthless to many—except to psychiatrists and bankers.

By developing late nineteenth- and early twentieth-century technology, the affluent aged and had children at an older age. There was no economic reason for the child to be weaned. Instead, to this day the affluent parents continue to pay for continuing education, mid-twenties "child" healthcare, and they often rent an apartment for the degreed adult "child" or the "adult child" simply never moves out of the parents' house.

Student loans are presented as a carrot to continue education, but student debt is the government stick the slave master uses to keep servants working.

More gadgets have evolved in the last forty years as discovery of truly novel concepts has slowed. Whereas, the previous half century developed electricity, radio, functional computing, atomic energy, outer space programs, air conditioning, the Internet, and so on.

Young twenty-first-century minds are not conditioned to remember, mentally process, produce, and implement novel ideas. Gadgets are considered innovative. In fact, smartphone texting was considered novel and adopted by many young adults although it was telegraph era technology. Samuel F.B. Morse (1791–1872) and Alfred L. Vail (1807–1859) developed the system to electronically send individuals messages in 1836.

It indicates young minds (who were not taught to use memory, history, or science in the current education model) are incapable of understanding the concept "novel."

Woe to the country when artificially supported young adults and those on the public dole become the majority. They will dictate political and economic policies—a sure sign of economic decline.

If many can feed off few, the many dictate to the few until its society dissolves.

When unwed girls and women can have babies, live independently with full government support for food, clothing, and housing, where is the incentive to get job-paying work? Even wants (like bus tickets, cable television, college, and cell phones) are given without work. What incentive remains to marry, be a responsible spouse, or get a job? Lacking responsibility, couples marry later—a sure sign of delayed maturity. Young men are also becoming shiftless. Those not supporting families have less incentive to work, volunteer, or take on societal responsibilities.

The school system breeds promiscuity. Morality is passé. Culture changed. Societies historically developed with strong wife/husband bonds. They are decaying without it. Couples provided for each other; now governments are the life-partner. Through grants, free college education is offered. Perhaps one personal benefit for attending higher education is that governments provide or subsidize child care—an excuse to get out of the house, socialize, and re-impregnate. Historically, it is a strange relationship. What is next, government-sanctioned sex shops next to abortion clinics?

With artificial (debt driven) affluence, society loses its moral compass.

Most countries are implementing national education with an international standardized system—a system that increases servants, delays innovation, and lacks business acumen. Is it wise?

How much education is too much? At what point do years in school become an economic drag? Western Europe, North America, Australia, New Zealand, and Japan appear to have tipped the scale to their disadvantage. More years in school become an economic dilemma. Graduates shun physical work and expect more services. Designed as stimulus, there is adequate proof around the world that excess formal education has failed. Simply measure service industry output against gross domestic production.

As an economist, I am not exposing a new trend. Two decades ago it was well known and explained by President Bill Clinton's U.S. Department of Commerce.

Compared with a generation ago, U.S. service industries now account for a larger share of real output, and a much larger share of employment. Service inputs also comprise more of the embodied value of all the goods and services Americans produce for final use.[2]

The cause was also identified in the 1996 report:

Powerful forces now at work in the United States and elsewhere give these changes overwhelming momentum. Some of these forces are demographic (e.g., women's increased presence in the workforce and the aging of the population). Some reflect long-term public choices (e.g., ... public education and health care programs). Others arise from the relentless expansion of technical knowledge (e.g., advances in computer and communications technology ...).[3]

The United States is not the only country experiencing the educations-to-services dilemma.

Recent experience prompts reasonable doubt about the growth potential of service-oriented economies. Since the 1960s, most G-7 countries[4] have experienced a gradual slowing in average output growth, coupled with steady expansion in the services share of economic activity and, especially in the United States, a sharp decline in service-industry productivity growth.[5]

As a reminder, President Eisenhower initiated the first college student loan program under the National Defense Education Act of 1958; President Johnson initiated many government social and educational support programs in the 1960s, like Head Start in 1965; and President Carter established the cabinet level U.S. Department of Education in 1979.

---

[2] Service Industries and Economic Performance, Office of Policy Development, Economics and Statistics Administration, United States Department of Commerce, March 1996, pp 5, http://www.esa.doc.gov/sites/default/files/serviceindustries_0 .pdf (Sourced January 27, 2017)
[3] Ibid., p. 5
[4] In 1996, G-7 countries included the United States, United Kingdom, Canada, Germany, France, Italy, and Japan.
[5] Ibid., p. 5

As the school system developed, the United States shifted from a production to a service economy. The mid-1990s Clinton era report continued:

> Compared with the 1960s, for example, many more U.S. workers have some post-secondary education. Teenagers and women who entered the labor force with relatively few skills in the 1970s are now more experienced. And new research suggests that, in some service industries, heavy investments in information technology since the mid-1980s have at last begun to yield high productivity returns.[6]

As cell phones, Internet, and global positioning systems developed in the 1990s and early twenty-first century, technical services provided an economic spurt to the United States and developed countries. To remain competitive, manufacturing and assembly of gadgets to use those services shifted to developing economies, especially China. That shift provided more proof that the school system did not provide enough innovative background for few developers to improve production efficiencies enough to offset low-cost, unskilled labor and transportation from underdeveloped countries. Engineers developed gadgets without the skill to manufacture more efficiently than those with no skills.

What has happened to wages in the United States during the decades-long shift to an educated service economy?

> On average, wage rates in the service sector remain below those in other sectors. . . . The evidence seems less reassuring . . . whether service industries are functioning the way manufacturing industries once did, as providers of well-paid jobs for mid-skilled workers. (Moreover) service industries have been unable to compensate for job losses by manufacturing workers in the middle range of the blue-collar skills spectrum.[7]

The modern school system has not trained efficiency or innovation, especially in manufacturing. Result number one: Manufacturing shifted to reliable foreign production, and low-skill domestic services were relegated to immigrants, many illegal, who took their responsibilities

---

[6] Ibid., pp. 5–6
[7] Ibid., p. 6

seriously whether that be in lawn care, landscaping, construction, or fruit and vegetable harvesting. Result number two: Education has become a substitute for responsibility.

Leaders often get responsibilities confused with causes. It would be like the historic practice of putting eunuchs in charge of the king's bedroom. When the world was blooming with twenty-first-century Islamic terrorism (September 11, 2001), the military leader of the free world, U.S. President George W. Bush, was reading to children at Emma E. Booker Elementary School in Sarasota, Florida. Earlier that year, January 23, 2001, contrary to any executive authority constitutionally given the president, George W. Bush proposed U.S. education reform which became the No Child Left Behind Act of 2001. Taking his focus off protecting the country (his job as commander in chief), his educational cause weakened his military responsibilities. Similarly, President Lyndon Johnson's signature legislation, the Elementary and Secondary Education Act was signed April 9, 1965 at the height of the Vietnam War.

Presidents should perform responsibly. They are public examples. Presidents have shifted from legal responsibilities to voter appeasement. Why? Likely it is because parents have shifted responsibilities unto paid servants—daycare and school teachers. Responsibility is a simple thing. It should not be a government or school initiated function.

As I think back on our Guatemalan guide, will Alex take my fatherly advice while raising his boys? Will he continue to give them responsibilities? I may never know. He seems to be making wise choices. I do know that children can do chores and take on responsibilities at two years old, way before most parents would even consider giving them independence and age-appropriate responsibilities.

Alex was a service worker and likely remained an outsider in his wife's Guatemalan village. He was not a business owner or employer. Consequently, he may be an outsider for decades. That will not prevent him from changing the village; making it better; and showing others how he was raising his sons to be responsible youth and eventually productive adults. Alex provided a service. He was a great servant and wise father.

Servants are a valuable resource to society. Those with post-secondary education do not want to be called servants, but most support society through medical, financial, nutritional, recreational, hospitality, and government services.

Historically, through smiles, tears, and threats of thrashings for a practical cause, cultured youth grew. Many became servants like their parents. When taught properly, servants, no matter their lowly beginning status, have become leaders.

Servants often took charge using their learning-dominated status as did eunuchs in Assyria (850–622 B.C.), Persia (550–330 B.C.), Ptolemy XIII of Egypt (<51 B.C.), and the Chinese eunuchs of the Sui (581–614 A.D.) and Ming (1368–1644 A.D.) Dynasties. Eunuchs were the most trusted servants. They wrote regulations, managed the countries treasuries, and at night watched the king's harem.

Today's school system of training servants seems to be a slow castration of young minds. Impotency developed over years is evidenced in university graduates who can only function in team environments, or clerking menial jobs. With modern charter schools, home, and online educational systems, more children are fortunately escaping the clutches of the brick-and-mortar school system to become managers, entrepreneurs, and leaders. Evidence: Toddlers are reading graphics by swiping cell phones and electronic tablets.

Identify a cultured adult. Does it matter what century? Does it matter if they are surnamed Johnson, Walker, Hodson, or Laycock? (Well, most would admit Laycock is a service name not requiring a college degree.) Whether three millennia ago or a hundred years in the future, parents have an obligation to teach independence and responsibility, which yields innovation and productivity. Output measures life's accomplishments. A degree does not.

To many parents and students, learning gets confused with education. One learns how to work; education does not produce work. One learns how to take on responsibility; education does not produce responsibility. One learns how to be productive; education does not induce productivity. One learns to innovate; education is not a substitute for innovation. One learns to use memory; those educated on artificial memory will always be an understudy.

Understudies are servants incapable of being in charge.

16

Wean or Whine

Riddle: What is protracted, yet measured in degrees without a protractor?

Do you know agriculture? Few people do. Culture originated as an agricultural term perhaps when 90 percent of the world's population was directly involved with producing food, fiber, feed, and fuel. As has happened with the breakdown of the traditional family, society (and the "educated" in general) has prostituted the meaning of "culture," both rural and urban.

Webster[1] defines "culture" as "1. Cultivation of the soil 2. Production, development, or improvement of a particular plant, animal, commodity, etc. 3. The growth of a bacteria or other microorganisms in a specially prepared nourishing substance . . ." (and finally the forth definition); "4. Development, improvement, or refinement of the mind, emotions, interests, manners, taste, etc."

"Cultured" as an adjective is defined as "1. produced or obtained by cultivation 2. refined in speech, behavior, etc."

If you took a random survey of twenty-five-year-olds with a master's degree, what percent would identify "culture" as primarily an agricultural term? Less than 1 percent?

Their ignorance, speech, and home location often are symbolic of those that lack culture. Years of education have also played a part of

---

[1] "Culture," *Webster*, p. 345

their naiveté. To puff up their narrow minds, rural citizens are often demeaned by the highly educated as ignorant, and urban dwellers are artificially segregated by color and ethnicity (e.g., "country hicks," "the hood" for black neighborhoods, and "Chinatown").

Throughout history, aristocrats who considered themselves cultured and learned, segregated themselves by dress, language, and education from servants and peasants. Interestingly, supreme leaders of the Chinese Tang Dynasty issued decrees in 779 A.D. and 836 A.D. against Uighurs forcing them to wear traditional clothing, and "Dark People" (i.e., Indians, Iranians, Arabs, and others) were prohibited from intermarrying Chinese. Like disease, irresponsibility has symptoms. It is easier to inflate personal or ethnic ego by demeaning others rather than through self-improvement.

Microcosms of irresponsibility can be identified. Adult, educated children seek sanctuary at their parents' homes. Without acceptance of cultural sustenance, couples age without wanting responsibility of rearing children. From a national perspective, cities likewise become sanctuaries for the carefree.

America's bastion of so-called acceptance, San Francisco, is a city highly segregated by color, ethnicity, liberal elitism, and a sanctuary for illegal roustabouts. The San Francisco Bay Area is home to digital techies who are experts at programing gadgets. Yet, they are incompetent at manufacturing those devices more efficiently than the uneducated and unskilled in undeveloped countries. Their gadgets are not sustainable without unskilled labor. Many work in Silicon Valley, a stronghold for self-aggrandizement, while they reside in neighborhoods that espouse elitism as named by those they elected.

Following is a condensed list of San Francisco neighborhoods followed by the percentage categorized by the 2010 U.S. Census as "white": Presidio, which means "fortified" in Spanish (80% white), Presidio Heights (75% white), Pacific Heights (81% white), Diamond Heights (70% white), and Upper Market (80% white). That census reported 54 percent of San Francisco's total population was white.

What about other areas of San Francisco?

Did the city council assign similar names to minority neighborhoods? No! Some San Francisco neighborhoods with minority populations are: Outer Richmond (44% white), Outer Sunset (35% white),

Outer Mission (31% white), Chinatown (12% white), and Visitacion Valley (12% white). Although Asians and others account for nearly half of the city's population, through neighborhood naming, minorities in San Francisco are considered outsiders and visitors.

According to census data, those mostly white neighborhoods named above had a median annual household income of $101,080 and 2.2 person per household with 91.6 percent over age twenty-five having more than a high school education. The minority neighborhoods listed had median annual household income of $57,533 with 3.1 persons per household, and only 54.6 percent had more than a high school education.

Obviously, there are significant differences in San Francisco neighborhoods often categorized by color, ethnicity, income, education, and the number of children. Similar to the educated of Silicon Valley, the city of San Francisco residents cannot produce a population to sustain itself. Primarily white neighborhoods established their elite culture but are not sustainable (producing only 0.2 children per two adults).

In a city with one of the highest education levels, even the names of neighborhoods are assigned to establish white elitism. Secondly, San Francisco maintains an established social class that discriminates against families with children. Educational institutions are designed for youth. Meanwhile, neighborhoods with the highest education generally had the least number of children. Hypocrisy at its height, San Francisco describe itself with pride:

> San Francisco's racial and ethnic composition remains diverse. The City's Asian population is growing steadily, but the number of Black residents continues to drop. San Franciscans of Latin or Hispanic origin are also increasing, although not at rates seen at state or national levels. San Franciscans are also getting older ... (and) San Francisco continues to be in the top three major cities with the fewest children. Our citizens are also better educated. ...[2]

---

[2] San Francisco Neighborhoods–Social Economic Profiles, 2005–2009 American Community Survey, San Francisco Planning Department, May 2011, http://sf-planning.org/sites/default/files/FileCenter/Documents/8501-SFProfilesByNeighborhoodForWeb.pdf (Sourced January 30, 2017)

Households without children are not sustainable, hence schools are not needed. San Francisco provides proof formal education does not convey sustainable culture. It segregates it. Established as a progressive city, it is dying. It cannot sustain itself unless working-age people temporarily move in, families and retirees move out, and servants commute making vehicle traffic congestion one of the worst in the United States. Necessities of food, water, shelter construction, and security are sourced elsewhere. The service sector is primarily high-tech gadgetry that nobody needs to survive. Even their gadgets are not produced locally–meaning the self-declared tech geniuses lack the ability to manufacture items more efficiently than the uneducated and unskilled.

Sociologically, economically, serviceability, educationally, and environmentally San Francisco's lifestyle is not self-sustaining. Existing any other time in history, San Francisco would be considered a city in chaos. Paradoxically, residents there think they are progressive. Unless its demographics change, it will be blotted out historically. Cultures crumble as buildings and infrastructure fall into disrepair. San Francisco is a replica of culture collapsing.

Throughout history, port cities, like San Francisco, became culturally unsustainable. Natural disasters take their toll as it did April 18, 1906, when a minute earthquake and resulting fires destroyed the city. A couple weeks after the earthquake, engineering professor Samuel Fortier wrote: "There is practically nothing left. . . ."[3]

Some cities, like San Francisco, eventually were rebuilt on top of old ones. For hundreds of years from B.C. into A.D. the Greek city of Piraeus, a city known for its temple of Aphrodite (pagan goddess of love and beauty), survived through earthquakes, wars, and toppled governments followed by 1500 years of decline.

Some cities, through human negligence, were never rebuilt. Ancient Ephesus was a port city on the Aegean coast (Turkey) known for its pagan Temple of Artemis (revealed as the twin sister of Apollo and goddess of virginity), considered one of the Seven Wonders of the Ancient World. That temple was built, destroyed, and rebuilt three times before being abandoned.

---

[3] Correspondence from Professor Samuel Fortier to Dr. Elwood Mead of Washington, D.C. May 1, 1906. https://www.archives.gov/exhibits/sf-earthquake-and-fire/earthquake-fire.html (Sourced March 24, 2017)

The ancient Library of Celsus had its home in Ephesus, and 2000 years ago performances thrived in one of the world's largest theaters.

When I was in the former port city of Ephesus twenty years ago, it remained an abandoned city of archeological ruins. Tourists lamented the past. It was completely depopulated, an ecological disaster, enclosed by hills of jagged rocks completely denuded of productive vegetation as soil, long since, had eroded into the sea then nearly four miles (six kilometers) from seawater. Many feet below the surface an excavated, huge paved marketplace bordered its abandoned harbor—a symbol of past affluence without a future. Ephesus remains soulless, and to this day without solace.

Directed by the highly educated, San Francisco provides an oblique pattern of the developed world in the twenty-first century where personal and cultural preservation is unstable. Relying on immigrants to provide mathematical, computer, and engineering skills, the unskilled to provide manufactured goods, and imported construction, healthcare, and other servants, the city provides a glimpse into the developed world and an unsustainable subculture.

A jobless twenty-five-year-old with a master's degree, who has traveled overseas a few times but living at home, under parents' health care is not cultured. Also, just because they order wine for dinner rather than having a beer, and wear an ascot,[4] does not change the fact that they are uncultured.

Need proof that parents with highly educated children are even less cultured? Many have not figured out how to wean an adult twice the age of puberty. Parents providing adult "children" with food, shelter, personal and financial security, and healthcare at age twenty-six is an historic abnormality.

Furthermore, living at home and jobless is proof that twenty, or more years of institutional training has not biologically or socially "... refined the mind, emotions, interests, manners, or taste ..." to satisfy the definition of culture because culture is "production" and "development."

To maintain a culture, reproduction must occur at the same rate as death. Western Europe, North America, New Zealand, Australia, Japan, Singapore, and others epitomize the formally educated developed

---

[4] Ascot is "a kind of necktie or scarf with very broad ends hanging from the knot, one upon the other. ..." *Webster*, p. 81

world, like San Francisco, with an unsustainable population which has migrated into an unsustainable egocentric, me-first culture.

Education may cultivate, but cultivation produces nothing–just the opposite. Cultivation is also designed to destroy. In agriculture, cultivation destroys pests (i.e., weeds and insects). In doing so, it also impedes natural soil structure. Whereas in society, does cultivation provide structured production and weaning, or imply ignorance, incompetence, and self-centeredness? It needs the former and cannot survive on the latter. Care must be taken to ensure cultivation does not destroy intended reproduction.

To produce and consume one must plant, nurture, control nuisances, and harvest. The school system has the ability to plant ideas, but spends more time nurturing. It is losing control of pests (i.e., nuisances like bullying, illicit drugs, and inappropriate behavior) without providing a system of producing and harvesting ideas. Nutrients in the field of formal education are found wanting.

PRIDE OF A TEN-YEAR-OLD

One spring evening I got a telephone call from our ten-year-old grandson. It was the first time he had ever called us. Somewhat startled, I said, "What's up Willie?"

Not chit-chatty like most calls start, he went directly into the purpose of his call. Ten-year-olds seldom waste time; they have not learned the nuances of social etiquette.

"Guess what I did today grandpa?"

"Well, let's see Willie, you're out of school. Hmmm. I don't know. What did you do?"

"I planted a quarter of sunflowers!" He burst out.

"That's fantastic! What planter were you using?" I asked.

"A 24-row with our new auto-steer," he blurted proudly.

"Willie, I'm so proud of you," I said empathetically as spring memories circulated my head. To show acceptance of his youthful responsibilities, I explained, "I have never planted a field of corn or sunflowers in my life."

We did not have sunflowers back then and the only row-crop we grew was corn. Back in the 1960s, the small 4-row planter we had needed to plant straight; practical Global Positioning Systems (GPS) were decades in the future. Later cultivation was our system to destroy weeds between corn rows. When planting, dad would shoot a half-mile line-of-sight and not turn. You could watch pheasants in the fall for a couple hundred yards down those straight rows.

Until we were teenagers, our father did not dare allow us boys to cultivate corn and our mother was rarely allowed to do so. All 15,000 plants in those 38-inch rows had to be saved. One chance per year was all we had to raise a crop. A couple years after buying a 4-row, 3-point hitch cultivator, we were changing shovels one night and dad realized why we had trouble cultivating without destroying some corn plants. Although the cultivator support brackets appeared uniform, they were off-center from the tractor tires that were to be centered between rows. A slight steering variation destroyed corn.

A child likewise needs to be straightened out occasionally to cultivate a respectable culture.

What parents would put a ten-year-old in a quarter-million-dollar tractor pulling a $100,000 planter sowing a 160-acre crop that needed to yield $50,000 just to break even? Parents who feel comfortable teaching and expecting responsibility from their son know when and what is appropriate.

Yes, I was proud of my grandson and just as proud of my son-in-law and daughter for raising such a respectful, culturally educated young boy.

Were there risks? Yes. Historically, boys much younger than ten were working in fields alongside their father and given responsibility to cultivate, sow, and harvest. Cost of equipment, automation, and area covered are the main differences in today's farming system.

Ancient cultures would be shocked to know a "modern" society lost the basic concept of raising a child to be self-sustaining. Responsibility was expected. Stories and fables have been passed on for centuries about irresponsible youth. It was unusual then. Why? Youth were expected to be responsible.

About 2500 years ago, Aesop told a fable that is still told today. It was about a young shepherd boy who cried, "Wolf!" "Wolf!" Neighbors who heard the screaming through the valley responded several times to the boy's cry for help only to discover the boy was playing a prank. Finally, when a wolf did appear, the boy cried in earnest. "Wolf!" "Wolf!" Nobody came to his aid and the boy was killed. The moral: Do not deceive. A liar is not trusted even when he tells the truth.

Parents taught their children to be honest and develop their minds using poems and songs to develop functional memory. Parents singing the A-B-C song to toddlers is an example. Activities to support the family, like drawing water, feeding animals, or caring for younger siblings were incorporated into rhymes, ditties, and bedtime stories. One old British lullaby, "Bye, Baby Bunting," first published in 1784, ties family activities together.

> Bye, baby Bunting.
> Father's gone a-hunting.
> Mother's gone a-milking.
> Sister's gone a-silking.
> Brother's gone to buy a skin
> To wrap the baby Bunting in.

Even more shocking to an ancient culture would be current society's inability to wean. The longer it takes a parent to discipline a child, the longer it takes to wean a child into perceptive reality of the world. One must develop an ability to accept discipline as responsibility quietly evolves. Otherwise, expect whining.

In the lullaby "Bye, Baby Bunting," the girl, whether older or younger, goes to weave silk. Her brother, too young to hunt and milk, is responsible with the family's money and caringly goes to market to buy a soft (likely tanned fur) carrier or covering for the baby. Today's parent directives, "Be responsible," or asking "Is that appropriate behavior" would be harsh and inappropriate words while swaddling a chubby little baby (bunting). Instead, the nursery rhyme sung to a baby by all family members reinforces parent and sibling responsibilities. Directly or indirectly family actions are learning experiences for toddlers, especially in the five-member (bunting) family.

A modern version may go something like this:

> Bye, baby woebegone.
> Daddy's nowhere to be found,
> After screwing mom around.
> Sister's playing with her phone.
> Brother's out buying pot,
> While baby's nose is running snot.

To the other extreme, parents who protect their preschool children should also accept responsibility for their ineptitude when their child has trouble adapting to classroom discipline.

A symptom of modern abnormalities may be autism.

Autism perhaps has grown as a childhood disorder perpetuated by school system structure. There must be a cause. Alternatively, if the society-wide disorder developed at home, why did the Autism Society form in 1965–the year the Head Start (preschool) program originated? Was it because kindergarten was implemented nationwide and pre-school (pre-kindergarten) was being pushed to toddlers who had not adjusted to an out-of-home environment?

About 10 percent of autism cases are identified as a genetic disorder; consequently, autism is more common in children with autistic parents. Why then is autism increasing beyond genetics? There are many theories as to why autism continues to increase (e.g., nutritional imbalance, lack of sleep, and family-life interruptions). Likely, because there is a better chance of getting research funding, autism is more often investigated as a medical condition rather than caused by a societal dysfunction of highly structured education.

Genetic autism is noticed by parents when children are usually under two years old. It is well known that genetics differ by race regardless of societal development. If autism was caused by parents (genetics), why does the U.S. Centers for Disease Control and Prevention state:

> Autism spectrum disorder (ASD) is about 4.5 times more common among boys (1 in 42) than among girls (1 in 189) ... (and) is reported to occur in all racial, ethnic, and socioeconomic groups.[5]

Furthermore, why has autism increased paralleled to school system dominance in early learning?

Historically, boys played outside and girls have traditionally played in their homes. Could it be that boys cooped in schools beginning at age three, four or five are more likely to develop anti-social responses to being institutionalized? Along the same train of thought, boys are more likely to quit before high school graduation, and less likely to go to

---

[5] Autism Spectrum Disorder, United States Centers for Disease Control and Prevention, http://www.cdc.gov/ncbddd/autism/data.html. (Sourced September 29, 2016)

college than girls who have adapted over centuries to confined domestic activities.

In fact, some studies indicate autism is more common in cities, especially high-tech areas, than in rural areas.[6] Autism has also been found to be more associated with education level of students and parents.[7]

In a 2014 study, it costs an estimated $8610 more to educate an autistic child, but their patients did not have more out-of-pocket costs nor did they spend more time giving care to those diagnosed with autism spectrum disorder.[8]

When it comes to analyzing the school system, follow the money. Where are the school systems' priorities?

Schools' determination of development disorders, like autism, is different than medical diagnosis.[9] Schools get funding based on the U.S. Individuals with Disabilities Education Act and therefore are financially incentivized to categorize children for special education. On the other hand, they do not get more funding for educating brighter or more talented children. Schools diagnose disabilities differently. Regulations vary state-to-state, and students are diagnosed differently between school systems and can segregate without a medical diagnosis. By government fiat, educators became clinicians.

Parents often foster more blame when they too were educated in dysfunctional, standardized, youth-restricted school systems.

Is it any wonder autism is the fastest growing childhood disability? Again, per the U.S. Centers for Disease Control and Prevention in studies of eight-year-olds, autism has increased from 119.4 percent in 2000

[6] Chait, Jennifer, "Autism more common in high-tech cities," July 6, 2011, Baby, http://www.pregnancyandbaby.com/baby/articles/935229/autism-more-common-in-high-tech-cities, (Sourced September 29, 2016)

[7] Cone, Marla, "Autism Clusters Found in California's Major Cities," Environmental Health News, *Scientific American*, January 6, 2010, https://www.scientificamerican.com/article/autism-clusters-california-highly-educated-parents/, (Sourced September 29, 2016)

[8] Lavelle, Tara A., et al., "Economic Burden of Childhood Autism Spectrum Disorders," March 2014, Volume 133, Issue 3, *Pediatrics*, http://pediatrics.aappublications.org/content/133/3/e520.short, (Sourced September 29, 2016)

[9] Burnette, Courtney, "Educational Eligibility vs Medical Diagnosis in Autism Spectrum Disorders," March 9, 2012, http://www.cdd.unm.edu/autism/Handouts/EducationalEligibilityVsMed.pdf, (Sourced September 29, 2016)

(1 in 150) to 2010 (1 in 68). Were their parents' education different in the 1960s (children surveyed in 2000) than later? Yes. Federal and state governments increasingly forced their policies on local school systems into the late twentieth century, and still do.

Child guidelines may be as simple as being in class, seated by 8:00 a.m.; keeping only one piece of paper on their desk; picking up paper clippings from the floor; and clearing their desk before leaving school.

Those responsibilities may be a stoical change from overly pampered, school-manipulated parents who have given their children no responsibilities.

Simple rules of the school world are unreasonable to an untethered child who could do whatever he/she wanted any time of day or night. Life has rules. Parents take heed. Civil War President Abraham Lincoln said: "You cannot escape the responsibility of tomorrow by evading it today."

It may be a shock to some mothers, but the umbilical cord was cut at birth. Freedom is not without guidelines. Ground rules apply when the kid begins to crawl and life expectations are set while in the crib.

A child gets teeth first on the bottom to warn the nursing mother. When the top ones appear, grinding and biting is a certain clue the child should have been trained to consume more than breast milk. Mothers: You know it is time to keep your blouse buttoned when the child undoes it and asks for a booby.

One reason it is illogical for grandmothers to raise infants is they cannot lactate.

Teething is a good grandparent discussion. Timing of teething is hereditary. Asking the grandma when you got your first teeth is an appropriate question for first-time parents. Expecting grandparents to care for your child while both parents work outside the home is inappropriate, especially when the grandparents are both currently working and provided financial support during college.

Expecting working grandparents to provide babysitting services is unusual; so is expecting grandparents to interrupt their retirement to help raise another generation. After having a child, young parents need to accept responsibility like they never had before.

Multigenerational parenting is a latent symptom of inappropriate weaning. Historically, grandmothers watched children up to age four or five to support young parents as they went about their jobs, to fields, or to do household chores. Now grandparents are expected to babysit to allow parents more free time. The world has changed. Irresponsibility is rampant. Culture has changed.

The laws of human biology guide production, rearing, and weaning. Age of grandmothers preclude them from becoming pregnant and nursing. Why then should they be involved with rearing and weaning their grandchildren?

Often, I've heard parents say raising their children has been a battle. For that, I will respond with a quote from Britain's WWII leader, Winston Churchill (1874–1965): "It is no use saying, 'We are doing our best'. You have got to succeed in doing what is necessary."

When grandparents get overly involved, it provides their children even more excuses to not properly parent their children. In a stark break from history, parents are not giving their children adequate responsibilities by ages two, three, and four. Today, many grandparents are not even expecting their children to be proper parents in their mid-twenties or thirties.

Grandparents are increasingly getting involved with rearing their grandchildren. Why? If they did not give responsibility to one generation, what gives them the right to screw up the next?

The progression is dramatic. In 1990, grandparents raised 3.5 million grandchildren. By the year 2000, the U.S. Census Bureau reported the number had grown to 4.4 million. "Nine percent of those under 6 years, 6 percent of those aged 6 to 11, and 4 percent of children aged 12 to 17 were listed as grandchildren of the householder."[10]

In 2012 using census data, the U.S. Department of Commerce reported:

> About 10 percent of all children live with a grandparent. Since 2007, about one-third of children who live with a grandparent also have two parents present. Grandparents maintained 67 percent

---

[10] Children and the Households They Live In: 2000, Census 2000 Special Reports, issued March 2004, CENSR-14, http://www.census.gov/prod/2004pubs/censr-14 .pdf (Sourced June 13, 2016)

of coresident households. About 1 in 3 grandparent-maintained households had no parent present.[11]

Although parents rely on grandparents to babysit and care for their grandchildren, there are corresponding benefits to the elders. As I mentioned before, my disabled paternal grandfather lived with our family from when I was in the first grade until he passed, five years after I graduated from high school. Children learn from grandparents and learn to care for others. With seven siblings, it was our responsibility to daily put on grandpa's shoes and socks, maintain his toenails and wash his feet, and each morning empty and rinse his bedside three-pound coffee can.

As with my grandfather, not all grandparents care for children; it may be the other way. According to the 2012 Census Report: "Coresident grandparents are also more likely to be in poverty and more likely to be unable to work due to illness or disability compared with grandparents who did not live with grandchildren."

However, inability to wean seems to be a growing issue in the United States. Grandmothers are especially vulnerable. They apparently feel a need to compensate for their children. Toys, gadgets, and stuff are guilt payments. It is like a gambling addict sticking another $20 into a slot machine and hoping the results are different from the last $20 or $100.

What is the difference if the government or the grandparent takes control of a child?

That is a cold question. Perhaps as cold as the Australian government's policy to forcibly remove aboriginal children from their parents under the specific policy of 1915:

> The Board may assume full control and custody of the child of any aborigine, if after due inquiry it is satisfied that such a course is in the interest of the moral and physical welfare of such child. The Board may thereupon remove such child to such control and care as it thinks best.[12]

---

[11] Ellis, Renee R., Tavia Simmons, Coresident Grandparents and Their Grandchildren: 2012, Issued October 2014, P20-576, U.S. Department of Commerce, Economics and Statistics Administration, U.S. Census Bureau, https://www.census.gov/content/dam/Census/library/publications/2014/demo/p20-576.pdf (Sourced June 13, 2016)
[12] Australian Aborigines Protection Amending Act, Section 13A, No. 2 of 1915. http://www.nma.gov.au/online_features/defining_moments/featured/aborigines_protection_act (Sourced September 9, 2015)

No proper records were kept, but it has been estimated that up to 50,000 Australian Aboriginal children were forcibly removed from their parents by various government entities between 1909 and 1970. Is it any wonder Australian Aboriginals remain a social obstacle a hundred years later?

American grandparents are stealthier. They often start out babysitting the infant when the mother returns to work. As the parent(s) must go out of town for work, or to get a break for a weekend or a week, the child becomes "at home" at the grandparents' place. Upon divorce, which is common with irresponsible parents, the grandparents take full responsibility, but not necessarily custody, of the grandchild. The Australian government was more blunt and forthright with Aboriginals.

In many cases, grandparents want their grandchildren around. When they do not have grandchildren to nurture, they often get at least one dog or cat to satisfy their fostering instinct.

If you were a grandparent and had an option, what would you rather do, have your grandchild live with you, or pick up dog shit morning and night for the next fifteen years?

Parents vary in ability—that's life. It was not right for the white Australian government to pull Aboriginal children from their parents and place them in foster care. Likewise, it is not right for grandparents to place grandchildren under their care when the parents are not incarcerated or institutionalized—which also may be a result in questionable rearing.

If grandparents have not weaned their children properly, there is a high probability they will also inappropriately wean grandchildren under their care. Grandparents will likely give them too much and expect too little.

Often one parent gives their child more responsibility than the other. Later in life, the child may consciously or subconsciously realize the differences. The mother may want to push their daughter out the door into the real life, while the father continues to dote over his daughter by continuing allowances into adulthood, maintaining her car, and paying her rent. Mothers are not exempt from weaning responsibilities with temptations to do laundry or cook and clean their daughter's or son's apartment while they are at college or work.

Quit whining. Wean. If you are a child-rearing grandparent, you missed responsible opportunities by at least two decades. Culture has parallels at home and in society. In the first three years of life, parents establish their child's ability to be responsible. Likewise, the careful in society struggle to support the carefree.

17

After Weaning

Riddle: What is easy to find, measures by age, and runs on time?

May 7, 2015, during a 7:00 a.m. coffee clique a retired marketer said, "A lot of kids are moving home and living into their late twenties and thirties with their parents."

I replied, "I don't think parents know how to wean their kids anymore."

"Yeah, when we were eighteen, we were expected to move out," he continued. My wife, Patricia, has made that comment many times. In my teens, I did not know that staying at home after eighteen was an option. I knew I was old enough to support myself. Why should my parents work extra hard to support me when they had six other mouths to feed (my younger brothers and grandfather)?

Throughout ancient history, children used to be employed fulltime in their teens. By my grandfather's era, grade eight was the highest graduate level expected for most boys. Girls began to stay in school longer. By the 1960s boys and girls were expected to complete high school before going to work fulltime. Basically, weaning started with bottle feeding but migrated to age eighteen as economies prospered from previous industrial, mechanical, and electrical innovations.

That morning's coffee group was smaller than normal. Only the marketer and I had farm backgrounds, but it gave me an opportunity to throw in a bit of practical agriculture.

One of the hardest things on the farm was weaning calves in the fall. I found it hard to sleep hearing a hundred calves bawling hours on end a couple days for their mothers. Mother cows would stand on the other side of the fence, wailing with almost tears in their eyes. My father knew it had to be done. After a couple of days, I would get off the school bus and the calves would be doing their job—eating hay, silage, and ground-feed from bunks. Mother cows would be grazing the nearby pasture. The next year weaning was easier for me.

Parents should put up with a whiny kid a couple days and they would be weaned.

A semiretired businessman sat across the table from me. He had just returned from his winter home in California. Then he added this little story:

One afternoon, my wife and I were invited over to a neighbor's back-yard party. Us guys were sitting around the pool, when the owner grabbed his running grandson and said, "I only have one rule: Don't run around the pool area." As soon as he let go, the five-year-old started running. The next lap, the grandfather said in a louder voice, "No running around the pool!" When the grandson finished his next lap, the grandfather grabbed him by the arm, whopped him on the butt and said, "I only have one rule: Don't run around the pool." His daughter was sitting in the ladies group and witnessed the multi-lap event.

The businessman finished the story by saying, "My friend's daughter was so mad because he popped her son on the butt, that she didn't talk to her father for several days."

His story was the perfect example of a daughter and her son not taking personal responsibility.

Irresponsibility is learned. It is taught by the irresponsible. Did that pool owner ever pop his daughter on the butt for inappropriate behavior?

It was easier for the parents to do nothing—let the kid run wild as if he was an animal. Alternatively, the grown daughter confused domestic abuse with love, concern, and safety.

Poet Samuel Butler (1612–1680) would not have been surprised by the story when he penned in a 1664 poem "Spare the rod and spoil the child."

It is quite likely Butler took liberty with King Solomon's (950–700 B.C.) quote: "He who spares his rod hates his son, But he who loves him disciplines him promptly."[1]

Too bad the businessman's friend was not able to quote Solomon on how much he loved his grandson and wanted him to be safe, so he disciplined him promptly.

One of my poems, "Rode Road," I wrote "for some it is the path; others it is the journey." Paths have borders–otherwise, it would not be a path. Those with no borders have no path and struggle in life's journey. Weaning is a corner we must all negotiate before we lead a content life. The question becomes, "Where is the road taking us"?

Weaning is learning.

I expect concurring readers have moved from childhood to adulthood–weaned into the world. Weaning methods have changed as schools became a fundamental obstacle in the normal learning process. Certainly, some will object to my premise. Likely, objectors will be those that want to protect children (even in the twenties) who are supported by someone other than themselves. Of course, government subsidies for necessities (food, water, shelter, healthcare) are included in "support"– meaning those living with outside support are not yet weaned into the adult world.

Children like to play with kitties–playful but often evasive–personalities with perspective. Nursing kitties are not yet required to catch mice for food. Birds are more visionary. Upon leaving the nest, they must find their own food. Birds are fun to watch. In particular, hawks are aerial acrobats, as they catch prey and chase other birds. At times, smaller birds follow hawks in whirlwind flight where size and maneuverability benefit the smaller, making tighter corners and drafting–a skill learned after weaning. Watching birds and playing with kitties is as old as civilization. Observing maturation, imaginations run rampant. Adult cats, birds, and people still play.

A couple boys that were apparently weaned appropriately, given an education, and independence still had childlike imaginations. Decades before sitting on the bleachers and watching television became a sports' substitute, Wilbur and Orville Wright were not on the beach playing.

[1] Proverbs 13:24, NKJV, p. 923

They could have made a living in their own shop in the new industry, bicycling. Instead, they spent years tinkering and engineering a dream and watching the sky.

Before their first flight, the Wrights removed debris from the beach; this time it was not for building but to clear a path. They used the beach for its uniform surface and predictable winds. Ever since their first flights, pilots take off and land into the wind to slow ground speed. It was as if King Solomon 2800 years earlier was watching. "To everything there is a season, a time for every purpose under heaven . . . a time to cast away stones, and a time to gather stones."[2] There is time for play and time for work. December 17, 1903, was work.

Wilbur and Orville were studying, but not in school. As business-men, they became engineers continuously calculating and evaluating other research. When systems were not commercially available, they built their own (e.g., wind tunnel and aluminum block engine). Using exist-ing technology, they built their own temporary rail line. Even a century ago, extended formal schooling was getting too rigid for many and did not present opportunities. It provided educational background, but not fliers.

Wilbur was taking notes on his younger, thirty-two-year-old brother who was practicing on skids so the flier would not have to land on his feet. Sometimes the paths we make and take are parallel. It was an unusual, theoretical road the Wrights built that day. Like weaning, the goal was to get rid of support. Life's paths are built with improvement in mind. Why build a permanent rigid rail if you can fly over it?

Some think parenting is nurturing rather than a responsibility. How can one grow if not weaned? Some also get school's educational founda-tion confused with the functional part–developing independence.

Descending from twenty feet in the air, Orville's outfit skidded to a stop after twelve seconds and traveled 120 feet. The game was on. "Let's do that again." With varying conditions, learning each flight taught Wrights from wrong.

December 17th is generally not the best day to head to the beach. Clothes in 1903 were heavier and bulkier. I guess the brothers (twenty and twenty-four years older than my grandfather) were tougher than we are today. Four times "Flyer I" cleared the parallel rails that day. Per

---

[2] Ecclesiastes 3: 1, 5, NKJV, p. 954

their notes, Wilbur won with a distance of 852 feet flying for a minute. Actually, it was 59 seconds. Like two competing brothers, Wilbur already had the record for their four flights that day and as meticulous engineers, Orville did not want to stretch 59 into a generalized minute.

Thirty-six years and 206 days after man's first powered flight, July 10, 1940, "The Battle of Britain" began as "The Blitz" of Hitler's German warplanes began the first battle (actually, months-long campaign) entirely conducted with airplanes. 1940 was a leap year. Only an extra day was inserted on the calendar, but 1940 was a leap year in war. Planes constantly leaped the English Channel, refueling and returning to bomb, bomb, bomb.

I can relate to the learning path of flight.

My grandfather was twelve when the Wright brothers made the first powered flight over a North Carolina beach, and my father was eleven when Germany began aerial bombing Britain.

I was five (1958) when President Eisenhower launched the civilian space flight and research agency, National Aeronautics and Space Administration (NASA); and nine (1962) when President Kennedy gave his "Moon Speech"; and I was sixteen (1969) when Apollo 11 took Neil Armstrong and Buzz Aldrin to the moon.

When Orville landed man's first powered flight, Wilbur, in his notes, could have lamented Biblically *"What hath God wrought"*[3] as did Annie Ellsworth (daughter of the U.S. Patent Commissioner) in the world's first official long-distance telegraph between Baltimore, Maryland, and Samuel Morse in the U.S. Capitol May 24, 1844.

During the century from the first telegraph past the first flight to the first all-air battle, was anything learned?

Ancient wisdom:

To everything there is a season . . .
A time to kill, and a time to heal;
A time of war, and a time of peace;
A time to break down, and a time to build up;
A time to keep silence, and a time to speak.[4]

---

[3] Numbers 23:23, Holy Bible, King James Version
[4] Ecclesiastes 3: 1-8, NKJV, p. 954

A time for change continues. Technology is perplexing. Is that why we send children to school earlier? Many believe we are learning faster and earlier than any generation. Based on historical accomplishments of people that lived a third, or half of our current life expectancy, we are weaning later, learning slower, and are less mentally developed upon entering adulthood than previous generations. Result: Innovation has slowed. Things seem be changing faster as technology utilizes previous innovation. It is an illusion compared to my grandfather's generation.

Completed a year before my grandfather was born, in 1890 an electric six-mile railroad ran over seven bridges to connect Sioux Falls, South Dakota, with East Sioux Falls (a suburb known for quarried quartzite). At the time, it was purported to be the world's longest electric transport service. The purpose of the Dakota Rapid Transit and Railroad Company was to efficiently and economically transport workers to the quarries so they could enjoy amenities Sioux Falls offered. A year after statehood, it also provided a boost to the city's population and outclassed supply cities like Minneapolis and Saint Paul. Electricity utilization and transportation efficiency was the order of the day.

A short seventy-four years after Dakota Rapid Transit became operational, my grandfather heard the news about Japan christening the world's first high-speed rail line in 1964, known as the "bullet train."

Sioux Falls leaders in 1890 thought their idea was novel as did Japan's railroad engineers. In modern times, they were considered quite advanced. However, using a stone roadbed line to transport people, rock, commercial goods, and military ships predated Dakota Rapid Transit and Japan's bullet train by at least 2500 years.

Diolkos was a paved line exceeding five miles operating at least 650 years crossing ancient Greek's Isthmus of Corinth. It was operational by 600 B.C. and used into the mid-first century A.D. Diolkos quickly railed whole war and commercial ships overland—not just cargo, sailors, and military supplies.

Technology adoption is not always rapid.

As detailed earlier, man's first flight to the moon landing took only sixty-six years. That is rapid adoption. People used aviation technology to develop rockets, and rockets to develop space flight. Although landing on the moon was a late 1960s' novelty, innovation of flight preceded eventual uses. Likewise, it took a relatively long time for electricity to become functional.

Experiments with electricity date back 5000 years before Benjamin Franklin (1706–1790) discovered positive and negative electrical charges, its equilibrium without power, and electrical storage batteries that helped develop the first, but short-life light bulbs in England around 1835. An electrical light bulb was not practical until Thomas Edison (1847–1931) made one long-lasting and manufactured 1200-hour light bulbs in 1880. Since then, the world has been using his type of light bulb and his replacement screw system—the Edison screw. For millennia, lamp and candlelight sufficed.

Without (Franklin's) constant supply of electricity, (Edison's) artificial memory systems, (Franklin's) electrical storage batteries, German physicist Heinrich Hertz's (1857–1894) transmission of electromagnetic radio waves in 1887, and (Edison's) telephone carbon microphone transmitter, today's cellular smartphones would not exist. There were many other developers of those systems in Europe and Canada that developed practical uses. Research is ongoing. Sure, there are new models of cellular phones and electronic gadgets appearing monthly, but it is a huge stretch to call them novel compared to their fundamental base of innovative technology.

An Olympic style space race manifested. From Russia's Yuri Gagarin's first journey into outer space April 12, 1961, until July 20, 1969, when Neil Armstrong stepped on the moon, the race was international. It was a race of imagination that put education to the test and technology to use. Those born in the 1910s, 1920s, and 1930s before "school system" showed up in the dictionary built mechanisms for manned space movement.

That was the same generation that fought and lived through the six-year war—World War II (September 1, 1939, to September 2, 1945). Halfway through that war British prime minister, Winston Churchill, said as if weaning his nation: "Now this is not the end. It is not even the beginning of the end. But it is, perhaps, the end of the beginning."[5]

---

[5] Churchill, Winston, "The Bright Gleam of Victory," November 10, 1942, Mansion House, London, England, The Churchill Centre, http://www.winstonchurchill .org/resources/speeches/1941-1945-war-leader/987-the-end-of-the-beginning (Sourced January 6, 2016)

Each of us have a beginning, a learning curve, and should gain experience to become independent adults.

In the fall of 1976, a year after I got out of the Air Force, I had attended college for a year and still did not know what was going to be my university major. Still considering teaching vocational agriculture, my favorite subject in high school, I started taking a "teaching block" (a set of classes designed for future teachers). Besides, being a single guy at twenty-three, it did not hurt that there was a choice of beautiful young women in those classes.

One teaching-class project was to prepare a half-hour lesson for third and fourth graders. Our purpose was to educate. The spring before, I completed military classes in radar prediction and analyzing aerial photography. I found shadows cast by objects and analyzing semi-transparent cover intriguing. Consequently, I decided my first teaching project was to give a lesson on shadows and transparency. It was fairly easy in those days when an overhead projector was a common tool used by all teachers. No materials had to be developed, no handouts, and no other equipment was needed.

I had never taught. Apprehensive. I had not been around kids that age for years; and I was a bit afraid of being intimidated by laughing kids who would embarrass me in front of two classes with good looking teachers about my age. The third grade teacher began the class and introduced me. She moved to the back.

Flipping on the overhead projector I began making a rabbit with my hands projected onto the whiteboard. I asked, "Is this a shadow or are you seeing a nontransparent object?" A few hands went up. Kids that age are very willing to take risks—to guess both answers. It is a part of weaning, to break out on their own. After explaining the differences, I scribbled on a transparency and repeated the same question. A coin was laid on the transparency. What was transparent; what was not? It was a simple class to teach. Only one question was asked each time I put my hand on top of the projector, in front of it, placed the transparency on the projector, in front of it and my hand blocking it. I moved to the window and did the same thing.

No laughs. Whew! Made it through that half-hour.

Next class was just down the hall about twenty minutes later. When I walked into the classroom there were three other young ladies, other teachers, already standing in back of the class. Like the first class, the teacher, an older lady (perhaps 35), began the class and introduced me. As I turned on the overhead projector, I realized the young teacher in my first class had recommended other teachers or assistants step in and watch my presentation of shadows and transparencies.

Just then I realized I had the attention of the class of fourth graders but also good-looking young teachers. Unfortunately, the flow of the second class did not go as well as with the third graders. Maybe it was because the kids were a year older. More likely, it was because I never had that many young ladies watch me for a half hour.

It was all part of growing into a seasoned adult–a learning experience for me, but the teaching block of classes I found quite boring compared to economics classes.

Junior and senior years of my high school were filled, no hour break for study hall, as vocational agriculture was then my priority. Unfortunately, I did not take algebra II, trigonometry, chemistry, or physics in high school making college chemistry, physics, statistics, and quantitative economics much harder for me than those that had taken extra math and chemistry in high school. I realized high school classes at that time were teaching usable math.

In case you are wondering, I never got back to that grade school; never saw those teachers again; but I did continue to look for a couple of them while I was getting groceries or downtown having a beer. Like the 1930s' vintage radio program "The Shadow Knows"[6] had a relationship developed, would I be a retired teacher? If so, would I be as harsh on them in my books?

Actual training and functions expected of each teacher must have been more detailed in later teaching blocks. I do know that many teach what they do not know, do not care to know, or are afraid to know. In order to cover mandatory classes, school superintendents often assign teachers to instruct classes they dislike or are ill-prepared to teach.

---

[6] "The Shadow" radio drama series was introduced in 1937 based on earlier magazine, comic strip, and radio programs about "The Shadow." The mysterious actor's (Frank Readick Jr.) whisking voice closed each program with "The weed of crime bears bitter fruit. Crime does not pay. The Shadow knows!"

Teaching is a job often in a location where the spouse must live. Some years, half my classes were taught by men; that seemed to switch to mainly female teaches in subsequent years.

Growing up in the 1960s we heard that women in the United States were a minority and that they were discriminated against even after given the right to vote. Men dominated everything.

Wrong!

Nineteen was a popular number for women. The 19th Amendment to the U.S. Constitution passed an all-male Congress in June of 1919 and was approved by enough voting men in the states to quickly become ratified by August of 1920. What was never taught was that more women in rural America had graduated high school than men from 1900 to 1920.

The midwest and western United States was mostly an open rural area back then. Farmers and ranchers would get their supplies in small towns, almost always connected to a railroad. Those small towns, like my hometown of Ipswich, South Dakota, started schools. Priority was elementary schooling. Then, it was known as "primary" school followed by high school known as "secondary" school.

My grandfather only went through the eighth grade graduating from it in 1904. There was a high school, but Ipswich never had a high school graduate before Ava Hodson in 1906. One graduate that year was multiplied to four from Ipswich High School in 1907: Mabel Bruce, Fannie Jaquith, Florence McEachran, and Genevieve Tate. Nineteen-hundred eight, (the year my grandfather could have graduated high school) had four more young ladies. Nineteen-hundred nine had one lady graduating, Harriet Chubbuck, followed by three ladies in 1910. In 1911 there were six high school graduates, Herbert Crissman and five young ladies. Yes, five years after the first young lady graduated from Ipswich did the first young man have a chance to graduate.

Nineteen-hundred twelve had eight ladies and two young men graduate from Ipswich; 1913: six ladies; and in 1914 three young ladies graduated. War affects schooling. Military recruitment for "The World War" saw a spike in boys staying in school: in 1915 five men and two ladies graduated Ipswich followed by 1916 with nine ladies and one man. The rest were either farming or at war.

Demand for food has always forced children to be weaned earlier and work at a younger age.

Graduation of women followed the World War I draft registration of June 5, 1917. Men were notified of their obligation to serve. My grandfather was a prime recruit as were some of his brothers. He turned twenty-six three weeks after the first registration that included all men between the ages of twenty-one and thirty-one. Being the oldest boy of the family he had to stay home and farm. Likewise, during World War II (1939–1945) my father, as a boy of ten to sixteen, helped supply wheat and flour for Europe.

My mother should have graduated in 1949. She missed one year of high school to stay home and help her father harvest crops, feed chickens, and milk cows because all able-bodied men were fighting the war.

School attendance used to be effected by food and economics. My Aunt Mildred, my grandfather's youngest sister, planned on graduating Ipswich High School in 1932 but because of the depression she had to stay out a year and graduated in 1933. My aunt was the first Wietgrefe to ever graduate high school. None of her older brothers had that opportunity between 1908 and 1930.

In 1917, three young ladies and two men graduated from Ipswich. The trend of having more young ladies graduate than men followed into the 1920s. Graduates followed: 1918: seven ladies, no men; 1919: eight ladies, six men; in 1920, two years after the end of World War I, Ipswich High School graduated an equal number: six young ladies and six young men.

It may be a surprise to many, but female college enrollment currently far exceeds that of males. According to the U.S. Department of Education: "Females are expected to account for the majority of college students: about 11.5 million females will attend in fall of 2015, compared with 8.7 million males."[7]

How many of you were taught in school that it was more important before 1920 for girls to go through high school than boys? How many

---

[7] "Back to School Statistics," Fast Facts, National Center for Education Statistics, Institute of Education Sciences, http://nces.ed.gov/fastfacts/display.asp?id=372 (Sourced January 28, 2016)

were taught girls got to stay in school while boys were sent off to work or war? How many are taught that more girls attend college than boys? Why isn't that taught now?

Had I only known what I was taught in grade school, high school, and college social studies, I would think that women had no role in American society until the 19th Amendment gave women the right to vote in time for the November 1920 national election. Republican Warren G. Harding beat Democrat James M. Cox. Harding was chosen by all states north of the Mason-Dixon Line and all states west of the Mississippi River except three southern states: Arkansas, Louisiana, and Texas. Harding also carried the state of Tennessee thanks to men giving women the right to vote for the first time only three months earlier.

I am certainly not against educating girls. I do not know anyone that wants women's education hampered. With the school system as it developed, I must ask, are we giving females the best education? After a century of giving girls more education than boys, it seems to me, our school system has stymied female entrance into the world rather than supported it.

There is much to living that is not taught in school. Work follows weaning. Opportunities exist to get a job or create one—mowing lawns, babysitting, washing cars, shoveling snow, pulling weeds are historic entry-level jobs for unemployed teenagers. For the money, they have to be better than doing it yourself, or the next person. Now they can be paid by us seniors to teach computer, operate a smartphone, and other electronic equipment operations.

There are expectations after weaning. Independence is part of the equation.

To get a job, a person must make himself or herself known and promote their skills. Just showing up for a job does not accomplish the task. A hatchling lays in the nest and expects to be fed. Once booted from the nest, weaned, birds are expected to get their own food. Most birds and people are rewarded for extra effort. Without it, self-satisfaction is worth more than pay. It is much better to get noticed for doing something extra than laying back and expecting to learn by osmosis or replaced by artificial memory.

Getting noticed reminds me of a ranch story. The rancher had one big older bull in a pasture of about seventy cows. He searched for more breeders and found a young bull and one of medium age with experience, which he delivered to the pasture. Upon opening the cattle trailer the two new bulls jumped out with excitement at all the cows wanting service. After taking a few steps both the new bulls noticed the monstrous older bull with huge horns standing by the cowherd. Immediately, the youngest bull started digging his little horns into the sod, grass flying, and pawed the dirt with his front hooves. The medium bull says to the younger one, "Are you crazy! You will never win against the horns of that behemoth." The youngest bull responded, "When I was weaned, my mother told me life has challenges. I want to make sure he knows I'm a bull."

Getting proper notice is one of the biggest challenges of getting employed. It is a learning experience, not a school experience. Two seldom get hired for the job of one. Therefore, the person hired must be at least slightly better than the second choice, which brings me to another story.

Two hikers were out in the woods continually looking for evidence of bear. After about an hour, both smelled trouble. One hiker immediately dropped his backpack and quickly tightens his shoelaces. The other hiker said, "You can't out-run a bear." "You are right," was the response. "I only need to outrun you."

It is natural to have apprehension searching for a job, especially the first one. We are in a different era now than the ancients—most were employed after weaning at a young age in the profession of their parents. Weaning sets expectations and is often learned from older, more experienced workers which reminds me of another cattle story.

An old bull and a young bull are released into a pasture overlooking a herd of cows. The young bull says to the older one: "I'll race you to that young heifer." The older bull says, "No. I'll walk and get the whole herd."

Job fit, getting noticed, picking the right battles, and learning are all part of having successful employment. It is better to have earlier experiences, thereby minimizing financial, social, and employment risks. Rather than getting work experience, students are now caught between job prospects and frustration with school. In the school system we have today, when does frustration develop?

When do teens drop out of high school?

Fifteen- to seventeen-year-olds made up 60.1 percent of the high school students in a 2012 study,[8] and accounted for 35.6 percent of the dropouts. Eighteen-year-olds made up about 27 percent of those in grades 10–12 and had a dropout rate of 25 percent. On the older end of the scale, 13 percent of all U.S. high school students (grades 10–12) are age nineteen to twenty-four and account for 39.4 percent of the total high school dropouts.

School system's frustration gap begins by age fifteen and increases thereafter. Dropouts are a warning system. They are an untapped resource. Rather than shun them, their minds have to be tapped for their innovativeness, willingness to take on risk, and acceptance of responsibility without a school system crutch. If parents let them live in the basement rather than be productive young adults, parents must share blame for vagrancy.

Traditional tutoring and online programs in a subject are designed to increase school grades or bring a student up to speed with the rest of a class. Why don't they prepare the student for life?

If roughly 20 percent of high school students drop out before graduation, why aren't 20 percent of the tutoring and online programs preparing former students to make a productive living?

Good teachers with entrepreneurial skills could develop programs to suit the dropout population.

On a tour of Chiapas, Mexico, we hired a guide to take us through a Mayan archeological site. Her parents were biology teachers in Mexico City. We asked if they were still teaching. "No," she said. "They used to be high school teachers, now they just tutor." Her parents took advantage of their teaching profession by preparing for retirement as tutors in the subject they enjoyed. All teachers have the same opportunity.

Many battles in the next couple of decades will pit a half-century old school system against world history. Two completely different learning systems will battle: the school monopoly's wired world versus the ancient and twenty-first century wireless world. One fears technology,

---

[8] "Trends in High School Dropout and Completion Rates in the United States: 1972–2012," "Table 1. Event Dropout rates . . . grades 10–12, October 2012," published June 2015, by National Center for Education Statistics, Institute of Education Sciences; U.S. Department of Education, p. 27, http://nces.ed.gov/pubs2015/2015015.pdf, (Source January 23, 2016)

the other accepts it. History proves technology wins. Will we have enough minds developed to functionally use it for learning?

Late 1880s wireless transmissions created opportunities for a twenty-first-century wireless learning system. Obstacles exist. We have entered another world movement—a school weaning process.

Bye school bus route. Bye school building. Bye, bye teacher standing in front of the classroom!

The school system is like a telegraph wire in a wireless world.

Currently, a wired versus wireless campaign is going on with many battles yet to be fought between the old-school world and wireless world, class and outclassed, children's imagination and school regulation, mental memory and artificial electronic memory, team sport and individualism, family time and school time, school work and creativity, and homework and work at home. Wireless will win.

It is an exciting time for parents and parents-to-be. Opportunities exist for their children like never before. Independent thinkers have always existed. They are the ones who were given responsibility as toddlers, chores as youth, respected elders, worked as teenagers, learned outside the classroom, had novel ideas, and teams-be-damned implemented them.

Parents' inability to wean tracks with countries that implemented monopolistic, mandatory, elementary and secondary school systems. Teachers, professors, and school systems that fear technology have built sideline conflicts between weaned and dependent, responsible and irresponsible, exercise and watching, street guards and guarded schools, prescriptions and drugs, religious and agnostics, educated elite and workers, school debt and debt free, office time and home office, agitators and implementers, organic and technology, beggars and feeders, obesity and hungry, local and interstate commerce, country of origin and international trade, immigrants and refugees, liberal and libertarian, nationalism and globalism, national identity and one world order.

When responsibility is someone else's venue, conflict is ripe.

Weaning must occur. Technology can be adopted or fought. Laggards, like the unweaned, are adopters, it just takes them longer than most.

The path ahead has been developed, but the journey can be one of headache or adventure. Happy is the one who arrives content.

18

School-age Migration

Riddle: Name what has an annual uniform rotation that cannot be measured by pi, but is likely the last place pi is used.

Does formal schooling repress innovation? Are today's schools designed to maximize learning?

If they are, can you, your parents, uncle, aunt, or adult friend take an hour math class five days per week? Can any of you take Spanish or another foreign language class offered by your local high school? Does your local public school system offer classes essential to the major business(es) in your area? If so, can any adult attend?

Although U.S. state laws require mandatory education, local school boards have the liberty to deny certain students in their district from taking classes. Adults are often restricted from taking secondary classes. On the other hand, those parents that choose to home-school their children are often penalized and denied use of public facilities and instructors.

Our friend's grandchildren are young skilled musicians. Because the parents chose to home-school their children, they are banned from taking music classes and chorus, nor are they allowed to participate in their local school's band.

In our home state, most school budgets are funded locally by property taxes. Parents, whether they rent or own their own home, pay indirect or direct property taxes. Parents of the home-schooled children mentioned above own their own home and annually pay property taxes. Their children's education is mandatory by state law, yet their children are banned from public school music classes.

High school classes are not available for the local community, major businesses, or home-schooled children. These examples provide adequate proof public schools are protecting teachers' and administration jobs, not trying to provide the best education for their community.

School systems object to public and private money being spent on education if it does not go through the school budget. Why? An educated public is not the goal of the public-school system; instead, it is to increase budgets and staff of schools.

Learning has many facets. To be successful, sustained focus is needed. Focus on a topic. Dream. Let the mind wonder. Refocus. Pursue.

Teachers may reprimand for such absentmindedness. Schools have imprisoned minds. Country and state laws require minimum sentencing—it is called compulsory education.

Sixteen U.S. states and the Virgin Islands have a minimum dropout age of sixteen; eleven states it is seventeen; and the other twenty-three states, U.S. Samoa, Puerto Rico, and in Washington, DC, the minimum compulsory age to quit school is eighteen. Fortunately, states with compulsory education above age sixteen allow for parental consent to have the teen quit school. Most, but not all, states allow the student to quit if he or she has completed all academic requirements before their minimum compulsory age.

Canadian Provinces set the minimum school-leaving age at sixteen except Manitoba, New Brunswick, and Ontario, which have set it at eighteen.

It stands to reason that if credits for the final two years of high school (junior and senior year in the U.S.) were offered to fifteen- and sixteen-year-olds, many would graduate high school sooner.

Second, if students age fifteen through high school graduation were co-enrolled in high school and college (e.g., community college or technical school), they would be more motivated to successfully complete high school, more likely to successfully complete post-secondary training sooner, and dual-enrolled students would be more likely to aggressively develop their career.

Third, businesses are seeking educated, aggressive, competent young workers and welcome their ideas and aptitude. If not actively employed early, by the age of fifteen to twenty that passion is often dulled.

Why do most high schools not offer morning classes with free afternoons for those enrolled in technical school or college classes? Likely, it has more to do with maintaining the high school's business monopoly and unions' dues-paying teachers than it does providing students advanced educational opportunities.

Since the 1950s, some high schools have offered, and an increasing number of colleges/universities have accepted, Advanced Placement (AP) tests as replacement for entry-level college courses. Most common U.S. AP subjects are English literature and composition, history, calculus/statistics, psychology, and biology with the lowest participation in foreign languages.

Increasing numbers of high school graduates with AP (college) credits indicate the school system is wasting student time and they are underchallenged. It also indicates entry-level college/university classes are remedial for many post-secondary students who are educationally disciplined. Plus, it emphasizes my point of educational depreciation of college-age young adults.

The historic goal was to graduate college/university with a Bachelor of Science (or Arts) in four years. To increase sales, colleges/universities often do not offer enough space or classes for entry-level (required) courses and those needed to complete a major in four years. Hence, they are able to sell another school year or two while students are encouraged (some forced) to borrow more money to complete their degree and delay entry into a workforce needing their skills and ambition.

Worthwhile high school classes allow AP takers to replace college credits, reduce college costs, reduce parent and student loan debt, and make it more likely the student would get a degree in four years or less.

Competition among colleges has forced them to give credit for AP as more high schools offer the tests. High schools with a monopolistic business structure have limited cost in offering those tests providing budgetary justification for holding young adult students. Some colleges are reluctant to accept an unlimited amount of AP tests as they have fewer years and less opportunity to sell classes, books, dorm rooms, meals, stadium tickets, sports paraphernalia, and refreshments.

In the last two decades, less than half those entering college or university get their degree in four years. Universities argue that students are often not prepared.

In many areas of the United States, colleges and universities are running out of students. The South Dakota Board of Regents and other university boards have discussed whether out-of-state students should get state-funded reimbursement for enrolling in state-owned institutions.[1] Besides providing a headcount, foreign students seem to be higher-level students. (Obviously, foreign parents are not going to go through the expense of sending their dumb, incompetent children to foreign schools.)

Apparently, many domestic students do not have the background to get a four-year degree in four years. Entry-level classes are needed to bring the average student up to speed with university standards. If truly the case, why would a respected university admit those students? Perhaps "respect" has less to do with it than money.

The graying line between high school and college begs the question: When did countries begin requiring school attendance to a maximum age?

Ireland was one of the first countries to require compulsory attendance for children ages six to fourteen upon passage of the Ireland Education Act of 1892. England began setting school attendance in 1870 but has continually risen the age, for example to fifteen in 1944 and sixteen in 1972. School age migration is an indication of a country's failing faith in their children's abilities–cultural retrogression.

To ensure school terms feel like prison terms, some countries set an actual date of release. For example, England's and Wales's students must remain in school until the last Friday in June for those that turn sixteen between September and June, which means a few students can still actually complete their term at age fifteen. Most Australian states have set the minimum school age at seventeen with a couple at fifteen. New South Wales, for example, allows exemption for those under seventeen but requires working at least twenty-five hours per week.

---

[1] South Dakota Board of Regents meeting June 28–30, 2016, Madison, South Dakota.

While spending several months in Australia, we befriended a single mother who was raising her teenage son. Her limited resources were the reason her son was employed after school and on weekends in a local grocery store. Lack of financial resources seems to increase the likelihood of rearing responsible children.

If you want someone to become a skilled laborer, would you allow him or her to participate in a trade part-time at age fifteen, or require them to attend school until eighteen before participating? By age twenty, who would be more skilled? Of course, it would be those who had formal education, worked their trade the longest, and learned from others.

Developed societies do not expect most citizens to be common laborers, unless they are seeking unrealistic communism and socialism as tried in the former Soviet Union, China, and North Korea where the state owned the money and bureaucrats determined how best to dole it out. Free enterprise societies, by their nature, are designed to allow each individual freedom to hone a skill at any age.

Minimizing work is natural. A cat lies around until hungry, then hunts for mice, or in most homes today, heads to the cat food dish. Is a fifteen- or eighteen-year-old any different?

As a teenager, around six every morning and every night, I would sit down under the first milk cow on an eight-inch one-legged stool. I could squeeze tits and fill a pail faster than most. Efficient. More interesting to me was how the cats sprang to action. Those that were full from catching and eating mice before milking were dozing on the hay while others jumped at the chance to get a squirt of milk in their mouth. Some cats got their own food; others expected a free meal.

Going back to developing a skilled person: By age twenty, who would have mentally refined the process to improve efficiency of their selected trade, a fifteen- or twenty-two-year-old? Who would be more likely to sit back and expect a free meal, the young worker, the working student, or the one that never worked?

Teenagers sitting around consuming what others provided are a positive reinforced system of institutionalized laziness.

Allowing teenagers to participate in the workplace should increase their life skills, increase their efficiency, increase the labor pool, increase attentiveness in school, decrease unemployment, and piss off teacher unions. Hey, if changing a system upsets nobody, it is not worth changing.

That reminds me of another Aesop fable from 500 B.C. It goes something like this:

A teenage boy and his dad were going to market with their donkey. The first gentleman they meet starts laughing and asks: "You fools, what is a donkey for but to ride?" Promptly, the father allowed his son to ride as they progressed toward the village market.

As they passed a shade tree where field workers were taking a needed break, it was obvious the father and son were being ridiculed. One says, "Look how that father raised a lazy son. He rides while the father walks." Overhearing their conversation, the father asked the son to walk while he rode.

Soon they passed some women talking about how lazy the father was and allowed his poor son to follow along in donkey dust. Interpreting that comment, the father had the son join him on the donkey. As they approached the city on the sway-backed donkey, they realized people were mocking their cruelty to the donkey. How could they sell a donkey if it was overworked?

Father and son quickly dismounted and discussed a plan. Finding a pole and cord, they bound the donkey's legs and carried it between them with a pole on their shoulders. As they approached the market the crowd was laughing at the pair. Crossing a town bridge, the donkey broke twine to free a leg, and kicked the son causing the donkey to fall into the water below. With front legs tied, unable to swim the donkey drown.

As with all Aesop fables, there was a moral: In trying to please everyone, you please no one.

Likewise, the purpose of this book is not to please everyone, but to compare current with past cultural systems. The donkey owner's son learned a lot about people on that one trip into the village.

Schools force children to learn with others their age. Innovation is inhibited.

Sitting in school constipates the mind.

Children learn from older workers and look for efficiencies to improve the system, to decrease labor, and excitedly they look to develop new products. Like a mental laxative, older workers and public comment allows contemplation, reflection, socialization, and opinions different from those the same age.

Let me give you an example of an historic person that planned to attend a prestigious university. Instead he changed the world.

Wilbur and Orville Wright did not become the "The Fathers of Modern Aviation" after graduating from Yale—Wilbur's planned alma mater. One might say high school sports knocked some sense into him.

In his senior year of high school (1885–1886) during a hockey game a player's stick hit Wilbur (1867–1912) in the face badly injuring him. (That reminds me of a sports cliché: I went to a fight and a hockey match broke out.) A hockey stick changed the course of transportation history.

Wilbur quit school but apparently read extensively during his depressing convalescence. Three years after he was supposed to graduate from high school; Wilbur and his younger brother Orville (1871–1948) started a newspaper in 1889 when the brothers were eighteen and twenty-two. If their name was Wright, they had one of the homonymic skills in publishing a newspaper. Right?

Publishing a newspaper at that time required writing and mechanical skills. Like the bamboo and cork rubber band-driven model helicopter the Wright boys received from their father in 1878 (ages seven and eleven), the brothers could not keep their mind focused on their newspaper. Instead the bicycle craze of my grandfather's generation wowed them into opening their own bicycle shop in 1892.

Wilbur and Orville were not satisfied with the bicycles they were selling so they developed their own designs.

Their newspaper was an early indication they were cosmopolites (actively interested in the world outside of their local community). As bicycles stretched their mechanical intuition, the news of the glider crash and death of German aviator, Otto Lilienthal (1848–1896) envied throughout the world as the "glider king," renewed the Wright brothers' interest in Frenchman Alphonse Penaud's (1850–1880) model helicopter. That rubber band-driven toy helicopter provided Wilbur and Orville endless fascination eighteen years earlier.

Penaud's father was a French Naval admiral, but more interested in engineering as a teenager, Alphonse started drawing, building, and flying model planophores, ornithopter, and helicopters. Children were expected to follow their family's career path. A hip disease prevented Alphonse from getting into the navy.

On the other hand, Otto Lilienthal, born a merchant's son, followed a more educated path. Attending technical school after grammar school allowed young Otto to get a job and training with the Schwarzkopf Company becoming a design engineer. After attending the Royal Technical Academy in Berlin, he received several engineering patents, but became famous for his book *Birdflight as the Basis of Aviation*. Published in 1889, when he was forty-one, the book incited the craze of flying for the Wright brothers and other imaginations around the world.

If Wilbur Wright had gone on to Yale University to get a master's or PhD, it is certain his first day of powered flight would not have flown 852 feet in 59 seconds in Kitty Hawk, North Carolina, December 17, 1903.

The Wright brothers' flights in North Carolina did not excite Americans. The press hardly found their flying progress newsworthy. Bishop Milton Wright, the famous brothers' father, a senior leader in the Church of the United Brethren in Christ, likely warned their sons what Jesus said: "Assuredly, I say to you, no prophet is accepted in his own country (Luke 4:24)."[2]

The Apostle Luke recorded that message one thousand nine hundred years before man's first powered flight. Nobody knew where that flight would take us. If one only accepts what is acceptable in their own hometown the world loses much potential knowledge. Scheduling children to attend mandatory school locally for thirteen of their formative years is counterproductive. Fortunately, free-access Internet now provides a learning resource.

The Wrights' hometown newspaper, the *Dayton Journal* (Ohio), published nothing initially and was not interested in the Wright brothers' first powered flight even though their father personally delivered a telegram with the news.

About five hundred years ago, French philosopher, Michel Eyquem de Montaigne (1533–1592), said: "It is good to rub, and polish our brain against that of others."

Too many people fear what their neighbors or family might think if they venture off on a tangent. Mr. Eyquem de Montaigne also provides

---

[2] Luke 4:24, NKJV, p. 1465

a rebuff to them: "My life has been full of terrible misfortunes most of which never happened."

Disgusted from a lack of American interest, Wilbur Wright boarded a ship (not airplane) to France in 1908 and wowed French officials, royalty and journalists by giving them rides and selling their simple airplanes. With success in his mind and pocket, Wilbur returned to the United States in 1909. With his brother, Orville, they became wealthy businessmen selling airplanes before Wilbur's untimely death by typhoid fever May 30, 1912–less than nine years after his initial flight.

Wisdom and a free mind to explore passed on by a father to son, generation by generation, is not something a lifetime of school can spawn.

My grandfather, Walter Wietgrefe Sr. (1891–1976), was a horseman. Stupid mechanical things like bicycles were dangerous and required replacement parts, not just feed and water like a horse. Replacing horseshoes was not considered a mechanical endeavor. Though my grandfather drove a car and tractor, he never changed the oil; that task fell to someone more mechanically inclined, usually my father or the equipment dealer in town.

Interests vary.

My grandfather had an interest in horses, and farming with them. That did not mean he was somehow stupid when he completed school (8th grade) in 1904. In the 1940s when he bought a threshing machine, he was behind the times; mechanical harvesting and threshing, called "combining," had replaced the labor-intensive thresh machine. It should be no surprise that my grandfather never flew and very likely never rode a bicycle.

Thirty-six-year-old Wilbur Wright spending his money messing with the impossible, a flying machine, was considered a stupid venture by nearly everyone in 1903. Only sixteen years later, several transatlantic "aeroplane" flights had flown from America to Europe including carrying mail.

At 10:56 p.m. Eastern Daylight Time July 21, 1969, an American Neil Armstrong, climbed down the famous Lunar Module, Eagle. As his left space boot touched the moon's surface, astronaut Armstrong said what Wilbur Wright could have said a short sixty-six years earlier: "That's one small step for a man, one giant leap for mankind."

For thousands of years people flew. That was not the hard part—it's landing alive. By the time I was in school, flying was no big deal. Armstrong's four words, "The Eagle has landed," to me (a sixteen-year-old kid) was far more amazing than an eagle known for strong flight.

Thankfully, the world has had people overlook stupid ideas, use and avoid standard education, and innovate. Five hundred years ago Italian painter, sculptor, scientist, and inventor Leonardo da Vinci said: "Once you have tasted flight, you will forever walk the earth with your eyes turned skyward, for there you have been, and there you will always long to return."

Work for a teenager should be considered a valuable opportunity, not a task or school assignment.

Parents, consider flight from a practical standpoint. If it were not for birds, many grandparents would be shivering from October until April. Birds fly south in the winter and trained us how to do it without spending twenty years in school learning how. Without learning how to fly as juveniles, birds would thirst, starve, and freeze. Why should our children be out of school before they learn to feed themselves?

Individuals developed ideas. Individuals dreamed the impossible. Individuals feared change—others changed.

All individuals are creative, some more than others. Forcing individuals, year-after-year, into a standardized school system removes individuality. Wilbur Wright liked flying; the senior Walter Wietgrefe did not. Is one better than the other? No. Each used their incomplete school skills differently.

Compared to today, the fundamental difference in the Wilbur and Orville Wright and Walter Wietgrefe Sr. generation was that they relied on memory, used the schooling they had, developed ideas, acted upon them, and took responsibility for the results. Things were done in earnest, with speed.

Where is the urgency today when adults who have never worked are still attending university in their mid-twenties?

19

Dog Trick

Riddle: Where are all going in the same direction, but all follow a different path?

Last year I was standing at an airport gate waiting to board with every other passenger on that flight. The gate attendant made the preliminary boarding announcement: "This is the preboarding announcement for flight —. Those passengers with small children and any passengers requiring special assistance please come forward to begin boarding."

A lady with a dog was the first in line. The dog appeared well trained and the woman had no apparent health issues. Why then was the dog, likely a "service dog," allowed to board before paying passengers?

A similar incident happened at another airport. While waiting in line for initial identification and boarding pass screening, a woman with a dog walked around the line of ten to twelve people. The Transportation Security Administration (TSA) agent looked at her information and the woman (it would be wrong to address her as a lady) walked ahead of the group and cleared security before the rest of us. Sure enough, as I was walking toward my gate, the woman and her dog were waiting for their flight at another gate. Why then was a dog, likely a "service dog," allowed to bypass the security line before paying customers?

In both cases, if the women would not have had their dogs they would have waited in line at security and boarding, just like other normal passengers. Were these women so abnormal that they deserved special treatment? If so, are they potentially putting the plane and passengers

237

in danger? I saw no apparent physical or mental issues. Therefore, I questioned whether the women were receiving special treatment or their dogs.

When did it become an airline policy for animals to take priority over people? About a month later I realized it was not the dog getting special treatment. The two women figured out how to get special treatment using their pet. I am sure thousands more will learn, or are already using, their dog trick.

Current airline policy is to charge full fare for children over age two. Should dogs be charged full fare if they are over two? If not, then it must be airline policy that dogs take precedence over children. Signaling a true change in culture, a child's body and soul is replaced by a dog' body without soul. It manifests into a physical versus spiritual debate.

To many, in today's culture people and animals are the same. Do you remember the most important "Commandment" in George Orwell's 1945 book, *Animal Farm*? It is relevant today: "All animals are equal."[1]

Assume the child and dog are both under age two. Consider for a moment servicing their physical needs. What if the infant's diaper had to be changed? No problem. Airlines provide a diaper changing table. What if a dog has an urgent call of nature on a plane? Plane toilets are barely big enough for a person. I cannot imagine trying to relieve a pet with toilet floor space hardly big enough to turn around. Then again, since many people treat their dogs as their children, is the airline diaper changing table used by dogs? Likely.

If dogs can ride in the passenger compartment of commercial airplanes, why can't other animals? In Orwell's book, pigs rule. After some flights, it appears some people are more comfortable in a pigsty.

A woman, of preretirement age, from Florida had flown to Mexico, she told us, to live more economically. "I cannot afford to live in my house in Florida, so I rent it out and figure I can afford to live down here (Mexico)." Obviously, she planned not to work. She told us her dog accompanied her on the plane. The big (50–60 pound) dog was likely half the weight of the woman. A Florida doctor, she also told us, approved her pet, I'll call "Trigger," as a "service" dog. I am not sure what service, in particular, Trigger was providing but somehow she was approved for it. If true, there was no way Trigger would have fit under an airline seat

---

[1] Orwell, George, *Animal Farm*, 1945, Secker and Warburg, p. 21.

and certainly his kennel would not have fit either. I had pity for the passengers that had to sit in front, back, and beside Trigger and the "fully serviced" woman.

People learn quickly how to take advantage of a situation. Increasingly, it is a cultural trend. Abusers ruin care for those that sincerely need it. Likely, Trigger's owner took advantage of her classmates and others through life. It happens when parents push care of their young children off to someone else, then blame someone else when their child is disobedient to authorities.

Although we later saw the woman at a fruteria (vegetable store), coffee shop, and restaurant, she never had Trigger. While visiting a neighbor of Trigger's owner, we realized the "service" her dog provided was protecting her apartment. Running loose in the patio area, Trigger barked constantly at the owner's little dog, luckily protected by a wall. The woman would not stop Trigger from the constant, loud, irritating bark, bark, bark. Trigger's owner was irritated that the property owner's dog was disturbing Trigger.

Rather than paying a higher monthly rent, the woman agreed verbally to commit to a year's rent at a discounted rate. She left town with Trigger unexpectedly after about a month. Mexicans are very trustworthy, and likely her landlord never required a deposit, but hopefully he was paid at least one month's rent . . . and enjoyed the pleasure of his dog without a constantly barking Trigger.

Trigger's owner found a way to have her dog fly in the passenger cabin rather than in the specially designed climate controlled and pressurized lower compartment airlines have for transporting pets.

Was Trigger's owner emotionally unstable? Perhaps. She was scamming the airline, her landlord, and had to ignore the stares of fellow passengers. That can be emotionally draining. What if her dog started barking on the plane? Could she even control the monster that was stronger than her?

I do not want an emotionally unstable person pulling Trigger on any flight I'm taking.

Was Trigger's owner any different from many pet lovers? It is obvious; many dog owners never discipline their animals. Trigger was not.

Watch dogs and owners walking in a park or down a sidewalk. Many dogs, if leashed, stretch it, and the owner's arm, to maximize freedom. Many run untethered even where signs specifically state "Leash Required." Untrained dogs are no different from untrained children. Someone who lets their dog have free reign, likely never disciplined their children either. Is that irresponsibility, laziness, or incompetence? It certainly is not good parenting or good dog training to let either run uncontrolled.

The next time you see a dog dragging its owner down the sidewalk, just imagine how their children were raised. Continue wondering ... do their grown children respect authority? Are they the ones imbibing illicit drugs just because they can? Laws and authority be damned. Nobody is going to tell them what is right or wrong. Why should they obey laws and public authority if the parents never disciplined them?

I pity the teachers that have to put up with children who have lived without discipline, just like I pity the people, especially with pet allergies, that had to fly with Trigger or other animals in adjoining seats.

Is someone ready for employment that has never been disciplined? All entry-level jobs are positions subordinate to someone. Are they ready for subordination? No. Who would want to hire such a good-for-nothing louse?

From my mother's family library, a grade school textbook I have mentioned before, *Sheldons' Modern School Fourth Reader*, first published in 1882, contained many short stories. Some were historical; many seemed to be practical support for parents and teachers preparing students for future employment and to be upstanding citizens. Of the 116 reading lessons, the more practical stories were more apparent in the beginning of the Reader. Schools used to allow reading and enforcement of moral principles. Even if children only progressed partway through the book, they likely would have read Lesson III, "Letters of Recommendation."[2]

---

[2] "Letters of Recommendation," Lesson III, Sheldons' Modern School Fourth Reader, Sheldon & Company, 1882 revised in 1885, p. 28, no copyright found.

Letters of Recommendation

1. A gentleman once advertised for a boy to assist him in his office, and nearly fifty applied for the place. Out of the whole number he, in a short time, chose one, and sent all the others away.

2. "I should like to know," said a friend, "on what ground you chose that boy. He had not a single recommendation with him."

   "You are mistaken," said the gentleman; "he had a great number:

3. "He wiped his feet when he came in, and closed the door after him; showing that he was orderly and tidy.

   "He gave up his seat instantly to that lame old man; showing that he was kind and thoughtful.

   "He took off his cap when he came in, and answered my questions promptly and respectfully; showing that he was polite.

4. "He lifted up the book which I had purposely laid on the floor, and placed it on the table, while all the others stepped over it, or shoved it aside; showing that he was careful.

   "And he waited quietly for his turn, instead of pushing the others aside; showing that he was modest.

5. "When I talked with him, I noticed that his clothes were carefully brushed, his hair in nice order, and his teeth as white as milk. When he wrote his name, I observed that his finger-nails were clean, instead of being tipped with jet, like the handsome little fellow in the blue jacket.

6. "Don't you call these things letters of recommendation? I do; and what I can tell about a boy by using my eyes for ten minutes is worth more than all the fine letters he can bring me."

Today, applications are filed online using computerized forms. Many applications likely are filed while the unemployed sit in their pajamas with bedhead hair and unbrushed teeth. The grade school reading lesson above was published well over a century ago. It could have been written for a Roman administrator two thousand years ago. The principles were the same. What we are gaining today with Internet efficiency, we are losing at least as much in personal observation before hiring someone. Hence, video conferencing attempts to bring personal connection compared to a phone exchange. Dress, manners, and background provide character clues.

How long does the average college graduate work in his or her first job? Does a resume establish job fitness, or is it just an employment ticket? For efficient operations, job fit is important.

However, it is important to get experience in drudgery. More is learned on what not to do than what to do. After a time, change, or change jobs are the best two options. Most managers do not have the guts to tell a subordinate their job is not right for them. Instead the manager or employee often moves on so he or she does not have to correct an inappropriate job fit.

Job fit often is like personal relationships. Alfred Lord Tennyson (1809–1892) in his 1849 poem "In Memoriam A.H.H."[3] wrote:

> I hold it true, whate'er befall;
> I feel it, when I sorrow most;
> 'Tis better to have loved and lost
> Than never to have loved at all.

Dogs used to provide support to families. They hunted, caught pests, were trained to protect property, and herded cattle. Children coddled them and ran them near and far. Now children can lay around the house like overfed dogs—neither with responsibilities.

Lines from the same Tennyson poem are seldom quoted but have relevance today for child and pet.

> The linnet (bird) born within a cage,
> That never knew the summer woods . . .
> To whom a conscience never wakes . . .
> But stagnates in the weeds of sloth. . . .

Thus, a handshake is no longer a mutual contract, with dog or adult. A loan is no longer secured by earnestly looking into the banker's eyes. Hiring is illegal without records and employees use worktime for social media.

Consider where children get most of their training. Basic trust has been removed and replaced digitally with artificial memory. What will

---

[3] Tennyson, Alfred Lord, "In Memoriam: A.H.H. Obiit MDCCCXXXIII: 27": poem written upon the death of his friend Arthur Henry Hallam.

restore both: The current school system? No. That is where trust and memory wane.

Dog owners cannot take a wild dog into a public dog park and expect other owners to put up with their untrained pest. Likewise, parents must do their part well before a child goes to school. Why should an unruly, wayward child be allowed attendance at a public institution if not trained with obedience needed for public exposure?

Some families raise children with responsibility and discipline. Should deviants get more educational time and attention from the school system? Both provide examples for others to learn or misbehave. Both types of children are expected, but in times past those out of line were few. School attendance is for learning while responsibility and discipline used to be prerequisites.

Unfortunately, in many cases parents have become the parenthesis (set apart) from rearing a child upon their reaching the ever-younger school age. Teachers, in many cases, are relegated to guardian of the kennel door.

20

Radar

Riddle: *What uses electricity, has a scanning system, and results are predictable without using radar?*

A blank, white 8 1/2 × 11-inch sheet of paper, pencils, rubber cement, compass, and several scissors lay on the large raised 5-foot × 12-foot table scattered with topographic map clippings. Multicolor, large-scale 1:25,000, medium scale 1:50,000 or 1:100,000, and a few small-scale trimmings of a 1:200,000 were scattered about. A couple of 4-inch × 8-inch pilot guides, completed, were stacked neatly at one end. Pilots would need the others tomorrow. Five work stools supported our hunched backs. One door. Locked. Always locked. A shadow passed the thick-plated opaque window. When someone strolled the hall outside, there was movement but no body—usually they were lost. Others knocked for permission to enter.

Nobody could see in the second floor windows of the smallest office on base although we could see fighter planes on the tarmac below. Intelligence is always confined to small spaces. Secret and Top Secret grey and olive green five-drawer legal-width filing cabinets protected the hall wall and map cases were against the back wall. Talk between the six of us was seldom quiet, entertaining when not serious. Everyone had separate jobs; one project: ensure maps were accurate, orderly, and targets clearly defined.

Four years of wearing headsets on two continents finding, listening to, and copying Top Secret messages in a large concrete complex with hundreds of receivers, printers, and double-reel tapes constantly humming 24/7/365 was physically and socially isolating. Thereafter, the four years I spent as an Air Crew Intelligence specialist with the Air National Guard was income and respite while in college and beginning my first career.

I pulled the white sheet closer; grabbed the compass and drew a perfect circle then a horizontal line. Only one place can a circle be divided in half by a horizontal line. That line has to pass through the compass dot in the center. Depending on the fighter plane's elevation, descent or accent angle, the radar screen may have more ground clutter or uncluttered sky. My job that day was to predict radar reflectivity with different shades and thicknesses of #2 pencil by unscrambling high-altitude aerial photography and matching it with topography viewed at 1000 feet five miles from the target.

Briefing and debriefing pilots was much easier when maps and radar screens were predicted accurately. It may seem archaic given today's technology, but in the 1970s it was a highly specialized field of aircrew intelligence. To my knowledge, I was the only person in South Dakota, and very few in the country, ever trained to accurately predict a radar image suspended one moment in time at one elevation for an airplane flying several hundred miles per hour.

Afternoon classes January through April 1977 offered specialized training for the various service branches and CIA operatives at an undisclosed base in Colorado. The paid military class allowed this poor college student to take one morning class at the University of Denver and still receive a discounted GI Bill to help cover my trailer house lot rent and utilities in Brookings, South Dakota, where I returned for summer school at South Dakota State University and eventually graduated the following year.

For nearly eight years the Air Force and Air National Guard kept my bank account balanced and mind focused on utilizing available intelligence. It is interesting what one can predict given tools and training.

A bridge is a highlighted line against a backdrop of water. Vehicles are dots; trucks are bigger dots on a dark straight wide line often flanked by faint vertical power poles and fainter horizontal power lines. At all cost, towers, arrow straight, narrow but bright, must be avoided at lower elevations. Shadows predict structure and height based on plane elevation and time of day. Like will-o'-wisps, never count on seeing a tower's shadow.

The U.S. military intelligence services trained me in radar prediction. A faint line on a fighter plane's radar means nothing unless its context is related to surrounding marks. That faint line (bridge) means something if across a squiggly black mark (river) running across the radar screen. From ten miles, the long series of dots and dashes approaching the faint line are nothing ... unless the pilot interprets them as infantry tanks followed by a supply chain of tanker trucks approaching the divide of friendly and enemy territory.

Predict. What is better: A.) Destroy the river bridge in two minutes before the first tank crosses; or B.) Wait ten minutes until the tanks are across but before the tanker trucks and supply chain crosses the bridge?

Most politicians, to keep enemy from friendly territory, would say the bridge should be destroyed before the enemy crosses the border bridge. Whereas a trained military analyst would want proof of incursion, a target predictor would destroy the bridge after the tanks cross the bridge and before the crucial fuel supply crosses. Tanks are inefficient when not moving forward and worthless when they run out of fuel. Military strategists want to prove invasion and would rather have useless enemy tanks on their side of the line.

At some point the inefficient system will run out of fuel.

Stop Wietgrefe. "This is a nonfiction book. Why address predictions?"

Predictions are everyday reality to all of us.

A mother predicts her children will run out of milk and cereal tomorrow morning, so she picks them up at the grocery store today. Drivers step on their brakes before rear-ending the vehicle in front of them—a prediction that a collision will occur if brakes are not applied. New automation has taken that responsibility from drivers.

Automation and communications have replaced brick and mortar schools—most do not know it yet.

Learning is always multifunctional.

As mentioned earlier after studying agricultural business, I eventually settled on an additional degree in commercial economics. It took me years to realize the study of economics is radar prediction on the same sheet of paper but analyzed and presented differently.

Military training is not worth anything. So claim many. Wrong! Enforced responsibility of teenage adults is a reality jolt to many. Applied studiously, a few weeks or a few months of intense training provide a lifetime of practical applications. I did not plan to make a living drawing radar screens. Thank goodness! That would have been a very short career. Technology would have replaced me quickly.

It is fine to eat an organic heirloom tomato. Perhaps it gives a sense of smells past. It is a dot of reflectivity on radar that has long passed its usefulness. We flew by that era every year for the past century. Heirlooms have been crossed and re-crossed; pollinated; infected by genetically altering bugs, fungus, and viruses every year; then reseeded, transplanted, and harvested. It is not the tomato my grandpa ate as a child. That does not stop me from imagining it was from his garden.

There is nothing wrong with an heirloom—however, society cannot base its livelihood on it any more than it can live without electricity.

From the late 1800s to mid-1900s, less than a century, U.S. schools provided biased, yet broad, but practical literacy and numeracy into adulthood. When my great grandfather, Henry L. Wietgrefe (1861–1918), sent my grandfather to attend school for eight years, there was little comparison to today's school system. It was similar when my father attended school for almost nine and a half years. (His farm chores and deep snow piled upon the teenager, not allowing his bike to make the daily ten-mile round-trip to town school). My father made a living at fourteen. Unlike my parents, I was able to attend school, uninterrupted, for twelve years. Changes were beginning to occur in the school system.

It is hard to plot learning, yet easy to plot a life. Three generations are buried in the Ipswich Cemetery. The fourth is where my headstone sits. What will change as I pass?

As I entered "town school" in 1963, team sports began to trump learning. School size and more area per child were considered requirements for better learning. A practical extracurricular activity, debate, was cut in 1968, and all vocational agriculture classes in our farming community were eliminated in 1971—the same year that school size doubled. Implementable education was cut.

It is different now. Worse. In America, implementation of secondary education is not the goal—college is.

Lunch rooms are now spacious, hallways wide, entries expansive, and schools are now built, expanded, designed, and maintained to maximize use and attendance in the gymnasium with a basket hanging on each end. What do a couple of empty baskets do for a few hundred brains bursting to learn and explore?

Why are hundreds of thousands of local dollars spent on a football field? How are "educational" funds prioritized? Electronic scoreboards, aluminum bleachers, broadcast booth with oversized speakers, and suspended flood lamps that can be seen from space are considered standard high school facilities. The field and parking lots have regular weed control and are mowed continuously but the playing field is used less than twenty hours per year. Education is obviously not the highest priority.

Earlier I told a story of four preschool Mexican boys taking turns playing on a cobblestone street thumb-pushing a marble—one marble, a shared marble. Was it a game? Yes.

Was it a team? No.

Was there competition? Yes.

Every minute or two one of them would land the marble very close to the leaf on the rock below the tree that provided shade on a hot sunny day. Did they have rules? Yes.

Did they make the rules? Yes.

Were they organized? Yes.

Did they share resources? Yes.

Were they moving? Yes.

Were they learning? Yes.

Were they respectful? Yes.

Did they bother anybody? No.

Are school football, basketball, and volleyball as efficient at learning? No.

A couple months later, I was walking down a different cobblestone street in the same Mexican town. One house had a concrete sidewalk the length of a house elevated about six inches above the cobblestones.

A young girl, perhaps eight years old, sat on the sidewalk with bare feet rolling back-and-forth over a couple of well-rounded rocks. Two boys, one perhaps a brother, maybe age six, were on their hands and knees each with a marble.

Obviously, these boys were at least twice as rich as the four boys with one marble I had witnessed earlier. The girl, waiting her turn, watched the technique to see how each boy rolled his marble toward a one-inch hole left from a small stone that had popped from the worn concrete sidewalk. They appeared to be golfing by finger-flicking marbles.

Quiet. Never a word. The girl looked up once. I took several photos with my camera/phone. As I continued my walk, a housedress-clad young lady stepped out of the doorway of the house across the street. She had been watching the kids. Watching me. I walked on. She returned to her home as I passed an Internet café with six stations.

I did not need radar or economics to predict the marble players would grow up with independent minds, be respectful, make and follow rules, be creative, inventive, make a decent living, and provide for their families.

Will they become scientists, homemakers, construction workers, physicians, businesspeople, or discover a disease cure? Maybe. When they grow up they will not need a team. Multimillion-dollar schools and sports facilities would be an expensive distraction rather than a support system. It was easy to see that those children playing with a couple of marbles were independent and knew how to interact with others to develop new things.

It is easy to predict as forward-looking radar. That night the three marble players likely sat down at the dinner table with their sister and brother excitedly telling what they learned at the Internet café stations a few feet from home.

One day I was visiting with a Canadian who had been in the overhead door business for forty years. His son was in college majoring in mathematics and his daughter-in-law was seeking her degree in physics. One weekend, while trying to figure out pressure for a special-order door spring, the father, with no college experience, gave the information to the young couple. They punched buttons on their smartphone and computer until they came up with no answer. Later that weekend, the father asked the college-bound children to take his problem to their professors.

The following week the father, based on his experience, estimated the door spring needed to exert 350 pounds of pressure. If he was wrong, the expensive, special-order spring would not be functional, potentially dangerous, worthless, not usable elsewhere, and it would have to be reordered. His customer would be upset and demurrage accessed.

When the university students returned the following week, they both reported their professors claimed they did not have enough information and could not compute the spring pressure needed.

Why is it that business decisions have deadlines, face repercussions, and taxed to support education, but schools do not have to support business? Answer: All eat, are clothed and sheltered, but some have responsibilities whereas others do not. Students, teachers, and professors do not have to answer to parents or businesses, yet remain supported by the latter.

What has changed? A century ago, it was a privilege to teach; a career teacher was not necessary. Throughout history, it was hard to find competent teachers. It still is. . . .

Have you considered that many children do not have to work before they graduate from college? Very few have parental responsibilities. Young minds are no longer conditioned to answer practical problems. University professors seldom have business experience. Consequently, they can teach, but not understand it. Calculators and computers have replaced memory and ability to reason. Computers, now considered mandatory, are not a substitute for keyboard (type) training. Slow input slows output, communications, and concept development.

Education changed culture.

As the garage door designer learned, neither computers, calculators, smartphones, the school system, professors, nor children require practical knowledge to exist.

Culture involves change.

Some skills in my generation would have been impractical for both my grandfather and grandchildren. Generational accomplishments include the basics of respect, responsibility, morality, and etiquette. Reading and writing came later. Just because my grandfather never used a calculator or computer and used a map rather than GPS did not make him less learned than my grandchildren.

Because I learned to pop a clutch by watching my father does that mean my grandchildren should learn it? They may never learn to drive a stick-shift vehicle. Automatic transmissions are much less energy efficient, but my grandchildren grew up in a world where efficiency was not something taught in school. To them automatic was a better substitute. Resource wasteful, but less effort. In fact, they may think "pop a clutch" is an elderly medical condition.

Having never experienced a typewriter, if I had mentioned a "hunt and pecker" to my great grandmothers, before explanation, I probably would have been drug to the wash basin and had my mouth washed out with soap. "Pregnancy" to them was a dirty word—such women were "in the family way."

Function, even words, mean something different to each generation. "Home keys" to my grandfather would have opened our house doors, except we never locked them. Sixty-five years before him, "home keys" to Beethoven[1] would have been piano finger positioning. I was exposed for the first time to "home keys" in high school typing, whereas, my grandson's computer has only one "home key" and his college dorm room was opened with a swipe of a plastic card rather than a metal key.

Life is a journey of change. You can either be a pessimist or optimist.

If you are a pessimist, what are the results of those formally educated since the 1950s? In a technology-savvier world, schools into the mid-twenty-first century will continue to follow custom while struggling to remain relevant. They will resemble a Christmas tree in January—adorned, but out of date. Education is no longer local; it is national and developing internationally. Is that good?

When uniformity becomes standard, originality perishes.

Students have become inconvertible. Debt unmanageable. Checkbooks nonexistent. Minds become translucent. Memory dwindles. Snippets remain undeveloped. Gadgets will be expected to answer problems although minds are not conditioned to properly synthesize input or output.

When the highly educated rule, government must educate and train government employees (previously called government servants). Lack of understanding has built resistance to older systems.

Computer manufacturers quit making parts after five years. Machines costing more than several months' food become worthless. What was stored in computer memory has moved to artificial clouds as

---

[1] Ludwig van Beethoven (1770–1827) was a German classical pianist and composer.

a business income source. Clouds come and go. They are more fragile than businesses that support them.

Commercial clouds have replaced novels, textbooks, student notes, architectural drawings, engineered plans, chemical formulas, atomic research, diaries, photo albums, health records, and money as online relationships appear and disappear. As clouds dissipate from bankruptcy, power failure and viruses, personal, economic, and research systems are not abandoned–they simply no longer exist. Culture will vanish with clouds.

What preceded disappearing clouds? Consumerism. Overconsumption diminished reserves. Children will be aborted while a hyena is rescued from an environment long since destroyed. Human height and obesity will peak–an early sign of dwindling food supplies, as large bodies replace small minds.

Artificial intelligence, like artificial memory, decreases creativity by reducing mental capacity. Automation created leisure. Local, national, and world leisure will decrease innovation as more time will be spent relaxing, not inventing.

When a smartphone becomes a need, food, water, and shelter become scarce. Anticipation languishes. Apathy matures. Clouds perish. Disease and pestilence abound. Pandemics. Systems unrepairable. Civilizations populated from cloud-holding technology collapse. Horizon of a new Dark Age dawns as the world starves for resources depopulates.

There is hope.

If you are an optimist, how will subsequent generations develop? Instantaneous communications will replace transportation. Automation manufactures and processes. Goods move without man. Innovation? Unlimited. Travel? Virtual.

As the world works from home, as in ancient times, families multiply and eat together. Families are teams. Children play with others while receiving neighborhood education without a room. Information? Instantaneous. Bond-laden schools and office buildings convert to residential community laboratories, training, and recreation centers for all ages.

Businesses, large and small, become micro operations, strategic, local, family, and community affairs. Concepts develop. Employment is worldwide. International conflicts become commercial not military and are resolved with balanced trade. Cultures relish their system of modernism. Medical and other services will be remotely administered. Delivery efficacious.

If you are an optimist, you know clouds are temporary. Temporary things have never sustained the world. The sun will shine for posterity as artificial electronic memory clouds are backed by micro hardcopy.

Energy is stored (think E=MC^2).[2] Exercise will be for physical conditioning, not work. More energy is spent thinking. Stress subsides as home life replaces work life. Shelter? Communal (think condominiums).

We are in transition.

Retail stores are outdated (think online ordering). Oregon, to my knowledge, is the only remaining state in the United States where state politicians think drivers are too stupid to pump their own gasoline. Other states, especially in rural areas, have fuel pumps available unmanned 24/7/365.

Efficiency eventually prevails.

There is always a job available in fast food and retail. Right? No.

A grill fries a burger, or a microwave warms one—not a cook. Interstate highway drivers in the United States pull into a rest area, slip in a credit card, punch a button, and out pops a piping hot sandwich, fresh cup of coffee, or ice cream bar. Banks do not need tellers—ATMs collect and give money. Within three decades, video retailers started and became extinct. Big box retailers have automated check-out counters. A clerk is not needed to check, count, and collect.

Likewise, fast food is now coming from kiosks that dispense automatically. To serve farmers day and night, more than a decade ago I developed an unmanned, automated dispensing system that stored, opened, and delivered packages and bulk products automatically. (See U.S. patents 7,640,075; 8,387,824; and 8,442,675.[3])

---

[2] A 1905 theory by Albert Einstein (1879–1955), E=MC^2, where E is physical system energy, M is mass, and C is the speed of light. Mass at rest stores and is equivalent to energy.

[3] Wietgrefe, Gary W., Apparatus and Method for Coordinating Package and Bulk Dispensing, U.S. patent 7,640,075, issued December 29, 2009. Apparatuses and Methods for Bulk Dispensing, U.S. patent 8,387,824, issued March 5, 2013; and Apparatus and Method for Coordinating Automated Package and Bulk Dispensing, U.S. patent 8,442,675, issued May 14, 2013.

Replacement parts will be made locally (think 3-D printing). Without stores, daily deliveries assure freshness. Drones up to 55 pounds (25 kg) are now licensed by the U.S. Federal Aviation Administration to observe, communicate, transport, and deliver goods.[4]

Wider becomes the gap between efficiency and laggards. If educated, school systems know their time is numbered. A competitor, the bureaucratic, labor-union dominated U.S. Postal Service has struggled by not adopting and endorsing decades-old technology like email. The Postal Service did not stop digital mail, nor will the school system stop digital learning. The Postal Service can thrive if adapted as online retailing replaces retailers. (Will schools allow wireless education or cling to brick and mortar?)

Preservatives will be minimized as whole grains are stored and strategically moved (think Egyptian Pharaoh's dream)[5]. Highest producing crops replace multiple crops with carbohydrates, oils, vitamins, and minerals refined to match cultural uses. (Review my U.S. patent # 8,641,910.)[6] One of the most valuable resources, water, is collected from plant material with highly efficient solar power, called photosynthesis. It is used for processing, before solids are efficiently transported to users, or reapplied to the field or hydroponic use for subsequent crops. Controlled and coordinated vegetable, berry, and fruit production match just-in-time delivery for processing into reusable packaging (think milk and milk bottles).

Urgency occurs only with open eyes.

Future: Matching historical norms, work, energy, shelter, water, and food sources are localized. Challenges become international, competitive, and shared.

Throughout history energy is minimized. Efficiency always wins.

Dawning: An Educational Revolution.

---

[4] Drone Registration, United States Federal Aviation Administration, https://drone-registration.net/ (Sourced March 27, 2017)

[5] Genesis 41:1–47:28, NKJV, pp. 60–73

[6] Wietgrefe, Gary W., Systems and Processes for Producing Biofuels from Biomass, U.S. Patent 8,641,910, Issued February 4, 2014.

21

Don't Never Know

Riddle: *What operates as William Shakespeare (1564–1616) wrote in his play, "The Tempest," "Whereof what's past is prologue; what to come, in yours and my discharge"?*

People today are confusing "education" with "schooling" and "learning." They are different things. Especially, fallacious are those who think that the number of years someone spends in school equates to their education level. It simply is not true. Years in the school system certainly does not equate to "learning" level.

One must *Relate to Ancient Culture* to juxtapose and demarcate education, schooling, and learning.

As I was writing this book, Patricia and I were having dinner with a group of people. A second-generation Canadian farmer whose grandparents emigrated from Japan was sitting across from me, and a sixty-five-year-old active business lady that has written several books on personal development was sitting next to me. The well-educated farmer asked me what were my activities while vacationing.

Rather than going into detail about Patricia and I not having a home, nor apartment, nor RV, nor vehicle, or explaining we have traveled for four consecutive years, I said, "I'm writing a book."

The author next to me asked, "What are you writing about?" I replied, "My books are about my experiences as they relate to ancients a hundred years ago, a thousand or several thousand years ago, but mainly since my grandfather was born."

As we were having our appetizers earlier that evening, the lady told us about her grandchildren and how her youngest, a two-year-old, would touch the computer screen and say, "I love you, gramma." Thinking of her grandchild communicating by computer, I said, "I believe children today are less developed than in previous centuries."

At the same time, the Japanese farmer and the business lady's eyes opened wide, heads tilted a bit, and they gave me a very perplexing look before the personal development author said what I consider a fundamental truth; "I don't think that is true until children start school."

It hit me then. People will understand my books, no matter how many years they have spent in school.

I have spent months writing thousands upon thousands of words. It took the business lady eleven words to explain the concept of my book, *Relating to Ancient Culture.* I don't think children are less developed than in previous centuries until they start school.

We should never, never underestimate the understanding of a two-year-old. They understand concepts but simply cannot explain them, or more likely, as ignorant adults we never explain concepts to them. They learn some things now with electronics. Today's school system was set up before electronic communications systems were developed to teach. One will survive.

When a two-year-old asks Why? Why? Why? Why? Why? Do not brush it off as pestering. There probably is no more inquisitive person, one willing to learn, as a two- or three-year-old. They would not ask why, if they did not fundamentally understand that three-letter word. Asking "why" reveals conceptual thinking.

Once children start preschool, pre-kindergarten, kindergarten, and progress through the numbered grades they are conditioned to sit in school, learning controlled, as their learning process is conflicted to match the content of the average student. Teachers train based on established lesson plans of the average student. Bright students are slowed to average and the others are frustrated, slowing their learning. Teaching to the average is more proof the personal development author was correct—children develop slower after starting school.

It is sad; brilliant individual little minds are conditioned to slow their learning to match that of pre-established education guides. Worse yet, teachers who want all students to graduate continue at the speed of slow learners. Teachers, knowingly or not, do it.

Think about classes you have taken. Think about how many years you have spent in school. I am setting you up to prove my point. Readers of this book will have likely spent at least thirteen to twenty years in formal schooling. A few of my readers were placed in preschool at age three and have received their doctorates in their late twenties, which equates to about twenty-five years in some type of classroom.

If only ten classes were taken each year, and my average reader spent fourteen years in school, then the average would be 140 classes taken. Now, I ask each of you: "Of all the classes you have taken, in how many did you complete the textbook or the whole lesson plan?"

I cannot answer that question for you, but of all the years I spent in school NEVER, NEVER once did my teacher cover all lessons in the class textbook. I am sure some of you think I am ignorant because I did not get to go to preschool or kindergarten and the class was slowed by my incompetence. So be it. You are right for my early grades. I was the slowest learner in my class. However, I was the only student in my class grades one through four in our one-room country school. Our teacher had seven other grades to teach.

Did I deserve more focus than others? No. Teachers, even then, were mandated many nonteaching responsibilities (i.e., building heating, cooling, cleaning, trash disposal, and student dress and hygiene). I seriously doubt that any of my teachers in grade school, high school, or college ever completed a textbook in any of their classes. That is over a hundred careers of my teachers that never completed the class lesson.

How long would a business survive if they only completed 75 or 80 percent of a product or project? Not long! Teachers do not complete their work. Why do we allow it? We should not; however, the school system does.

One of my teachers jumped a hundred pages or so toward the end of the school season to cover a chapter at the end. I don't remember the class, but I do remember how unusual it was to actually get to the back of a textbook. Like almost all students, I never took the time to read what I should have learned.

If textbooks (or lesson plans) are written for the average student, and the teacher never completes the textbook during the class, that provides confirmation that teachers are teaching to those below average. When textbooks or lesson plans are not completed, the class should be considered incomplete. The class and the teacher failed.

It does not happen that way. Very, very few students are failed each year. They can flunk a class but are still moved to the next grade level. The result: our school systems are set up to train to a level below average.

During my twelve years of primary and secondary training, only one kid was flunked. Likely he was not above average intelligence, but he disrupted every class, presumably in an effort to get attention. Finally, he was flunked (to what I remember as repeating his freshman year). While in my brother's class, the flunky began to apply himself and started dating a very nice girl. Bam! All of a sudden he started studying and graduated with the rest of that class.

As a career, what did the former high school flunky do? He became a science teacher and taught my younger brothers. Was he a successful teacher? In 1992 he was awarded "Outstanding Physical Science Teacher of the Year Award" by the South Dakota Department of Education. He was the only science teacher from our school to ever get the honor in the thirty-five years in which it has been awarded.

An average student, even a flunky, can apply him- or herself to a subject and be good at it. Just because many, perhaps most, teachers are below average intelligence does not mean they are not good teachers in their specific subject. Many would make excellent tutors in an hour or two setting with children and young adults segmented based on ability and interests of the student and teacher. Everybody learns best at their learning pace.

This era of electronic media gives us access to very creative minds that can expose anybody to all levels of education. On the downside, Internet search engines narrow the scope of intellectual engagement and become a hindrance as they get paid to feature their advertiser's web sites. The Internet is increasingly being used in primary and secondary schools.

Like manipulated commercials, why are we allowing children to be taught by average teachers, in average classrooms, disrupted by below-average students, targeted by Internet advertising, and taking lessons that are never completed?

Why do we have guards walking the halls of schools, protecting the doors, and school administrators seeking measures to physically subdue students? Is it because the system is broken and too many children do not want to be there?

Do you want your child trained to be average in a guarded environment and to have average expectations? A prisoner has more time to think independently.

Is it acceptable to train for the average?

One might call it a mean average—and I don't mean the arithmetic mean. Mean to the parents, mean to the teacher, mean to the student, mean to their career, and mean to society.

If you do not agree with average expectations, what has to change?

I personally struggle calling our present school structure "education." It is structured derangement—upsetting the order of natural learning. Sad.

If you want to use a sports analogy, how many high school sports teams in your hometown have won the state tournament, or have been in the top two in the past fifteen years? Has your school? Likely not.

That means that a school may spend tens of thousands of dollars each year on football, volleyball, and basketball, but a student can go from preschool through high school and never see their home team win any significant title. Just as they treat students, the school system is spending gobs of money on the average or below-average sports program.

What is the purpose of sports? To keep kids in school; or is it to give them the best education?

No society in history has trained so many of its population and spent so much for so long with so many average instructors. Throughout the developed world our youth are trained to expect to graduate school with an "education" below average, leaving them unprepared for work.

Contrarians (likely not teachers), if they caught the "developed world" in my previous sentence, will say the "developed world" is developed because of the standard twelve years of primary and secondary education. If our school systems were not great, our world would not be developed.

Interestingly, the United States developed long before the school system was consolidated in the 1960s. The same is true for other developed countries.

Contrarians are behind the times. They are thinking wrong. They do not understand my book. The world has changed! We are not living a textbook world anymore. Our current school system has slowed youth development and it is getting slower. Schools do not even keep current on computer technology.

Teachers use standardized computer formats to ease test and quiz correction. Why? It saves teachers time, improves grading accuracy, and ranks students automatically. Since typing is not taught, students use the slowest method, hunt-and-pecking computer keyboards, which slows student learning down enough to keep them in school until eighteen.

My father had to quit school at fourteen to run the farm. When I graduated high school my class of eighteen-year-olds with twelve years of formal schooling were expected to make a living on our own. Some were drafted into the Army, others joined the military or family business, some farmed, some worked construction, a few borrowed money and worked summer jobs to attend college. Everybody I knew was employable at eighteen with twelve years of schooling.

Now, a large percent of our population have learned enough from their delinquent parents and indolent friends that they can make a living off government give-away programs, private or semiprivate nonprofit organizations, or simply continue to live with their parents into their late twenties and thirties. Free food, housing, and medical care are an expectation for many without working. Is that progress? Is that what our present school system is teaching? Who is satisfied with a listless culture?

Canadians, Australians, New Zealanders, Japanese, Russians, Spanish, Germans, Brits, Swedes, etcetera, and etcetera—you too are training your youth in a school system that is slowing your children's development. Look at your young adult unemployment and crime rate in recent years. It is high and climbing. Why? School systems failed.

The same is true in the United States. The average age of workers is climbing. If we were truly educating our youth, they would be out of trouble and employed, or at least employable, at voting age. They are not. Why? School systems failed.

Viable workers, acting as vagrants, are a drain on society rather than a macro-economic stimulus. Societies cannot survive without workers. Toddlers are too young, those incapacitated are nonfunctional, and most old seniors are beyond contributing to a country's energy, transportation, communications, medical, and food needs.

A civilization is not sustainable when most people expect to work only a third of their life, or not at all.

How should we educate our youth to make them employable?

The German kindergarten has become a worldwide term. It was developed to prepare students to speed education in school. Once accepted worldwide, kindergarten has slowed individual development and set the expectation that children need to go to school not just twelve years but at least thirteen before they begin to learn a trade. What a pathetic failed system—efficiency in reverse.

Governments only survive on workers. To keep older people working, countries lessen the tax on their government's senior pension (i.e., Social Security). In the United States, low-income, part-time working seniors age sixty-five, currently only pay income taxes on half their annual Social Security income, but the tax may raise to 85 percent taxable if senior income is too high.

Higher paid workers, including seniors, are taxed the most—that discourages work.

What do governments do when their eighteen-year-old adults are unemployable? Rather than encourage them to work, governments have created preschool and pre-kindergarten classes for the very young and hire more teachers at the wrong end of the learning spectrum.

If the school system was not failing, it would not need to extend public education.

Compulsory education until seventeen or eighteen has become a worldwide standard. Governments heavily subsidize community colleges, trade schools, and universities to keep students in school longer, hoping that at least some of them will someday have employable skills.

At twenty, except for the disabled, there is no excuse for anybody, no matter how stupid they are, to get a job and contribute to a developing society. Even an employed simple person will intrigue fellow workers with simple concepts.

Remember, the Internet has reached every corner of the world. It has reached our infants. Preschool grandchildren, throughout the world, are playing with technology. That technology, by the time they are teenagers, should make them useful contributors to a world of personal freedoms unimagined by our grandparents.

Fundamental knowledge does not come from only those who spend two decades in school with below average part-time teachers, but those who have minds not imprisoned by a standardized, average schooling system.

On the current path, what will our future look like? What will we be building? What will our world's energy, communications, transportation, medical, and food system look like a hundred years from now?

I should ask Owen Williams.

Who is Owen Williams?

The Owen Williams I am referring to was a friend, I believe grade school classmate, of my father. It was my understanding that Owen and his brother, Richie, had to quit school early to make a living farming just like my father and many rural youths in the 1930s and 1940s.

One day in June 1975 I had ridden five miles into Ipswich with my father in our old farm pickup truck to make stops at the post office and bank. When my parents got married they started getting the *Aberdeen American News*, our daily newspaper. It came in the mail and we did not have rural mail delivery, but instead grandpa or some family member usually picked up our mail daily in our Ipswich post office box. Checks from selling grain, cattle, cream, and eggs and from my dad's employer had to be endorsed and taken to the bank.

I had just got out of the Air Force. After getting our mail, we drove to the bank. I remember it was a beautiful spring day when I was re-introduced to Owen and Richie Williams. I was proud to have served my country as a Vietnam Era veteran and even more proud to walk the streets of Ipswich with my father—a well-educated man with only nine years of schooling.

I was always amazed at the volume of books, newspapers, and magazines my father would read. Someone would give him a paperback book and he would read it in a day or two. He always read our daily paper, and several bi-weekly and monthly farm magazines: *Successful*

Farmer, *Farm Journal*, and *The Dakota Farmer* to name a few. How could dad do that when he was out doing cattle chores before 6:00 a.m. when us kids would get up for twice daily milking, feeding the calves, hogs, and chickens.

When did dad have time to read when he would leave the farm at 7:15 a.m. after feeding the cattle and eating breakfast? He could not read at work building pole barns and other structures throughout the Ipswich area until 5:30 p.m. He had no time to read before eating supper and heading to the field, checking for new calves, or fixing something in the rain or snow until the 10:00 p.m. television news. Did he read in his sleep?

My father, Walter Frederick Wietgrefe, was differentiated in our community from Walter Frederick Wietgrefe, my grandfather, by adding "Jr." after his official name. Grandpa, with only eight years of formal schooling, eventually signed his name ending in "Sr." I had never seen my father, grandpa, or my father-in-law ever compute with a pencil. They did all arithmetic in their heads.

Unofficially, my father was known as "Sonny"–being the son of WFW Sr. Thirty-five years after my father's death, my mother still referred to dad as Sonny. Mother said she was adamant that I should not be named Walter Fred Wietgrefe III. Walter Fred Wietgrefe the third or Sonny's Sonny was just too much. Instead, as the oldest boy, my middle name is Walter, in honor of my father.

Sometimes our mother would get frustrated, usually it was with at least one of us seven kids. Okay, honestly, she often got mad at us–this I cannot always put the blame on my older sister, Susan, or five younger brothers, Mark, Wayne, Wesley, Neal, or Kent. If I am to be honest, it was not always because they made me do it (as some claim).

Dad, however, was the ultimate disciplinarian. "Wait until your dad comes home," was mom's threat. Whew! A good break because it might be several hours of respite, or as diplomats call it, "a cooling off period." More times than not, we minded mother, all was fine, and my father did not have to carry out the sentence.

We often said something we did not mean. Sometimes we said something mean that we did not mean; or mean something we did not say. Try explaining it to your angry mother in the heat of discipline–homographs just do not work sometimes.

Dad would often make a joke of small things or just laugh it off. Work, finances, a cow dying, hogs electrocuted, crop failures, and machinery broken down were enough stress that dad often smiled and brushed off the little things with us kids. When dad would say something comical, grinning with a twinkle in his eye, mom would just say "Oh, Sonny." He was dead at fifty-one. I look back at those memories as a pleasant homonym and think of my Dad as "Oh, Sunny."

As we approached the bank that June day, Owen wanted to talk to my father. Everybody knew Sonny always had a positive attitude, and there was nothing that he would not tackle successfully, be it cash cropping, cattle, construction, motors, math, marketing, or teaching children's Sunday school after church.

Owen and Richie had just come out of Ipswich State Bank, then a prominent rock building on Main Street, when dad and I got out of our pickup. Owen quickly stepped forward, first stuck out his large hand to shake Dad's. "Gary, do you remember Owen and Richie Williams?" Dad asked.

I stuck my hand out and shook two very callused farmers' hands. After four years in the Air Force, I still had a very strong grip from milking cows as a youth, but I only had two calluses. They were between my index and middle finger on my right hand from turning knobs on radio receivers. Like secret communication messages I received, the calluses were hidden where nobody would see or feel them. I gave each man a strong handshake as my father and the Williams brothers were in active conversation . . . like hard working friends that seldom met.

My mind draws a blank of the topic of their active discussion. Likely, at twenty-two I was just enjoying a beautiful spring day, the freedom of small-town America, and soaking in the pride of being seen with my father like I used to when I was a little kid. At age four, five, six, or seven when hauling a load of grain to the local elevator, I would search our pickup glove-box for a nickel to buy a bottle of pop. If one or two of my brothers were along, we would all drink from the same bottle. I would get to stand proudly with my father as the grain emptied into a pit while sipping a bottle of pop.

Anyway, that spring day in 1975, Owen Williams said something that has stuck clearly in my mind for the last forty years: "You don't never know. You just don't never know."

Owen, I am sure, never claimed to be a thoroughly schooled man, but he, like my father, knew more about people, the world around them, and how to do their jobs better than the college-educated Ipswich school teachers then on summer break. Until much later, I did not appreciate Mr. Williams's command of an audience.

In a chapter of my other book *Relating to Ancient Learning*, a poem of homonyms, "Rode Road," is a story of two lives; one is compassionate; the other is not. A compassionate parent is not one who always disciplines or is always making excuses for their child's erring ways. Financing your child through twenty years of school is not compassion. A compassionate parent tries to educate their child, not just send them to school—it is really two different things.

Compassion and discipline can be two negatives but should make for positive parental education. Likewise, contrary to proper English usage, two negatives do not make a positive statement as Owen Williams used such to reinforce his point.

Those schooled in English may say of Owen, "What a dumb country hick. You can tell he wasn't schooled properly."

On the other hand, I have told the story of Owen Williams several times. Why would I want to put down somebody for improper use of English?

Like the person that does not delineate between "schooled" and "educated," they do not understand the astounding literary tools Owen used. William Shakespeare (1564–1616) is reported to be the greatest writer ever of the English language. Shakespeare, I'm sure, dreamed of people memorizing and moralizing his words simply by meeting him briefly on the street.

During a brief introduction, handshake, and chat with my father on a street in small town America, I live to pass on Owen's words without having the ability to pass on his command of conversation. Having an audience remember your exact words for forty years is quite a linguistic accomplishment.

Second, good writers, like great speakers, try to convey the same concept using different words. Repeating them in quick cadence for emphasis, "Don't never," "Don't never" was Owen's literary trick of conveying the same concept (a negative) by using two different words followed by what could be a negative homophone "no" or "know." Poets write their whole life for such a concise phrase.

"No" can be said diverse ways. Verbal is different from written when homophones are used. Owen's words spoken by a mother fearful of her toddler touching a hot stove might cry out: "Don't touch that hot stove. YOU DON'T! NEVER! NO!! YOU JUST DON'T!!! NEVER!!!! NO!!!!!" Owen used a play on words blending negatives and even a homophone of a negative (know vs. no).

Owen's third literary tool sharpened his casual speech. He used a speech trick, repeating key words, only great speakers use. For example, as a twelve-year-old fifth grader I was astounded at the speaking ability of African-American civil rights activist, Martin Luther King, Jr. King became more famous by repeating four words continuously in a speech, "I have a dream." His 1963 "I have a dream" speech has been immortalized as one of the greatest speeches of our time. What did he say about the education, not schooling, of his children? "I have a dream that my four little children will one day live in a nation where they will not be judged by the color of their skin but by the content of their character."

Thinking back now as I was standing outside the Ipswich State Bank on a spring day in 1975, I conceptualize better than ever what King was saying about our country and the treatment of people, especially poor people with different skin color, different hair, different accents, different dress, and different education levels: ". . . America has given the Negro people a bad check, a check which has come back marked 'insufficient funds'."

Reverend King was right in 1963 and it took me fifty years to realize America's school system is graduating millions of bad checks every year giving them limited ability to make the check good.

Owen used a fourth communications tool: Those with command of language personalize their point succinctly. Owen used *"you"* twice in nine words, personalizing his address. Owen pleasantly said *"YOU"* are the one that needs to remember my words.

Fifth, one does not have to be a lexicographer to make a statement memorable. Mr. Williams repeated four words and threw in *"just"* in his second sentence to jolt the attention of the listeners (dad, his brother, and me). If we all could be so succinct, we would need fewer books and would not have to talk so much. Even William Shakespeare, the greatest

English writer of all time, used a fifty-one-word sentence when only six survived as memorable: ". . . Brevity is the soul of wit. . . ."

Mr. Owen Williams on the Ipswich street theater in front of a rusty pickup truck with a three-man audience was far, far briefer than Shakespeare. Mr. Williams, without much formal schooling, had character you could believe and command of the English language.

On another point, one must realize Mr. Williams's philosophical statement is still awing for its simplicity and profoundness. Finally, he did not learn the nine-word combination in school. Although it is not proper English, everybody understands what Mr. Owen Williams meant. On the other hand, discuss a topic with the most learned teacher: The longer they talk, the more confused the listener. Likely, they continue talking to convince themselves of their random thoughts.

It may not be proper to give definitions toward the end of a book, but have you ever looked up the definition of "school system"?

The dictionary I used throughout this book and my working career was the *Webster's New World Dictionary*, Second College Edition, republished and copyrighted in 1982. It defines school, school age, school board, schoolbook, schoolboy, school bus, schoolchild, schoolcraft, school district, schoolfellow, schoolgirl, school guard, schoolhouse, schoolman, schoolmarm, schoolmaster, schoolmate, schoolmistress, schoolroom, schoolteacher, school tie, schoolwork, schoolyard, and school year. It does not define "school system."

Some time in the last three decades, "school system" entered our vocabulary. To find the definition of "school system," I used the Internet (that has an artificial memory of recent usage) and received 10,200,000 results. The first, according to Merriam-Webster's online dictionary, a "school system" is: "The aggregate of the public schools of an area under the administration of an executive officer who represents and is responsible to the board of education for that area."[1]

Never once in the definition does "school system" mention children or students. It is not a child or student system; it is a legal organization managing divisions of labor.

---

[1] "school system," Merriam-Webster, An Encyclopaedia Britannica Company, https://www.google.com.mx/webhp?sourceid=chrome-instant&ion=1&espv=2&ie =UTF-8#q=define+%22school+system%22 (Sourced December 14, 2015)

Rather than trying to establish the best education system for children, fights erupt between kindergarten through twelfth grade "school systems," usually based on revenue sources.

Throughout the United States conflicts arise between school districts. A recent noteworthy example happened in eastern South Dakota between a large school district (Madison) and a small school district (Chester). In 1997, the South Dakota Legislature allowed "open enrollment." Since then, South Dakota children could choose a school. Determined by property lines for taxation purposes, previous strict school district boundaries assigned students. Like any law with good intentions, exceptions develop.

In this example, a Hutterite Colony (a religious farming commune) chose to provide a location for their children to be educated by the farming community of Chester and its school district. Although the Colony property was located and taxed by the Madison school district, the Graceville Colony open enrolled all their students into Chester, which receives tax funds allocated to each student enrolled in their district.

Since the Madison and Chester school boards could not come to amiable terms, a bill was introduced into South Dakota legislature to resolve this exception under a joint powers agreement.

School systems claim to operate for the best interests of the students. They do not when it comes to legalities, money, and managerial control. The South Dakota Department of Education did not consider the place a "school" where all Graceville Colony students attended because they all were "open enrolled."

Like in any case before the courts, someone is the victim. An attorney involved in the case questioned if the school or the Colony children were the "victim." The children were the victims, except in the minds of those administering the two schools.

Since school systems are a labor management organization, "Education" on the other hand is defined as: "The process of training and developing the knowledge; mind, and character, etc. . . ."[2]

There is a strong push by the pre-kindergarten through high school system to co-opt the definition of education, that is, to pull it completely

---

[2] "Education," *Webster's New World Dictionary*, Second College Edition of the American Language, Simon and Schuster, 1982, p. 444.

away from parents and students. Parents must resist temptations and threats by those in the system. A half century of trying has proved the current school system has been wrong for parents, wrong for students, and wrong for our country.

There is so much talent freely accessible, or accessible at very low cost, to educate children in homes or community grouped with children of similar abilities, interests, and intellect. Money spent on school systems could be parent-focused, personalized with small classes, tutors, and tutorials far more effectively than on school buildings, upkeep, labor to run them, and lawyers to protect school systems' vested interests.

Those who now want to condemn the school system need only point at themselves. It was allowed to happen over a period of decades. Worse it will get as couples have fewer children and when both parents work outside the home.

Multilevel governmental school systems were an experiment that initially appeared promising. As federal and state governments regulated control from local schools, it failed. Failure is not just a grade; it is a breakdown in purpose and function.

Never should a child be publicly discriminated against because they are brilliant, average, have developmental disabilities, or have a religious preference. Our school systems are an environment that breeds divergence and dissidence. Worldly educated brilliant, gifted, and average students should be supporting the underdeveloped, not competing with them in standardized testing.

Over 2300 years ago, a father died. His son was placed under the care of a guardian, Proxenus of Atarneus. Without a school system, Mr. Proxenus educated his guarded child the best that he could. At eighteen, the young man had such an ability to understand and communicate, he was accepted into the most notable academy at that time, Plato's Academy in Athens Greece.

Immersing himself in the study of music, poetry, theater, philosophy, politics, government, and the sciences of physics, biology and zoology, he was awarded the highest honor in 343 B.C. of tutoring the thirteen-year-old son of Philip II, King of Macedonia. When King Philip II was assassinated in 336 B.C., his son was age twenty. In the following decade, he became one of the most well-known world leaders of all time, Alexander the Great. By age thirty, Alexander ruled an empire from Pakistan and India to Egypt on the south of the Mediterranean Sea throughout the Greek empire of the northern Mediterranean, thereby becoming one of the largest empires in the Ancient world.

Who began tutoring Alexander (the thirteen-year-old son of King Philip II)? It was a thirty-seven-year-old university professor, Aristotle (384–322 B.C.). What university professor today would quit his tenured post to educate a thirteen-year-old?

Just because Aristotle was fatherless at a young age did not stop him from becoming a tutor of one child, or eventually become the world's first documented scientist. Some of his inconsiderable theories did not become facts for over two thousand years–like the reproduction of octopus. Aristotle did not limit his mind to octopus, teaching a teenager, or any particular subject. Aristotle, believing in a broad fundamental education wrote: "Educating the mind without educating the heart is no education at all."

Why, in the last fifty years, are we expecting our school system to be our educational system? Why have schools become in loco parentis (in the place of a parent, or of a parent's authority)? Will parents again educate rather than school their children?

Has the school system pulled a dog trick on us?

What will our world's energy, communications, transportation, medical, and food system look like a hundred years from now? Educated or schooled? What will we build? Will it continue to be a school system or education? Will we be a lost civilization? What traces will remain? Will we change for the better? Mr. Owen Williams would say, "You don't never know. You just don't never know."

22

Sustainable Culture

ALLEGORY: SCHOOL SYSTEM

Everybody has feared the boogeyman–parents before children. Every country has a boogeyman. All meant to teach children a lesson. He used to take only naughty children away. "Babau" in the Mediterranean area would take kids away as punishment. Spanish-speaking countries have "hombre del saco," and in Latin America with sack on back, "El coco," the boogeyman, taught potentially naughty children lessons. Throughout history ancient Romans, Chinese, and Native American Apache had a spiritual being in physical body that children feared.

In the twentieth century, disguised as gentlemanly, just down the block, he captured more and more children over the years without fear. Children went on their merry way as he kept getting bigger with free food–consuming more every year. By that time, he was a cultural icon. All children were under his influence. He was clever and blended into every city, every state, and in every country.

With public support, boogeyman took custody of children during weekdays. He permanently took them from the home they knew. Occasionally, he hosted evening events, but for many years not on Wednesdays–that was church night. Then, with the pretense of freedom (separation of boogey-church with boogey-state), he banned children bringing religious materials. Eventually, he brought younger children into his fold and hosted events every night and on weekends.

His doors were guarded to keep out the public and he instructed those under his care to fear parents–to fear anybody outside his care. Revealed by those who enjoyed family activities before he came of age, and aided by technology and access to information, a few parents started noticing unease in their children, but nobody suspected . . . only the boogeyman did such things.

Eventually the boogeyman became secretive. After puberty, more and more teenagers quit going to see him daily. Showing age-inappropriate material to young boys and girls was enough for some parents to fear the boogeyman and keep their children away. Meanwhile, free condom giveaways did not prevent orthodox boogey-children. Boogey-believers bred.

Childhood psychological diseases ran rampant. Parents noticed their children were no longer motivated around home. They became self-centered; shunned church; avoided family meals, household chores, and even paying jobs. They just hid out in their room and boogeyed in bed. Substance abuse, disguised at first, became prevalent by crime.

Things were not calculating, but then psychologists, psychiatrists, and sociologists were never that good at math. Boogeyman was real and finally exposed as the common denominator of cultural decline.

Parents found other ways of teaching their children a lesson without boogeyman . . . but not until boogeyman became the most powerful being on earth as boogey divisions of labor. Boogey-believers feared competition, feared technology, feared the outside world, and wanted control by working for boogeyman. With boogey-support, they passed laws and infiltrated government to maintain boogey-control. When confiscated tax money was not enough to satisfy boogey's ethno-cleanse, boogey-bonds were sold to the unsuspecting public.

When boogeyed-out children no longer went to boogeyman, he became evermore fierce and demanded more children. Starved for a few years, his appearance shrunk. Eventually, boogeyman returned to the instructive gentleman he had been for thousands of years, but parents in every community, in every state, in every country still teach their children the lessons of boogeyman.

. . . and they lived happily ever after.

As a fictional generalization, an allegory has hidden meaning. Something designed to improve civilization, is perpetuating its decline. There is one fundamental reason why those entering the twenty-first century are different from any in human history. First, some manifestations:

- Culture changed with delayed marriages by extending formal education.
- Young adult needs, supplied by parents and the public, developed into families without spouse.
- Working youth declined.
- Without an age-blended workforce, culture changed.
- Youths' novel ideas were not mingled into the workforce.
- Freedom to use past innovative technology created economic prosperity.
- Interpersonal combat became impersonal wars.
- Culture changed by extending formal education, allowed by past prosperity, to create a service economy inflating educated egos beyond servant roles.
- Physical labor was for those without higher education. Ignorant immigrants could do those jobs.
- Textbooks taught ignorance and encouraged racial divides.
- Rather than improving after the American Civil War, racially and ethnically skewed textbooks were written by white, elite, university professors to perpetuate the divide.
- Sports was used to keep slow learners in school. Eventually it took precedence over education.
- National control of curriculum to raise the average cut innovation, stymied individual progress, and encouraged convoluted teams.

Although I realized many changes *Relating to Ancient Culture*, ultimately, with a slowing pace of production and reproduction, culture became unsustainable, as divulged in highly educated subcultures.

Everything must be sustainable.

Let us close after review of *Relating to Ancient Culture* with a few questions about the developed and developing world compared to known human history. In the1890s, many things were still done as in past centuries. Since extensive records do not exist for those thousands of years, for the questions below consider changes between the beginning of the twentieth century (1900) and today.

1. Are there more people in the world? Yes.
2. Are people living longer? Yes.
3. Are people eating more and do they have better shelter? Yes.
4. Will people subsist without electricity, running water, indoor bathrooms, vehicles, computers, phones, gadgets, public healthcare, education, and other wants? No.
5. Is there a higher or lower percent of people in the workforce? Lower percent.
6. Are people working as many hours as in the past? No.
7. Are boys and girls entering the workforce as early as they have in the past? No.
8. Are people spending more time in school rather than working? Yes.
9. Are people working as hard, as diligently, and are they as conscientious about their work and employer needs as in the past? No.
10. Does delayed workforce entry delay retirement? No.

After reviewing the half-score of questions above, it appears today's needs and wants are not sustainable with today's workers for tomorrow's lifestyle. Everybody wants to know, what is the ending score.

Those a bit sharper would immediately suggest much of the human and beast of burden energy employed a century ago has been replaced with synthetic energy (energy of human synthesis) of usable products. True, but how were existing energy sources (e.g., wood, coal, petroleum, gases, nuclear, geothermal, gravity, magnetism, wind, sun, and etc.) converted to usable energy by humans? Learning.

If we are to continue feeding and sheltering an increasing world population at current or improved standards, learning systems that convert knowledge to usable product therefore must continually improve. Given transferable knowledge, without depleting resources and lowering expected lifestyles, more energy sources must be discovered, and energy efficiency must improve continuously.

Alternatively, with a higher world population and an aging workforce that created prosperity, young people must work diligently, harder, more efficiently, and for more years than in the past. Given the ten questions above, these alternatives are unlikely.

Although some lament "the good ol' days," few, if any, want to go there. As reviewed throughout this book, culture is changing. Given the allegorical school system (the answer to each chapter's riddles), you must read my next book, *Relating to Ancient Learning*.

What may be—RIP

A marble bounced twice and rolled past my shoe. A dark-haired six-year-old stumbled as he scrambled like a cat after a mouse. It had popped out of the table-mounted screen.

"Never seen anything like it," I said.

The rush was on to get it before it rolled under Patricia's chair.

"What? The bounce of Micah's marble?" she asked.

"No," I said. "That thing on the table the kids are playing with."

Patricia glanced at the table.

"Oh, the kids got that the other day. It's a new Analyzer."

"What can you put into it?" I asked.

"About anything, I guess, if it's smaller than your fist. It is a kid's version," she explained. "You could walk into the new adult size."

"Yeah, I suppose if I could walk better. Walking several hundred miles a week back in '17 I used to wear out a pair of shoes in six months." Half joking, I continued, "Now shoes wear me out in six steps."

"Oh, get off your butt and go down to the community room. Our association just bought one. Try it out you ol' bugger," she pestered.

As I moved to the Magcurtain, Micah's older sister and brother were already gathered around the marble that had settled into a small divot, probably where our Harmony Center desk once sat.

My parents bought that desk in 1963 when our township's only school, Harmony Center, closed its doors for the last time. Consolidation.

The township, with thirty-six square miles of farm ground and decreasing farmsteads, had no town. Thereafter, not one school remained.

The vote was close. Town school, Ipswich, was offering free child bus pickup at each farm door.

Elementary and secondary education switched to a fully tax supported school system that drove kids from small schools into larger ones and kept them from being exposed to their family's business. If schools would have adopted communications rather than wasteful transportation, we would not have these huge school skeletons.

Those voting against consolidation feared taxes would go up (as if they ever go down). Most farm families were already taking their children to town school.

Harmony Center did not have running water. Never did. Hoffmans delivered it every day—they got the crock water cooler. Somebody brought cartons of commodity milk from town when I was in the fourth grade. Some days we got chocolate milk for morning recess.

Everything was sold, including the building and the money reverted to Harmony Township to grade the roads an extra time during the year, maybe a culvert or two were replaced, or perhaps someone on the Township Board got their road re-graveled—one of the few benefits of being elected to the board.

I used that desk for many years during my career after Patricia and I bought it at Mom's 1998 farm auction. Teacher's desks were small then—two drawers, but it looked big to me as a kid when called up to give a report. I suppose teachers were smaller then also. With just one teacher, she took the time to teach each of us in all eight grades. No computers then. I learned more from listening to the older kids give their reports than I learned from my own books.

Likely, throughout history people learned more from older people than from those their own age. It is no wonder the school systems disintegrated so quickly. Desire to learn will always override laws that force children into schools where they learn only with kids their own age.

A strange sensation, goose bumps I guess, rippled through my arms and mind as I blinked for clarity.

This happened before—more than once. Yogi Berra was right: "It's like déjà-vu, all over again."

"That's it! That's it."

"What's it?" Patricia asked.

"Oh, that marble reminded me of Mexico," I mumbled reminiscing. "Remember when I told about the kids playing marbles on a cobblestone street under the shade tree in La Penita? A couple months later three other kids, a girl and two boys, were trying to shoot a marble into a sidewalk hole?"

"First," she responded, "all the streets were cobblestone. Except for the gravel. I think you have déjà-vu, because you also wrote about those kids."

"Oh, I know. That was the most amazing realization for me. Kids were not tied to school there. They learned in a completely different system: maybe four hours in various classes, then on the street playing or helping their parents. Hard questions or arguments were settled by going to those computer places. What did they call them? Internet cafés?"

"Schools and teachers were efficient. One batch had classes in the morning, the other in the afternoon—even grade-schoolers. When schools have lots of money, they can waste space and even worse, they can waste time. It took decades for the rich countries to realize a few focused classes taught three or four times per day were far more effective for learning and efficient use of buildings and utilities.

"Scarcity breeds resourcefulness."

"I like this complex," Patricia said. "This old school building really isn't that old. All on one level, mixture of old and young families, it is good. How many rooms are there for workshops and labs?"

Scratching my bald head as if I still had hair, I responded, "Let's see, there are two for biology if you count the medical projects, one for chemistry and physics, one for convertibles, a fabrication area, two for culinary including the service training area.

I almost forgot the two music rooms and literatim area—interesting how they make copies of any document. I think there are fifty reusables to check out in that converted library. Texture of pages and cover feels like the books we used to have. I probably read a hundred from mine. Come to think of it, I should upload another today."

"I like those group classes. You never know what age group will show up," Patricia chimed in. "Wireless learning was just catching on then. Hmmm, remember when we use to have phone lines, cords running appliances, and those rectangular electrical boxes with two outlet holes to plug stuff into?"

"You know, I even saw a plug-in in one of our hallways the other day," I added. "A century of technology is a blip of time. It's hard to find them these days. Plug-ins are dangerous in case they turn on the old generator. Some fool may still run a buffer or vacuum in the hall using the plug-in. 'The plug-in'—stupid term wasn't it?

"The kids could get killed poking something into them. These kids have no idea what those boxes were used for. Boy have things changed," mumbling as I walked to the Magcurtain.

"How many years since we spent time in La Penita? Now we are living in the old Ipswich school. Might as well. Taxpayers are still paying off bonds when they put on the last addition six or so years before no kids showed up for school one fall.

"We had a lot of teachers sitting around twiddling, until they realized the kids were not coming back. At least they get to use their own homes now. Yeah, adults, us seniors, and kids hardly walk a block or two to get a special class."

A standing doze . . . Hmmmmm?

Remember when they used to have school buses running around, sometimes a hundred miles each day, picking up farm kids and kids from Mina, Cresbard, and Loyalton? Those big orange things . . . gas-guzzlers they were. Five miles to the gallon, or was it five gallons to the mile?

I wonder if they are still running them as chicken buses in the mountains of Guatemala. School buses finally shut down, I guess, a month or so after nobody showed up for classes that fall.

Since toddlers, kids had been playing with phones, tablets, and computers, whatever they call them now. What did the schools think? The kids would sit in a classroom all day, every day, for fifteen or twenty years. When they could not come up with any reason to stay in school, adults moved back in with their parents. Education changed before politicians realized someone must work.

It took a few years for teachers to reemploy themselves. Many never worked for themselves before, nor planned to work every month.

At least teachers do not complain about pay. Now, they get what they are worth. Those of little value do not get paid, or have appropriate audiences. No more forced standing in front of a class and having kids throw gum or blow spit-wads when the teacher turned; or did spit-wads go out with manual typewriter and paper? It is easy to lose track.

Community classes, even virtual, are interesting. Instructors are actually vested in their students. It is amazing some of the projects that come out of those classes. Us old buggers can keep current on changes, and occasionally get to throw in some expertise from the old days.

I like it here.

It is almost like our country schools as kids; only now anybody can take classes–any age. There are different things to learn. Some of those little kids have such interesting ideas . . . and they try to prove they are right. Some are.

I guess in the 1960s they were already trying to keep parents out of school. Too many used school to get out of work. No wonder it had to change.

Teachers were always stressed out. Always griping for more pay. Always wanting more time off, as if the summer, Thanksgiving, Christmas, New Year's, and spring break were not enough; they had those "in-service" days. In-service to whom?

Oh, and then there were ball tournaments even if the football, volleyball, or basketball team did not make it into the state tournament. Everybody was off. No wonder academic performance waned and a new definition developed for "empty baskets."

Sport of empty baskets, empty net, and two uprights allowed schools to exist for decades.

Why did they call them "baskets"? They were holes with a metal ring around them. A basket at least holds something. Empty baskets . . . emptied minds.

Some schools existed for two holes. When athletics, not academics, became the tack that held up education, the definition for "school" was already lost.

Now teachers teach because they want to. Teach what they want; when they want. Education is available any time. Teachers get to pick their subject. Specialize in one thing. I guess even average teachers got tired of not completing their lesson plan.

Look at this huge beast. Nobody in their right mind would build something like this with their own money. Kids had too many other opportunities to learn.

I blinked, and mumbled. "More practical now. I think that young family down the hall just had a baby the other day. Kind of funny when I heard they delivered it online. When was the last time we had a line?

"So easy now on the kid and the mother. They don't have to be exposed to all those institutional germs."

Patricia finally interrupted. "You are rambling again. You know what? I think that is the same lady that may have talked about the new Analyzer–that adult one in the community room. It used to be a science room when this was a school.

"Maybe she will give us a demonstration. I really shouldn't call it an adult version, because the kids can use it, too.

"Come on kids. Rip Van Winkle[1] is awake. Let's beat grandpa South Dakota down to the Analyzer!"

We exited through our Magcurtain into the hallway. Turned right. John had just returned from his morning walk.

"Chilly out this morning. Never know it once you pass through the Magcurtain," he said.

Just like each Magcurtain has a different transparency, they all function the same–just like the Analyzer.

"Do you like it here, John?" I asked.

"Sure do! I just spent my whole walk thinking about this place and how education, businesses, and families changed since schools went under."

He continued.

"I lamented knowing that several decades, from the mid-1960s to the 2020s, most families hauled their kids to babysitters six weeks after birth.

"Parents simply woke them, sometimes fed the kids, dropped them off at daycare, picked them up after work, fed them high-fat, high-sugar, drive-through, fast-food before putting them to bed and repeating that every day, every week, every month, year on end. On weekends the

---

[1] "Rip Van Winkle" is a short story and the main character. Published in 1819, Washington Irving's story tells of a married man who avoided his wife's nagging by walking into the Catskill Mountains, falling asleep, awakens to find he had been sleeping for at least twenty years. RIP often written R.I.P. (meaning Rest in Peace) in the epilogue title is a play on words to finalize this nonfiction book with a twenty-plus-year gap until the fictional epilogue.

parents were too tired to play with the kids. They needed a break, so they would go off and do adult stuff while the kids were dropped off at grandparents for the weekend. My children were no different.

"I saw several families on the way to the park this morning.

"It wasn't long ago parents could not even take their kids to city parks in the evenings or weekends because all the bathrooms were removed—just drug-trading vagrant dwellings for school drop-outs.

"Since man's first pee, there was a place to go until parents let the school system raise their children. Bladders won. One might say failed schools took the pee out of parks.

"For thousands of years parents worked out of their homes. Now they do it again. In the last decade, nearly all classes are virtual. Work is virtual. The parks are full during the day, evenings, and especially weekends.

"It is no wonder the parents and grandparents were worn out. Children, the first three years of their life, from the first day they can remember they had a continual transition. Sleep at parents. Play at daycare. Sleep at parents. Play at daycare five days followed by two days with grandparents—sometimes three, then back to the day/night shifting cycle. Those in school had more schedules than a clock.

"Something had to give. Kids were put on a school on-off cycle from infants through university. They did not have the time to process non-schedules. That is why they had to fill free time with organized activities. They could not think on their own. Teams became the home for those that could not think individually."

"You're right, John," I broke in.

"Teachers were not fools. They knew community based, virtual learning was inevitable.

"Do you realize there wasn't a school in the country that didn't have bond payments?"

"You are right," John added. "Some newer schools had $60 million in twenty- or thirty-year bonds with attendance of 200 students, $300,000 per student. Ridiculous! That was enough to build a fancy house for each student.

"When parents started working at home ... Telecommuting I think they called it back then, they realized their children were more techno-literate than they were.

"Telecommuting is another stupid term. Children finally got to stay home. Home games, contests, instruments, appliances were their learning tools, not school. And, parents went about their work just as they did when this country was founded."

Excited, I interrupted because this tied in with books I had written years earlier, *Relating to Ancient Culture* and *Relating to Ancient Learning*.

"It just didn't make any economic or logical sense for husband and wife to leave for work at 6:30 a.m., stop by daycare, burning up gas, stuck in traffic, having businesses up-charge to cover office expenses. If workers were lucky, they returned home by 6:00 p.m. and were only paid for an eight-hour work day.

"No wonder parents were stressed out and had little time with their children. Even when in the office, many meetings were done by 'video-conferencing'. Conferencing now. 'Video' went out with the taped camcorders—a 1990s plaything, but they were still using that term decades later.

"At first, schools thought it was a home-schooling trend and tried to ban, or heavily regulate community learning.

"When more and more parents both worked from their homes rather than go to the office, it was no longer a virtual system. It was the real economical and practical way to do things.

"Office space started freeing up. Big money bond-managers sitting in their New York offices didn't have a clue back in the 2000 teens that the traditional office was as antiquated as school systems soon would become.

"When news hit one fall that a school ... Wasn't it in Minnesota or Nebraska? Only about a dozen kids out of two hundred high schoolers showed up for fall classes.

"Football practice had been going on for two weeks as normal and the first game was the last Friday in August. School started on Tuesday and only about twelve kids showed up for classes.

"Janitors and kitchen staff outnumbered the kids that week. Some teachers had no students in their class. Thursday the superintendent called in the principals and school board for an emergency meeting. What were they going to do?

"Of course, by Friday night's game. Social media overloaded the system. There was no way of controlling what would happen next.

"The game was packed. A half hour before kickoff the parking lot was full and cars were parked out to the highway. Television vans and reporters were everywhere trying to get interviews.

"That night was the death-knell for the American school system and American football. That is why junior and adult leagues started what was more like a combination of rugby and Australian Rules football. Schools could no longer justify sports without classes.

"Basketball continued with traveling leagues. That was not new. They had traveling basketball, baseball, hockey, golf, tennis, and swimming teams for years outside of school. The school system, without team athletics, was a nonentity. It was like Elmer's®[2] without glue.

"Most towns didn't bother even calling football practice the following year. The well-groomed fields, stands, broadcast booths, scoreboards were worth nothing on the one-year anniversary of that night.

"Broadcasts went viral. The week following that football game every state, every country had some empty schools, empty hallways, empty classrooms. It did not matter.

"Social media had connected every student in the world. There was no way to force the world back to high school buildings. Virtual schools became the norm within months.

"Grade schools hung on a year or two longer until parents could arrange to work from home, or find different jobs.

"Literacy and numeracy became the base standard.

"Of course, the economy tanked.

"No school attendance meant there was no need for school teachers. Teachers' unions collapsed for lack of funding. Good teachers had student followings. They started virtual classes out of their homes and held specialty training, more like tutoring, in their converted garages, basements, or community rooms. Of course, they had access to the best teachers and lessons in the world.

"No school meant taxpayers no longer could justify paying tax-exempt bonds.

"Bond-holders were in a scramble to unload billions-upon-billions of worthless paper. There was no value in school or office property without students and without commuters.

---

[2] Elmer's® is a registered trademark of Elmer's Products, Inc.

"Commercial property, especially inter-city offices, became worthless. It would have cost more to tear down those buildings than the property was worth. Just like schools, it made sense to convert offices to residences with all the labs, workshops, music rooms, and theaters we have here in this old school.

"Why commute when all office workers could work more hours and communicate more effectively while their children studied in community rooms. Manufacturers became fully automated. Operators worked from home. They were able to spend four or five more hours a day enjoying family activities."

Patricia smiled as she said, "Home cooking reappeared. Neighbors started meeting each other again. Community barbeques turned into casual planning sessions on how to best educate their children. Many mothers and fathers stepped forward to use their back yard, basement or garage to hold classes and activities until network learning evolved to fill the gap."

"Yes," I continued, "education quickly turned into international NET programs. Languages converted automatically.

"Didn't some teacher in China come out with the most popular math program for fifth graders? Or was it the guy out of South Africa and his geography program that set the trend in international language converted to age-by-age training?

"Teacher talent popped out of the woodwork. There was so much teacher talent hidden in classrooms. The world was literally shocked at how fast the new system of home and community learning came about.

"Unemployment soared with the world economies in shock over the collapse of schools, offices, and the bond market. The world was adrift as the economies collapsed around us."

John said, "Yes, to say the least, it was going to pot and fast."

"No kidding," I went on. "Your wife was a teacher—a good teacher. She knew the system.

"It was good teachers, like her, that brought us quickly back into the post-digital age.

"Most teachers love their jobs. They care about the children they teach and many spend their life trying to find better ways of educating.

"When the students walked out of schools because technology allowed them to, teachers quickly found ways to feed them information in a system that defied the school.

"Buildings, four walls, sports fields, and a teacher standing in the front of the room was too ancient. Outdated. Kids knew there was a better way. It was not adults that faced reality; it was teenagers."

"And teachers identified their market...."

"... And found their place quickly!" John finished my sentence. "We should all be proud of them and their profession, especially now that they are not forced into the school system that collapsed because of inefficiency and redundancy."

"Let's head down to the lab and check out the Analyzer. Maggie, oh yea, Magcurtain," Patricia halfway apologized, "is waiting for us.

"I'm just so used to calling our great-grandniece Maggie. All I know now is that she prefers to go by one name, the name of her first invention, the Magcurtain."

"Quite a girl," John added.

"Her father is the Ipswich area molecular technician for the Analyzer. She must have inherited molecular interest from him. Older teachers stepped in to help her—more like tutoring.

"With free access to the world of science thorough NET research and our labs, she came up with tiny programmable molecules, like magnets that act as walls, windows, doors, even containers that detect the presences of only authorized users and blocks others. Amazing—just amazing for a teenager."

Patricia motioned for us to follow. "She is probably in the lab already teaching other younger kids—and us old gals. She has to be eighteen or nineteen now."

"How did she come up with Magcurtain?" John asked.

"Corn!" My one-word response needed explanation.

"One day, as a little girl, maybe eight, she was with her dad and me discussing how corn has improved over thousands of years. She didn't seem that interested at the time. Starting from plants in Mesoamerica, adoption spread into nearly every growing environment in the world—just like people. Corn improved just like people.

"No matter if the plant produced 50, 100, or 500 seeds, each generation remembered everything the parent seed passed on. Sure it crossbred, changed colors as mutant genes modified it for survival.

"Way better than us," John chimed in.

"Way better than us is right," I continued. "Each kernel remembered to set roots, stand proud, and mature every year no matter the changes we've bred into it or the environmental pestilence it has had to endure over the years. Young corn remembered what it learned from ancient ancestors." It did not need electronic artificial memory.

"What does that have to do with Magcurtain?" John asked.

"A Magcurtain is like corn: Each kernel, each plant remembers how every part fit back together. Magcurtain develops back to its original programmed form. It is like corn that knows how to block out insects or repair from disease damage. As a growing plant, it detects what is near, how close, and guards against intruders, sun, water, and drought," I explained.

"Little Maggie said to her dad, 'Why can't a window do that. You would not have to fix the one I broke last week.' Her dad said, 'Maggie, you should develop a window like that so you can fix it.' 'Ok', she said.

"It took her a few years constantly quizzing her dad, teachers, all of us how plants and newer versions of the Analyzer worked. She obviously picked up tips and product sources in community biology and studying NET physics.

"One day, parts in bottles started arriving at the back door of this old school, cases of them. The next thing her parents knew she had a working model of all those tiny, yet uniform, many nearly invisible parts. Were they parts? Pieces? Not sure.

"Simplified, it is something like how oxygen and hydrogen molecules stick together to form water. On an atomic level, it is like two electrons rotating in such a way as to form stable equilibrium—when disrupted they reform. It is like water parting.

"It is a combination of electromagnetism and biomagnetism.

"No matter how she shook it or poked her finger or fist through it, it would reassemble just like the original. The key was to program it into any form needed. For example, to let something or someone in or out was the key.

"As a young teenager, she started working with teachers in the community lab. Her friends, some my age, helped design and assemble models. She was a great teacher too; always teaching others her process and asking for suggestions."

"It makes a great doggie door," Micah said as he grabbed great grandpa South Dakota's hand as we all walked down the hall to the lab.

The end.

BIBLIOGRAPHY

Ag In the Classroom, "Growing a Nation, The Story of American Agriculture," http://www.agclassroom.org/gan/timeline/1860.htm (Sourced February 9, 2017).

Age of Paleolithic, Neolithic, Stone Age, https://en.wikipedia.org/wiki/Bronze_Age (Sourced August 22, 2015).

All in the Family, https://en.wikipedia.org/wiki/Archie_Bunker (Sourced September 30, 2015).

Atkinson, Nancy, "Who Discovered Electricity?," *Universe Today,* March 3, 2014, http://www.universetoday.com/82402/who-discovered-electricity/ (Sourced September 30, 2015).

Ben Ki-moon, "Global Education First Initiative 2012–2016," United Nations Secretary General, United Nations, http://gefidr160719.businesscatalyst.com/index.html (Sourced January 3, 2017).

Blixen, Karen, *Out of Africa,* no current copyright found, 1937.

Bread and Circuses, https://en.wikipedia.org/wiki/Bread_and_circuses (Sourced September 28, 2015).

Burnette, Courtney, "Educational Eligibility vs Medical Diagnosis in Autism Spectrum Disorders," March 9, 2012, http://www.cdd.unm.edu/autism/Handouts/EducationalEligibilityVsMed.pdf (Sourced September 29, 2016).

Chait, Jennifer, "Autism more common in high-tech cities," *Baby,* July 6, 2011, http://www.pregnancyandbaby.com/baby/articles/935229/autism-more-common-in-high-tech-cities (Sourced September 29, 2016).

Churchill, Winston, *The Bright Gleam of Victory,* London, England: The Churchill Centre, November 10, 1942, http://www.winstonchurchill.org/resources/speeches/1941-1945-war-leader/987-the-end-of-the-beginning (Sourced January 6, 2016).

Cone, Marla, "Autism Clusters Found in California's Major Cities," Environmental Health News, *Scientific American,* January 6, 2010, http://www.scientificamerican.com/article/autism-clusters-californiahighly-educated-parents/ (Sourced September 29, 2016).

de Trobriand, Philippe Regis Denis de Keredern, *Army Life in Dakota* (1867–1870), translated by George Francis Will, Chicago: The Lakeside Press, R.R. Donnelly & Sons Co. (1941): 223–225.

Ellis, Renee R., Tavia Simmons, "Coresident Grandparents and Their Grandchildren: 2012," P20-576, U.S. Department of Commerce, Economics and Statistics Administration, U.S. Census Bureau, October 2014, https://www.census.gov/

content/dam/Census/library/publications/2014/demo/p20-576.pdf (Sourced June 13, 2016).

Embury, Emma C., "Lesson XIV: Humanity Rewarded," *Sheldons' Modern School Fourth Reader*, New York: Sheldon and Company (1885): 46–47.

Fast, Howard, "A critic is a eunuch working in a harem. He watches it, but he knows he can't do it." Brainy Quote, http://www.brainyquote.com/quotes/keywords/failed.html (Sourced September 30, 2015).

Fortier, Samuel, Correspondence to Dr. Elwood Mead of Washington, D.C. May 1, 1906. https://www.archives.gov/exhibits/sf-earthquake-and-fire/earthquake-fire.html (Sourced March 24, 2017).

Friedman, Jane, *Publishing 101: A First-time Author's Guide*, Amazon (2014): 212.

Galland, Antoine, *Aladdin*, https://en.wikipedia.org/wiki/Aladdin (Sourced November 18, 2015).

Global Fire Power, "Active Military Manpower by Country," http://www.globalfirepower.com/active-military-manpower.asp (Sourced January 12, 2017).

Hawthorne, Julian, *The History of the United States from 1492–1910*, Volume III, New York: P.F. Collier & Son (1910): 836–838.

Hewitt, Katie, "How to win the kid v. veggies battle," Toronto, ON, Canada: The Globe and Mail Inc., August 16, 2010, http://www.theglobeandmail.com/life/parenting/how-to-win-the-kid-v-veggies-battle/article4267723/ (Sourced October 13, 2015).

History of Education in the United States, https://en.wikipedia.org/wiki/History_of_education_in_the_United_States (Sourced October 12, 2015).

Holy Bible, King James Version, Numbers 23:23.

Institute of Education Sciences, National Center for Education Statistics, Fast Facts, "Back to School Statistics," http://nces.ed.gov/fastfacts/display.asp?id=372 (Sourced January 28, 2016).

Irving, Washington, *Rip Van Winkle*, June 23, 1819.

Jurkowitz, Mark, "7 facts about White House press secretaries," *Fact Tank*, June 19, 2014, http://www.pewresearch.org/fact-tank/2014/06/19/7-facts-about-white-house-press-secretaries/ (Sourced September 30, 2015).

Lavelle, Tara A., et al., "Economic Burden of Childhood Autism Spectrum Disorders," *Pediatrics*, Volume 133, Issue 3, March 2014, http://pediatrics.aappublications.org/content/133/3/e520.short (Sourced September 29, 2016).

Law and Criminal Courts, South Australian Advertiser (August 10, 1985): 139, http://trove.nla.gov.au/ndp/del/article/31852449 (Sourced July 20, 2015).

Localite, http://www.merriam-webster.com/dictionary/localite (Sourced November 5, 2015).

Luddite, https://en.wikipedia.org/wiki/Luddite (Sourced October 10, 2015).

Lugaila, Terry, Julia Overturf, "Children and the Households They Live In: 2000," United States Department of Commerce, U.S. Census Bureau, Economics and Statistics Administration, Census 2000 Special Reports, CENSR-14, March 2004, http://www.census.gov/prod/2004pubs/censr-14.pdf (Sourced June 13, 2016).

Lynn, Richard, Tatu Vanhanen, and Jelte Wicherts, "National IQ Scores–Country

Ratings," http://www.photius.com/rankings/national_iq_scores_country_ranks .html (Sourced January 3, 2017).

Mahfood, Julie, "10 College Subjects With The Lowest Average IQs," March 10, 2014, *The Biggest, the Richest, Part of the Premium Network* http://www.therichest.com/ rich-list/the-biggest/10-college-subjects-with-the-lowest-average-iqs/ (Sourced April 27, 2016).

Manhattan Project, https://en.wikipedia.org/wiki/Manhattan_Project (Sourced October 12, 2015).

McCarren, Andrea, "Parents in trouble again for letting kids walk alone," Washington: WUSA-TV, April 13, 2015, http://www.usatoday.com/story/news/nation/ 2015/04/13/parents-investigated-letting-children-walk-alone/25700823/ (Sourced September 18, 2015).

Merriam-Webster, An Encyclopaedia Britannica Company, "school system," https:// www.google.com.mx/webhp?sourceid=chrome-instant&ion=1&espv=2&ie= UTF-8#q=define+%22school+system%22 (Sourced December 14, 2015).

Miller, Mark, *The Singing Wire, a Story of the Telegraph*, Philadelphia: The John C. Winston Company, 1953.

Mongol Empire, https://en.wikipedia.org/wiki/Mongol_Empire (Sourced September 19, 2015).

Mulqueen, Maggie, "The Book of Love, to Maggie Mulqueen a Tattered Old Journals Holds a Lifetime of Comfort," *AARP Magazine*, Washington, D.C.: American Association of Retired People (August/September 2016): 74–75.

Murphy, Sherry L., Kenneth D. Kochanek, Jiaquan Xu, Elizabeth Arias, "Mortality in the United States, 2014," National Center of Health Statistics, Centers for Disease Control and Prevention, U.S. Department of Health and Human Services, Data Brief No. 229, December 2015, http://www.cdc.gov/nchs/data/databriefs/ db229.pdf (Sourced August 20 , 2016).

Myers, Philip Van Ness, *Ancient History*, Boston: Ginn and Company (first revised edition 1904): 5, 6.

——. *Ancient History*, Boston: Ginn and Company (second revised edition 1916): 1, 4–5, 7–8, 15, 18–20.

Näth, Marie-Luise, *China After the Cultural Revolution: Politics Between Two Party Congresses*, Oakland: University of California Press (1977): p. 68. https://books .google.com.mx/books?id=YyT9pxmcmxgC&pg=PA77&source=gbs_toc_r&cad =3#v=onepage&q&f=false (Sourced September 30, 2015).

National Museum of Australia (an Australian Government Agency), "Aborigines Protection Amending Act," Section 13A, No. 2, 1915, http://www.nma.gov.au/online_ features/defining_moments/featured/aborigines_protection_act (Sourced September 9, 2015).

News Wire Services, http://assignmenteditor.com/news-wires/ (Sourced September 30, 2015).

Officially Amazing, Guinness World Records, "Most Living Generations (ever)," http:// www.guinnessworldrecords.com/world-records/most-living-generations-(ever)/ (Sourced December 9, 2015).

Orwell, George, "*Animal Farm*," London: Secker and Warburg (1945): 21.

Panama Canal, https://en.wikipedia.org/wiki/Panama_Canal (Sourced October 12, 2015).

Pew Research Center, "Americans Changing Religious Landscape," May 12, 2015, http://www.pewforum.org/2015/05/12/americas-changing-religious-landscape/ (Sourced February 13, 2017).

Preston, Thomas, "Hey, Diddle, Diddle," *Mother Goose Rhymes*, https://en.wikipedia.org/wiki/Hey_Diddle_Diddle (Sourced October 14, 2015).

Ritholzt, Barry, "Why Are Young Adults Living with Their Parents and When Will They Move Out?," *The Big Picture*, August 4, 2014, http://www.ritholtz.com/blog/2014/08/why-are-young-adults-living-with-their-parents-and-when-will-they-move-out/ (Sourced September 30, 2015).

San Francisco (California) Planning Department, "San Francisco Neighborhoods–Social Economic Profiles, 2005–2009 American Community Survey," May 2011, http://sf-planning.org/sites/default/files/FileCenter/Documents/8501-SF ProfilesByNeighborhoodForWeb.pdf (Sourced January 30, 2017).

Sanderson, Edgar, et al., *Six Thousand Years of History*, Volume 1, 1899, E.R. DuMont Publisher, Philadelphia, Chicago, and St. Louis (1899): p. i, iv–v, 1, 3, 7–9, 10–15, 16.

Schneider, Gary, Jessica Evans, Katherine Pinard, *The Internet–Illustrated*, Cengage Learning, 2009 https://books.google.co.uk/books?id=YHwQ9WpvHfEC&pg=PA6&dq=ARPANET&hl=en&sa=X&ved=0CEAQ6AEwBjgKahUKEwiUh5yyhKvHAhVKF9sKHessDV0#v=onepage&q=ARPANET&f=false (Sourced August 22, 2015).

Sheldons' Modern School Fourth Reader, "Aladdin and his Lamp," Chicago: Sheldon & Company, no copyright found (1885): pp. 61–64.

——. "Letters of Recommendation," Lesson III, Chicago: Sheldon & Company (1885): p. 28.

South Dakota Board of Regents meeting, June 28–30, 2016, Madison, South Dakota, http://dlsd.sdln.net/cdm/ref/collection/BORMinutes/id/1687 (Sourced March 29, 2017).

Temüjin his life's summary as Genghis Khan, https://en.wikipedia.org/wiki/Genghis_Khan (Sourced September 28, 2015).

Tennyson, Alfred Lord, "In Memoriam: A.H.H. Obiit MDCCCXXXIII:27."

Thomas Nelson, Inc., Ecclesiastes 3:1, 5, *The Holy Bible*, New King James Version (NKJV), Nashville: Thomas Nelson Publishers (1994): 954.

——. Ecclesiastes 3:1–8, 11, Nashville: Thomas Nelson Publishers (1994): 954–955.

——. Ephesians 4:28, Nashville: Thomas Nelson Publishers (1994): 1665.

——. Exodus 20:12, Nashville: Thomas Nelson Publishers (1994): 108.

——. Genesis 4:8, Nashville: Thomas Nelson Publishers (1994): 5.

——. Genesis 41:1–47:28, Nashville: Thomas Nelson Publishers (1994): 60–73.

——. Luke 2:42–43, 46, 49, Nashville: Thomas Nelson Publishers (1994): 1462.

——. Luke 4:24, Nashville: Thomas Nelson Publishers (1994): 1465.

——. Proverbs 13:4, Nashville: Thomas Nelson Publishers (1994): 921.

——. Proverbs 13:24, Nashville: Thomas Nelson Publishers (1994): 923.

——. Proverbs 22:6, Nashville: Thomas Nelson Publishers (1994): 936.

——. 2nd Thessalonians 3:8–11, Nashville: Thomas Nelson Publishers (1994): 1683.

Tiffany, Erwin Milton "E.M." Tiffany, "FFA Creed," Lyndon, Kansas, https://www
    .bing.com/images/search?view=detailV2&ccid=iwcAEvdv&id=50B754728DE2
    7E1802C4FE0FE99AF365033C5A9C&q=FFA+Creed+PDF&simid=6080313231
    40130117&selectedIndex=0&ajaxhist=0 (Sourced March 27, 2017).

Toilet paper, https://en.wikipedia.org/wiki/Toilet_paper (Sourced October 12, 2015).

United Nations, United Nations Development Programme, Human Development
    Reports, "Education Index," November 15, 2013, http://hdr.undp.org/en/content/
    education-index (Sourced January 3, 2017).

United States Central Intelligence Agency (CIA), *The World Factbook*, "China,"
    https://www.cia.gov/library/publications/the-world-factbook/geos/ch.html
    (Sourced February 13, 2017).

United States Department of Agriculture, "2007 Census of Agriculture, Small Farms,"
    https://www.agcensus.usda.gov/Publications/2007/Online_Highlights/Fact_
    Sheets/Farm_Numbers/small_farm.pdf (Sourced March 13, 2017).

United States Department of Agriculture, Natural Resources Conservation Program, ,
    "Brief History of the USDA Soil Bank Program," http://www.nrcs.usda.gov/wps/
    portal/nrcs/detailfull/national/about/history/?cid=stelprdb1045667 (Sourced
    September 18, 2015).

United States Department of Commerce, Economics and Statistics Administration,
    Office of Policy Development, "Service Industries and Economic Performance,"
    (March 1996): 5–6, http://www.esa.doc.gov/sites/default/files/serviceindustries
    _0.pdf (Sourced January 27, 2017).

United States Department of Commerce, U.S. Bureau of the Census, "Average Popu-
    lation per Household and Family: 1940 to Present," Table HH-6, September 15,
    2004, https://www.census.gov/population/socdemo/hh-fam/hh6.xls (Sourced
    October 6, 2015).

——. U.S. Census Bureau, Economics and Statistics Administration, "Public Educa-
    tion Finances: 2013" (June 2015): pp. XVI, 6, http://www2.census.gov/govs/
    school/13f33pub.pdf (Sourced January 28, 2016).

——. U.S. Census Bureau, "Living Arrangements with Children Under 18 Years Old,"
    http://www.google.com.mx/url?q=http://www.census.gov/population/socdemo/
    hh-fam/ch1.xls&sa=U&ved=0CB4QFjACahUKEwj6-N3ur67IAhVLmoAKHea
    WBHI&usg=AFQjCNE4DfhfcR4MfVhwW2DLoBfkzEumwA (Sourced Octo-
    ber 6, 2015).

——. U.S. Census Bureau, "Number, Timing, and Duration of Marriages, and Divorces:
    2001," February 2005, https://www.census.gov/prod/2005pubs/p70-97.pdf
    (Sourced November 12, 2016).

——. U.S. Census Bureau, "Number, Timing, and Duration of Marriages, and Divorces:
    2009," May 2011, https://www.census.gov/prod/2011pubs/p70-125.pdf (Sourced
    November 12, 2016).

United States Department of Education, National Center for Education Statistics, Institute of Education Sciences; Trends in High School Dropout and Completion Rates in the United States: 1972–2012, "Event Dropout rates … grades 10–12, October 2012," Table 1, June 2015, http://nces.ed.gov/pubs2015/2015015.pdf (Source January 23, 2016).

United States Department of Health and Human Services, United States Centers for Disease Control and Prevention, "Autism Spectrum Disorder," http://www.cdc .gov/ncbddd/autism/data.html (Sourced Sep. 29, 2016).

United States Federal Aviation Administration, "Drone Registration," https://drone-registration.net/ (Sourced March 27, 2017).

The Voyage of Hanno, http://www.metrum.org/mapping/hanno.htm (Sourced May 20, 2016).

Webster's New World Dictionary, Second College Edition, "Adult," New York: Simon and Schuster (1982): 19.

——. *Ascot,* New York: Simon and Schuster (1982): 81.

——. *Cosmopolite,* New York: Simon and Schuster (1982): 321.

——. *Culture,* New York: Simon and Schuster (1982): 345.

——. *Diddle,* New York: Simon and Schuster (1982): 392.

——. *Education,* New York: Simon and Schuster (1982): 444.

——. *Punt, Punter,* New York: Simon and Schuster (1982): 1153.

Wietgrefe, Gary W., "Apparatus and Method for Coordinating Package and Bulk Dispensing," U.S. patent 7,640,075, issued December 29, 2009.

——. "Apparatuses and Methods for Bulk Dispensing," U.S. patent 8,387,824, issued March 5, 2013.

——. "Apparatus and Method for Coordinating Automated Package and Bulk Dispensing," U.S. patent 8,442,675, issued May 14, 2013.

——. *Relating to Ancient Learning as It Influences the 21st Century,* Sioux Falls, South Dakota, GWW Books (2018).

——. "Systems and Processes for Producing Biofuels from Biomass," U.S. Patent 8,641,910, Issued February 4, 2014.

Wietgrefe, Seth, "Raising our children (letter)," North Pole, Alaska, July 16, 2015.

Wolfson, Arthur Mayer, *Essentials in Ancient History, from the Earliest Records to Charlemagne,* New York: American Book Company (1902): 91–92, 95–96.

INDEX

Continue your journey

of understanding current society by reading
Gary Wietgrefe's subsequent book:

Relating to Ancient Learning as it influences the 21st century

With provocative insight, Wietgrefe explores
societies' underlying truths of learning.
The school system is a recent phenomenon
and thereby could not have been the basis
for societal development.

What will be the product of
current learning systems?

Blending subtle humor, illustrations
from the illiterate, originality, and historic
examples of independent thinkers like
Aristotle, da Vinci, Franklin, Edison, and
Einstein, readers find Wietgrefe's audacious
exploits into 21st century learning intriguing
and highly controversial.

Find out why academia will be unnerved.